PROBLEMS OF INDIA'S DEVELOPMENT

Edited by

R.C. DUTT

GYAN PUBLISHING HOUSE
NEW DELHI-110 002
in collaboration with
India International Centre

Problems of India's Development
(Development Issues, Economics, Sociology, Applied Technology)

ISBN : 81-212-0453-4
Library of Congress Card No. 93-900318

Published 1994 in India by
Gyan Publishing House
5, Ansari Road
New Delhi 110 002
in collaboration with
India International Centre, New Delhi

Laser Typest by Specturm Media, Ph. 3262540 and
Printed at Goyal Offset Works, Delhi

PREFACE

The volume contains the proceedings of three seminars organised by the Social Affairs Group of the India International Centre on the problems of India's development. The procedure followed was to invite one or two scholars to write theme papers on the subject chosen for a particular seminar.

While the seminar was open to all members of the India International Centre the theme paper or papers were circulated to a group of participants who had shown interest in the subjects under discussion by participating in similar seminars earlier or who have expressed a desire to be included in the mailing list. Such participants were given about three weeks' time to peruse the theme paper or papers and send their Critical Notes, if they so desired, on the views expressed in these papers. These Critical Notes were again circulated to the enlisted participants a week before the seminar was to be held, so that they may come fully prepared for a meaningful discussion on the subject.

The three parts of the volume contain proceedings of the three seminars held on this broad topic. Each part has been divided into two portions. The first part contains the theme paper or papers and the critical notes as edited while the second summaries of the observations made by the participants in the deliberations that followed.

The first seminar (as contained in Part I of the volume) is on the Social and Economic aspects of Development, for which the theme paper was written by Dr. Kamal A. Mitra Chenoy of Jawahar Lal Nehru University. It was followed by ten Critical Notes, The second portion of this part contains summaries of the observations made by the twelve participants. Part II records the proceedings of the second seminar on the Application of Technology for which there were two theme papers. The first was by Dr. A. Rahman, the well-known science historian, and the second by Dr. Ashok Parthasarathy, at present Additional Secretary, Department of Scientific and Industrial Research, Ministry of Science and Technology, Government of India. The theme papers attracted eight Critical Notes and in the seminar that followed twenty-two delegates participated in the discussions. The third and the last seminar in this series, as contained in Part III, was on Secularism and Social Transformation. The theme paper was written by Prof. Rasheeduddin Khan which was followed by ten Critical Notes. Twenty-eight participants took part in the discussions.

The importance of the subject chosen, namely problems of development, hardly needs to be emphasised. Development is a matter on which not merely the well-being but the very existence of our polity depends. It is, therefore, not a subject which can or should be monopolised by scholars or "experts". Scholars and "experts" have undoubtedly a role to play, but the more important aspect of this role is to popularise the scientific and rational outlook on the problems, and to remove popular misconceptions, often generated by vested interests, rather than work on complicated models of development which few outside their fraternity would understand. This requires interaction of scholars with laymen and it is in this respect that the three seminars were organised and the volume that incorporates the proceedings, can claim to make a contribution.

The seminar brought together acknowledged thinkers and scholars with journalists, social activists and retired bureaucrats. The level of comprehension and even of expression of the participants has not been the same. Some popular views, rational and not-so-rational, have been expressed, but no attempt has been made to play down any of them in the interest of uniformity. The object of the seminars and of this volume, based on the discussions which took place in the seminars, is not to arrive at a consensus for any action, but to discuss frankly the different possible views in order to stimulate thinking, and enable the reader to exercise his/her own judgement to decide what he/she regards as the correct view. It is our earnest hope that the insights provided, the points of view presented and the data adduced in support thereof, will help broaden the outlook and ultimately remove the misconceptions which still plague our thinking on this important subject of development.

To what extent the purpose is likely to be achieved will be for the readers to judge, but there is no doubt that when cataclysmic changes have occurred and are still taking place in the world, involving not only the collapse of the economic cadre in a group of powerful countries, but the rise of such re-actionary forces as ethnicism and religious fundamentalism, there is a need, as never before, of clear thinking. The danger of being swept off our feet by these changes is as great as the danger of rigidly hanging on to the past, refusing to recognise these changes. If the volume contributes to clear this thinking the effort would have been amply rewarded.

Acknowledgement

My thanks are due to the Director, Shir A. Madhavan, and the Secretary, Shri N. H. Ramachandran, of the India International Centre who provided all the facilities needed to organise the seminars, and subsequently to prepare the papers for publication. In particular, I would like to thank Ms. Lalsawmliani Tochhawng, Asstt. Programme Officer, and Shri Anil Kumar Gupta, of the Programme Office who rendered all the help needed to arrange and edit the theme papers, critical notes and the summaries of the observations of the participants. Without their help it would not have been possible to handle the large volume of work involved in arranging the papers for publication.

R. C. Dutt
Convener

made to play down any criticism by the [illegible] of [illegible]. The [illegible] recommended the volume [illegible] but the [illegible] [illegible] took place in the [illegible] [illegible] to a [illegible] [illegible] [illegible] [illegible] and [illegible] [illegible] [illegible] [illegible] [illegible] [illegible] on this important [illegible].

To what extent the purpose is [illegible] [illegible] [illegible] [illegible] [illegible] [illegible] made.

[illegible]

[illegible] [illegible] [illegible] the papers [illegible].

CONTENTS

PART I

POLITICAL AND SOCIAL ASPECTS OF DEVELOPMENT

PART II

APPLICATION OF TECHNOLOGY FOR DEVELOPMENT

PART III

SECULARISM AND SOCIAL TRANSFORMATION

Part I

POLITICAL AND SOCIAL ASPECTS OF DEVELOPMENT

RE-THINKING DEVELOPMENT — I

Kamal A. Mitra Chenoy

Development has once again become a buzzword in influential circles. Earlier radical scholars had sharply critiqued the dominant mainstream theories of economic growth, political development and modernisation. Largely as a consequence of this critique and the liberal acceptance of its validity, the notion of economic growth was discarded in its old form and the notion of development which emphasised the distributive imperative became accepted. Those years of the late sixties and early seventies were also the heydays of the Group of 77, UNCTAD and the New International Economic Order. Much has changed in the world since then, and so old notions of economic growth, free market, the minimal state and a west-oriented modernisation have once again become increasingly acceptable.

The World Bank, for example, in its latest report incorporates all these neo-conservative ideas. The current ideological legitimacy of a neo-conservative notion of development is largely based on the political successes of the Reagan and Thatcher administrations in the last decade. Ronald Reagan, the old hero of the American Westerns, a former sportscaster, and even in his liberal days, an informer against his fellow Hollywood movie people during the Mc Carthyite witchhunts, contributed very substantially to the legitimation of this market-oriented development approach. It was Reagan after all, who coined that resonant, if illusory phrase, about the "magic of the market place" which underpins current mainstream development theory. The "Iron Lady', heroine of the Falkland War, provided further legitimacy to neo-conservatism. The fact that these leaders became embarrassments to their own parties, with the "Old Gipper" found to be fibbing on Irangate while the Tories actually forced out Maggie, has not tarnished their ideological achievements. Nor has the fragility or short-lived nature of their economic achievements.

The World Development Report 1991 presents the most recent restatement of this kind of theory. It starts, somewhat grandiloquently, by stating that : "A central issue in development and the principal theme of the report, is the interaction between governments and markets". It, of course, finds that : "A consensus is gradually forming in favour of a "market-friendly" approach to development". The prescribed relationship between the State, government and the market is most clearly stated in the chapter (number seven) on "Rethinking the State". Ironically, the chapter has as its epigraph a quote from John Maynard Keynes' book on *"The End of Laissez-Faire"*. Keynes, that famed proponent of State intervention in the economy, is cited in support of a conclusion that re-discovers an ancient truth pointed out in a fourteenth century Arabic treatise that argued. "Commercial activity on the part of the ruler is harmful to his subjects and ruinous to the tax revenue .... " Thus the Report, after hailing the "rediscovery of these ancient truths" as "one of the most striking legacies of the 1980s" goes on to aver that "Many governments are reconsidering their involvement in the economy, reviewing their spending priorities, and undertaking fewer commercial activities". Poor old Keynes, all his successes forgotten, is now refuted by a scholar no less than six centuries earlier, when the great depression could not even have been an opium-induced dream. But this is only one of the more striking examples of the kind of historical, political and logical analysis triumphant proponents of currently dominant development theory indulge in. More shockingly, this sort of shoddy analysis and argument is accepted by key policy-makers and opinion-builders, not least of all in our country.

The World Bank, IMF, G-7 and the governments of most developing countries accepted this model well before the last decade. Others, including India, have hitherto resisted foreign pressures to reduce sharply State intervention in the economy and to jettison regulations directed at securing the interests of the poorer strata. Current changes in the erstwhile 'socialist' world and the widespread acceptance of the purported virtues of the market economy (read capitalism) there, have sharply reduced the legitimacy of the so-called public sector, state regulations (including anti-monopoly, environmentalist, welfarist, etc.) and indeed any institutional arrangement which might indicate a non-capitalist path of development. The evident failures of what are, or were, State capitalists institutions and structures have further eroded the public acceptability of these statist measures.

The ideological offensive of current neo-conservatism is so overwhelming that earlier basic postulates accepted as truths have been forgotton, or dismissed as obsolete. Any number of Third World theorists and leaders, including the founders of the Non-Aligned Movement (NAM) had found the dynamics of the current international economic order (commonly known as imperialism or the capitalist international division of labour), to be a central cause for the under-development of their countries. This after all, was the political and ideological basis for the radical Third World unity displayed in the UN, UNCTAD. et. al. in pursuit of a new international economic order (NIEO), the development decade, etc. While much of the old radical thinking is clearly obsolete, this basic postulate remains relevant. In other words, despite the much touted 'universal human values' and the end of the second cold war, imperialism and the contradictions of the world economy remain.

This was clearly recognised in the report of the South Commission (1990) : "The Challenge to the South." The report noted that, "The widening disparities between South and North are attributable not merely to differences in economic progress, but also to an enlargement of the North's power vis-a-vis the rest of the world ... The fate of the South is increasingly dictated by the perceptions and policies of governments in the North, of the multilateral institutions which a few of those governments control, and of the network of private institutions that are increasingly prominent. Domination has been reinforced where partnership was needed and hoped for by the South."

In fact, as has been noted in a large body of literature, neo-conservative development prescriptions are doubly historical. In the first place, they propagate a path of development which is, historically speaking not feasible. For instance, as Eric Hobsbawm and others have shown, the industrial revolution in Britain would not have been possible without what Pierre Jelee has picturesquely called the 'pillage of the Third World." It was this imperialist exploitation of colonies that provided the necessary 'primary accumulation of capital' to take place; which in turn enabled the kind of rapid industrialisation which allowed the imperialist countries to develop into the industrial giants they now are. Such an option is not available to the Third World, even if it has some historical case as Iraq did for its aborted annexation of Kuwait. In fact, as shown earlier, the opposite is the case. Third World countries, as it were, are on the wrong side of imperialism being subject as they are now to the inequities of a world order skewed against them.

The mainstream development prescription is historical for a second reason. The kind of open door, anti-protectionist and non-interventionist policies advocated by the World Bank-IMF were not followed by the so-called success stories of the Third World i.e. the Asian Tigers, which at crucial stages of their development had highly protectionist economies with substantial State intervention. There could have been no Japanese miracle without the directive role played by MITI and the almost hermetically sealed nature of the Japanese economy, which even today is much less open than most. There is, therefore, no historical justification or validation for the kind of economic policies being forced on indebted countries, including our own. And as many number of studies and documents have revealed, including the South Commission Report, the consequences of such policies have been disastrous, economically, politically and culturally.

Virtually all countries following this development pattern have authoritarian forms of government. The elitist nature of development advocated, necessitates the suppression of the democratic rights of under-privileged strata. In India, for example, to cite the most democratic case, the Essential Services Maintenance Ordinance (ESMO, later ESMA), preceded the 1981 IMF loan. Currently there is much concern about an 'exit policy', which will permit industrialists to dismiss workers, without providing them the retrenchment benefits now necessary by law. The economic and social dislocations caused by such policies lead to fierce political resistance by those most severely affected : the poor and under privileged. It is to enable the efficient suppression of such movements, that authoritarian measures become imperative. So democracy becomes inimical to development. Even when say, parliamentary institutions exist, these are denied their participatory and democratic content, to conform to what is termed 'parliamentary authoritarianism.'

The impact on culture is no less negative. As it is, in the kind of capitalist development underway in the Third World, there is a kind of 'cultural imperialism' operating from the dominant local metropolitan centres. The 'great traditions' tend to obliterate the 'little traditions'. This tendency is of course, often vigorously opposed, and is the basis of many regional, linguistic, ethnic, religious and separatist movements. Ironically, these movements often provide the ideological justification for authoritarian measures in the 'national interest'. But there is a larger, much more powerful cultural imperialism. This is the domination of metropolitan culture of the advanced capitalist countries. The belief that what is foreign, or western, or more specifically American (read of the USA), is best reflects the uncritical acceptance of the superiority of the West. It also accompanies a profound distortion of local, indigenous cultures, where an imitative Westernisation is considered the epitome of true advanced culture. Such an imitative and derivative culture not only increasingly separates the ruling elites from the rest of the populace, it also helps provide the required consumer preferences for the new patterns of production necessitated by this elitist development model.

The most tragic aspect of the neo-conservative development model is the profound irrationality of the project itself. As the World Commission on Environment and Development

(Brundtland Commission) noted, the pattern of development is not sustainable. As its report clearly puts it : "The future — even a sustainable future-will be marked by increasing risk. The risks associated with new technologies are growing. The numbers, scale, frequency and impact of natural and human-caused disasters are mounting. The risks of irreversible damage to natural systems regionally (for example through acidification, desertification, or deforestation) and globally (through ozone layer depletion of climate change) are becoming significant."

The need to rethink development is, therefore, inextricable linked to the very survival of the planet. The most tragic aspect of the failed so-called 'socialist' model was that it had internalised the parameters of the capitalist model, to which it was supposed to provide a viable alternative. Parameters like per capita income, labour productivity, GNP, etc. do not indicate the basic problems of development discussed above. There is, therefore, nothing specifically 'socialist' about that failed pattern of development, since its indices were so completely capitalist. This criticism applies even more strongly in the Indian case. In sum, therefore, a truly humane, sustainable model of development will have to be based on totally different indices and premises. It is surely high time that this task was more comprehensively attempted in this country.

RE-THINKING DEVELOPMENT — II

Kamal A. Mitra Chenoy

In the earlier paper circulated for the seminar, I had ventured a critique of dominant. mainstream development models. Friends* have pointed out that no alternative model with its social, economic, political and cultural dimensions has been sketched out. I am, of course, guilty of this grievous error, for very obvious reasons I did not venture in these parlous times to theorise an alternative, especially since many from Grigory Yavlinsky to (the early) Manmohan Singh have so obviously failed. However, since Marxists tread where angels do not, let me venture some not so stray thoughts :—

Any viable model of development must be both people and nature centred. In other words, it must represent a path of development quite different from that of the earlier 'modernisation' model. Experience of earlier 'socialist' experiments has starkly highlighted the imperative need for participatory i.e. democratic political structures to help direct State activity and to re-orient the same when necessary. But substantial State intervention in the economy and polity, there must be, particularly in less developed countries as ours. Yet this intervention would be less bureaucratic and more participatory. For instance the 'public sector' would be made really public as distinct from state-bureaucratic capitalist as at present, through participation of workers in management, etc. A truly socialist model would involve a very significant decentralisation of power, all the way down to the lowliest panchayat level. Guarantees and checks ensuring the protection of the powers of the federal units and of all the plural political formations would have to be built into the Constitution. Emergency/centralising powers would be limited and carefully specified, and subject to judicial and legislative review.

Since the experience of our country points to the increasing penetration of the electoral system by black money, elections would be State funded. There would be the right of recall of legislators at all levels. Thus the legislators would be made truly accountable to their electors. The re-assertion of the powers of the legislature vis-a-vis the executive would be constitutionally sanctioned, in order to reverse the decline in legislative supervision of the executive. The working of government would be made transparent and public access to all but the most sensitive information would be ensured. Of course while one would prefer a socialist-oriented model, this choice itself would be open ended; with political parties, depending on the popular mandate free to espouse or implement any programme, within the limits of the Constitution. This presumably is what is meant by 'socialist choice.'

A democratic political process institutionalised by a pluralist, participatory political structure would have to address itself to the most ancient and insidious form of oppression : gender oppression. Despite the relatively recent rise of feminism, the sexist oppression of roughly half of the human race, women, continues. Despite legislation, not very advanced in countries such as India, discrimination against, and oppression of, women continues. Wide-ranging affirmative action consciously directed at upliftment of the female community, empowering them to exercise their ever-so-long denied rights, is indeed a minimal condition for any true democracy. Needless to say, this indispensable pre-condition for an alternate developmental form would require political will and enlightenment of the very highest order. And the major share of that impetus will have to come from women. As Germaine Greer once wrote : "How can men liberate women, when they themselves are not free ?"

In sum, a political structure built on democratic, pluralist principles would be the basis for any alternative model. What is often not adequately realised, especially on the right, is that the so-called socialist models failed not only because of bad economics, but primarily because of bad politics. Political authoritarianism masquerading as the dictatorship of the proletariat, ensured an unwieldly bureaucratic State apparatus which was incapable of responding efficiently or swiftly to economic signals. Moreover this sort of increasingly arbitrary and corrupt regime rapidly lost legitimacy and popular support, further strengthening authoritarian tendencies and further increasing wasteful expenditures. Problems in civil society instead of being solved were suppressed, often accentuated, only to explode later. A striking instance is the nationality problem in the Soviet Union and Yugoslavia today.

A particular feature of an alternative model must hence be a democratic policy on culture. As had been argued in the theme paper, and is generally well-known, the mainstream arguments relating to development are themselves prone to a kind of economic determinism. Vital historical, social, political and cultural pre-conditions and determinants of development are generally ignored. In line with the ethnocentric bias in pro-West models, there is an 'orientalist' bias towards Third World cultures. These cultures are, in the main, seen as backward, as impediments to development. But this is only half the story; indigenous cultures also contain the best of indigenous civilisations, and thus are a vital resource for development. Yet even in Third World countries, including our own, there has been a kind of cultural imperialism, in its own way no less pernicious than that associated with the West.

There has been a tendency for the so-called 'great traditions' to swallow up the 'little traditions', for urban, upper class (in our case also upper caste) cultural traditions and forms to displace, and ultimately efface local, often reformist or democratic, traditions and forms. Thus the Ramjanambhoomi movement glorifies a Rama which is not the "maryada purushottam' of popular culture, but a militant, unforgiving Rama who has an accommodation problem. Arguably the demand for the worship of a Ramajanamsthan itself reflects a semiticisation of Hindu tradition, since the birthplace of one of the avatars of Vishnu cannot in itself in earlier 'Hindu' tradition be such a hallowed place. Symbolically enough, the VHP/BJP have proceeded to demolish existing Hindu temples around the site, not merely because these belong to 'lesser Gods' but because they represent subordinate, 'little traditions'. So the Bajrang Dal has quite self-righteously demolished a Bajrangbali temple. Moreover the architectural but Shaivite, again reflecting a sectarian bias even within 'Hindu' traditions.

This cultural domination often reflects existing, or attempted political and economic domination. Popular resistance to such domination or oppression thus also takes cultural forms and tends to emphasise if not exaggerate cultural distinctiveness, the differences from the 'other' dominant culture(s). This cycle of reaction and counter-reaction is damaging to the cultural development of the society concerned, which makes the case for a democratic, non-sectarian cultural policy even more compelling in any conceptualisation of an alternative development model.

As indicated earlier, the economic dimension of the alternate model has to be substantially non-capitalist and pro-socialist, though this must be a product of popular choice and hence reversible. The profit principle cannot be the only determinant for economic decision-making. History is replete with instances to show that individual profit is often inimical to social welfare. But the profit motive cannot be ignored even by the capitalist, who generally is loath to share his/her profits with his/her workers. The accent in the people-oriented development path should, therefore, be on a combination of social welfare and individual profit. The notion of social welfare would have to take into account the environmental and ecological dimension, as indicated in the earlier paper. Consequently there would be a 'mixed economy' of a new sort. The public sector would be made truly public through popular, including workers' participation and control, and the private sector would be made socially accountable. All economic decisions would be subordinate to social welfare considerations and distributive justice would be given priority. In a sense the capitalists would follow the Gandhian 'trusteeship' principle, combining the individual profit motive with societal imperatives.

The stress on societal imperatives implies that the private sector would be responsive to the requirements of the 'national economy,' i.e. to the demands of domestic development. In other words, the emphasis on profits would not be to the detriment of national interests, in as much as the imperative of private profit should not over ride the welfare interests of the larger indigenous community. In the current operation of the neo-conservative development model, ruling elites have in instance after instance, forsaken local interests in their pursuit of profit, at the behest of MNCs and the World Bank-IMF.

In the context of current developments in several multi-national, multi-ethnic countries, including our own, it is perhaps necessary to elaborate a little more on the operation of the federal principle in the alternative development paths. Not only would there have to be democratic decentralisation of power, enabling the protection of the identities and autonomies of local and regional communities, there would have to be a constitutional provision for the normally unthinkable : the right of self-determination including the right to secession. This understandably goes against the grain of many nationalists; but nonetheless, the absence of such a right makes a fiction of the essentially voluntary and democratic essence of a federation or a confederation.

Such an alternative development path would quite obviously attract imperialist ire, a la Cuba. Countries venturing on these paths would require substantial international support. A foreign policy aimed at putting together a 'rainbow coalition' including pro-socialist, democratic rights, women's rights, anti-racist, environmentalist and other democratic movements that are generally non-governmental voluntary movements, could help in welding together a counter-vailing force that could carry the fight to the lions den : to the heartland of imperialism itself, to the USA, the EEC countries and Japan. The governments of imperialist countries are imperialist, not their own people, the bulk of whom, especially women, are oppressed. These people remain potential allies of all liberation strategies and theologies/ideologies.

In sum, the battle is far from lost or over, whatever may happen in the former USSR or East Europe. That there is no alternative to the IMF is an argument that is doubly false. Not only is there an alternative, but, as we have seen, the bank-fund provide no realisible alternative. Theirs is a prescription for disaster.

At the end it is necessary to sound an important note of caution : there cannot be, and must not be, any ONE MODEL of development. All this very brief and necessarily sketchy note has tried to do, is to attempt to merely indicate the broad contours of alternative development strategies.

RE-THINKING DEVELOPMENT

Kamal A. Mitra Chenoy

A CRITIQUE

E.M.S. Namboodiripad

I agree with Dr. Chenoy that "a truly humane, sustainable model of development will have to be based on totally different indices and premises. It is surely high time that this task was more comprehensively attempted in this country."

The model of development adopted by the Narasimha Rao Government will lead the country to the same debt trap into which the Latin American countries have fallen. The process began during the last years of Indira Gandhi when the first loan from the IMF was taken. It will be recalled that the Left and other Opposition parties, as well as a good number of well-known economists in the country, had then warned that, far from resolving the IMF loan would worsen the situation. That is exactly what has happened. The post-IMF loan years of Indira Gandhi and the 5 years of her son as Prime Minister have worsened the economic situation in the country and its foreign economic relations to the extent that the Narasimha Rao Government has today to seek a far bigger IMF loan with far more stringent condition-alities than earlier.

The question, therefore, arises whether the earlier model, originally adopted by Jawaharlal Nehru in the 50s was better. The superficial answer to this question would be that it was far better: not only did it lead to relatively rapid industrialisation but, compared to the present model, there was far greater freedom from the foreign imperialist bondage and far greater amount of social control over Indian capitalists. Foreign capital was not allowed free entry into the entire field of Indian industry, while the process of turning a handful of Indian industrialists into monopolists was curbed. That was why 'protectionism", together with the state sector industrial units in the Nehru model, became the targets of attack from the Indian and foreign capitalist circles.

The Nehru model, however, had its weak point in its failure to adopt radical land reform measures as key to the rapid development of the country's economy, social life and culture. We, Marxist-Leninists, have always pointed out that radical land reforms do not constitute a purely economic measures, though its economic implication is extremely important. Radical agrarian reforms are calculated to emancipate all aspects of social life—polity, family relations, education, culture and so on—from the iron grip or feudal and capitalist class domination in the entire gamut of socio-cultural and political life. Together with the emancipation of the peasants, agricultural labourers and other sections of the rural poor from economic exploitation, agrarian reforms lay a sound basis for political democracy, social emancipation and cultural advance.

This, however, requires an all-sided attack on the rural gentry which was unthinkable for the social democratic liberal, Jawaharlal Nehru. The agrarian reforms carried out under his leadership did not amount to more than the ending of the most obnoxious forms of feudal exploitation (zamindari and its various forms). Feudal landlords were allowed to transform themselves into modern landlords resorting to capitalist methods of exploitation through wage labour. The bulk of the rural masses continued to remain subjected to the exploitation of the old feudal landlords turned capitalist landlords. A handful of rich peasants also grew from the former tenant class. The old-type money-lenders who transformed themselves into the owners of modern banks, whole-sale merchants who paid less to the peasants for their produce while they charged high prices for the peasants production and consumption goods—these dominated rural society after the Nehru "land reforms". Over and above all this was the force of the capitalist market, ultimately controlled by imperialist capital.

The failure of the Nehru model to put an end to the feudal-capitalist exploitation of the peasantry (who constitute 70-80 per cent of the population) meant that the internal market could not be so developed as to ensure a steady growth of small, medium and large scale industry. It also meant that the mass of rural people could not save a portion of their annual income so that it could be used as the nation's productive capital. This continued exploitation of the rural masses also meant that the millions of people who could form the basis of a vibrant political democracy could not be developed in that direction. Above all, the continued grip of the rural gentry on the rural poor meant that a handful of them (the rural gentry) could resort to organised and brutal atrocities on the weaker sections of the society—the Scheduled Castes, the scheduled Tribes, the other backward classes, the religious communities, the women, etc. Here, therefore, was the basis for that all round socio-political crisis in the country in its various forms and manifestations which has continued since the last years of the Nehru era.

There is therefore, no question of merely going back to the Nehru model, that model itself has to be re-shaped. Revolutionary changes in the agrarian relations should be considered the axis on which all round development of the nation can be organised. This, however, will have to be supplemented by a programme of self-reliance which will give up all ideas of relying on foreign multi-nationals for technological and financial help in modernising the economy.

The spirit of Swadeshi, widespread in the years of a freedom struggle, has to be revived. The talents of our own intelligentsia should be relied upon and developed for the indigenous development of science and technology to which of course has to be added technological and other assistance from any foreign country which is prepared to provide it on honourable terms. Surrendering to the foreign multi-nationals and their institutional agencies like the World Bank and the IMF has to be ended. On the basis of such a policy of self-reliance, business relations can be established with such countries as are prepared to provide assistance on acceptable terms.

RE-THINKING DEVELOPMENT

Kamal A. Mitra Chenoy

A CRITIQUE

R. C. Dutt

In his paper, "Re-thinking Development", Kamal Mitra A. Chenoy has focused attention on the current wave which threatens to drown concepts like equity and sustainability, associated with non-capitalist development, with the triumphal re-assertion of private initiative and of "the magic of the market". The focus is timely if it were only to show that the wave is ephemeral. As Chenoy has rightly pointed out ".... imperialism (in a new form) and the contradictions of the world economy remain".

The Capitalist Wave

There is indeed no finality, or even long-term stability, about this wave. It is based on nothing more substantial than the failure of a particular model of development which Chenoy (in his last paragraph) refuses even to regard as "Socialist". The fact is that a similar wave, though in a different direction, had appeared six decades ago when the Great Depression had been widely regarded as a demonstrable proof of the failure of capitalism. The only alternative model then available was the Soviet model which was based on the recently launched Five-Year Plans. The wave then swept thousands, if not millions, as uncritically into the Soviet fold as the wave to-day threatens to sweep them back into the folds of capitalism.

The danger of this ebb and flow of tides is that while it cannot drown reality it drowns rationality. Socialism arose out of perceived weaknesses of capitalism. While some of these weaknesses, such as exploitation of workers associated with early capitalism, and the neglect of the weak, were cured in mature capitalism by a more enlightened view of the workers' efficiency and by a measure of welfarism, other weaknesses inherent in capitalism remained. The main weakness inherent in capitalism is that its progress is dependent on private initiative, which in its turn is based on private profit as its motive force. Private profit does not, however, always, in fact does not often, coincide with the good of the community, or in the larger context with the good of the world. This is the principal contradiction of capitalism, and as long as this contradiction continues the search for an alternative order, referred to as socialism, will continue. The failure of a particular model of development, as has now happened, does not end this search and make a reversion to capitalism inevitable, just as failure of fascism in Europe did not dry up the springs of capitalism and lead to the universal adoption of socialism. In either instance the failure of a model imparts a temporary impulse to the alternative model, but the impulse fades away as the realities of life assert themselves.

The Alternative Path

Kamal Chenoy has dwelt on the contradictions of capitalism and has shown how historically the path followed by capitalism is no longer open to developing countries. It is, therefore, not necessary to dilate on this aspect. In re-thinking development, however, it is not sufficient to negate the capitalist path. It is equally necessary to indicate the parameters of an alternative path, especially because an alternative path, hitherto acclaimed as the socialist path, has failed. Failure to do so can only lend support to those who proclaim that whatever the deficiencies of capitalism, there is really no alternative to it. It is to fill this lacuna that the rest of this critique is devoted.

Contradiction of Capitalism

The principal contradiction of capitalism, as has been noted, arises out of the fact that resource utilisation in a community is determined by prospects of profit as signalled by the market. The market signal, it is claimed, reflects the free choice of the consumers. So it does, but only on the assumption that the purchasing power in the hands of the consumers is equal, or at least near equal. Where it is not, and where, on the other hand, the disparities of income distribution arc acute, the market acting on effective and not on actual demand sends out wrong signals. In India, for instance, where more than 300 millions do not have enough purchasing power to buy food sufficient for their nutritional requirements, the effective market demand for say an extra metre of cloth, reflects not the real demand for cloth but merely the fact that large numbers of people cannot afford to buy it. Going by market signals, therefore, the available resources are utilised not to manufacture more cloth, but to manufacture perhaps four-wheel or two-wheel automobiles which are in demand from the section of the population who can afford to pay for them.

Market signals are particularly weak, and in fact unreliable, when they relate to infrastructural needs, and even more so for investments on human resources, such as education, health and sanitation. These promise no immediate return, and do not, therefore, attract resources through the market. And yet, they are essential for national development, if development is to be based on social justice and to cater to human rights in the broader sense, that is, if such rights are to include not only right to life and personal liberty, but also freedom from want, as also right to income in proportion to the quality of work performed.

State Intervention

State intervention is, therefore, necessary, more so, for a more economically backward country as greater is the prevailing inequality among its people. Such State intervention has been generally accepted since the thirties with the theoretical backing of Keynesianism and the practical steps taken by President Roosevelt in his new deal. The only dissent now comes from the World Bank and the IMF whose objectives are suspect on that account. They appear to be interested not so much in the development of the underdeveloped countries as in their integration with the global capitalist system so that they might continue to supply cheap raw-materials to the developed countries, provide opportunities for the investment of their surplus capital, and markets for their finished products.

Welfarism has also been accepted as a form of progressive capitalism, as in the Nordic countries of Europe, though voices are sometimes raised against this system too, as wasteful and an incentive to laziness. The main weakness of welfarism, however, is that it is not an integral part of the productive system but an optional adjunct to it. As such it is subject to cuts, as was demonstrated during the recession in the early eighties.

Planned Development

The essence of an alternative non-capitalist path of development, call it socialism or by any other name, is planned development where market can still be a useful index, but is not the guide to productive effort. The concept of "social good" takes the place of the market, and forms the basis of planning. There is, however, a danger in this procedure, for "social good" is not a precise concept. It can be interpreted in a variety of ways, and when decisions are taken on this basis by a comparatively small group of persons, alienated from the persons for whose good the decisions are purported to be taken, problems arise. Indeed, it was this alienation which resulted in what came to be known as command economy and wrecked the Soviet system.

Not only democracy but decentralised, participative democracy, therefore, is of the essence of planned development. This is especially so when development reaches the stage in which consumption, instead of being dictated by the very needs of existence, becomes a matter of choice. At this stage the market has a limited role to play, but planning continues to be paramount. It is still for the planners to decide whose needs are to be met—for society as a whole in such matters as security, capital accumulation et al. or for certain sections of society or groups of individuals. It is still for the planners to decide what priorities should be attached to each of these sets of needs.

The Public Sector

Planned priorities can be and often are supported by appropriate fiscal policies. There is nothing wrong in doing so, but fiscal policies have their limitations. The incentives and disincentives they provide function within certain limits. In situations of serious disparities in income distribution where the gap between real need and effective market demand is wide such fiscal incentives are powerless. In such situations there is no alternative to the public sector acting as the main vehicle of planning. This is so because the public sector alone can function without considerations of profit, the only limitation being the extent to which the State can and should appropriately subsidise demands.

The public sector serves another very useful purpose in the process of development. It is a matter of common experience that those who own means of production acquire considerable influence over the State. This happens for a variety of reasons not excluding the corrupting influence which wealth and money bring with them. Even apart from that, the owners of the means of production take hundreds of decisions every day regarding investment, employment et. al. which effect the lives of the people. It is for this reason that the Directive Principles of our Constitution warn us against concentration of wealth and economic power in private hands. Nevertheless, as experience has shown a tendency towards increased concentration is inevitable in the capitalist process of development. This can be restrained only by a judicious use of the public sector.

International Economic Relations

Turning to international economic relations, a good deal is being said about globalisation of the Indian economy in order to benefit by the comparative advantages of the international division of labour. It is overlooked that this concept of "comparative advantage", derived from classical economics, is a chimera in the real world, and that the prosperity of the advanced capitalist countries is based on a disproportionate consumption of the world's resources, by denying them to the weaker countries. The New International Economic Order (NIEO), which the developing countries have been sponsoring for the last two decades to provide a basis for fair international competition, has been repeatedly turned down by developed countries without even a serious discussion. In the circumstances, "globalisation", or opening "India's Womb", as Asoka Mehta once put it, to large scale foreign investments, including investments by powerful trans-nationals, would amount to opting for a subordinate role in the world capitalist system. The only way open to developing countries, including India, is to develop sufficient economic strength of their own to bargain for a better international economic order. This means self-reliance, for no country dependent on others can bargain for themselves on equal terms. It does not, however, mean, as it is sometimes wrongly criticised, autocracy. It is only a country which is basically self-reliant that can enter into mutually advantageous international trade.

Conclusion

Nothing that has happened during the last two years in the Soviet Union or in East Europe has either resolved the basic contradictions of capitalism, or rendered invalid the parameters of an alternative path of development. The failure of the Soviet model has been largely attributed to the fact that it denied democracy. To a large extent this is true, for alienation of the rulers from the people not only distorted policy-frames but encouraged corruption and elitism among the former, which became intolerable in a world of growing democratic consciousness. By the same token, however, capitalism with its Darwinian undertone of survival of the fittest and "Devil take the hindmost" is hardly the appropriate answer, especially in poor, under-developed countries where large proportions of the population are too weak to join the race for survival. The resurgence of capitalism has already led to growing unemployment, poorer social services, and even more dangerously to ethnic chauvinism, religious fundamentalism and in Germany to racialism, reminiscent of Nazi-ism. These are not ailments that can be cured by parliamentary democracy and by assured personal human rights as long as sizeable proportions of the population are too poor, weak and ignorant to take advantage of these rights. As Mahatma Gandhi had said that even God had to appear before the poor in the form of food.

Socialist humanism based on a wider concept of human rights than those assured only in law is as relevant today as it was earlier, if democracy is to be real and vibrant. Denial of democracy in the name of class struggle was indeed a grave error for which the socialist movement has paid heavily. It was an error committed in spite of stalwarts like Rosa Luxemberg having warned the movement against it. That should not, however, blind us to the basic humanism of the socialist movement which alone holds promise of a better tomorrow for the starving millions.

DEVELOPMENT PARADIGMS : SOME CONCEPTUAL CLARIFICATIONS

Dr. Paulose Mar Gregorios

Theoretical discussions on development paradigms seldom go deep enough. The discussion is usually about such important major factors as governmental control versus liberalisation, proportion of mix between public sector and private sector, free market economy versus socialism etc. The concept of development itself is taken for granted. One can make distinctions between economic development and cultural or spiritual development, or between one paradigm of development and another, but in all cases the concept of development itself is assumed without question.

Even those who argue for alternate paradigms of development or talk about 'another development' or 'development alternatives' do not feel the need to question the very concept of development. This paper wants, among other things, to raise some of the questions involved in the very notion of development.

Development is an English word, and has its own etymological and praxiological history. It seems to arise in the European languages at about the same time, that is, with the Industrial Revolution in Europe. German "*Entwicklung*', French

'Development' and Spanish "Desarrollo" as currently used, go back to the 17th and 18th centuries. But even then it did not have the connotation we have now given it in the last half century or so. The classical meaning of 'develop' is in contrast with the word 'envelop'; to envelop is to pack-up and conceal; to develop is to unpack and reveal.

We, in India, have chosen *Vikas* as the Sanskrit or Hindi equivalent, but we also have no pre-capitalist tradition of using that work in the sense of social or economic development. In fact I could not find the word *Vikas* in my Concordance to the Principal Upanishads and the Bhagavadgita. Our Vedic hymns do speak of a cosmic order, but they did not conceive of a process in which human beings are the actual developers. Their notion was best expressed in the following hymn:

> "May Heaven and Earth, honey-dropping, honey-dispensing, honey-rivered, rain down honey for us, bringing unto the gods sacrifice and wealth, and for us great glory, reward and heroic strength.
>
> "May Heaven and Earth swell our nourishment, the two who are father and mother, all-knowing, doing wondrous work .... bringing to us gain, reward and riches."
>
> Rg. Veda 6.70

The idea here is not that of human beings engaging in a corporate programme of developing nature, but rather of offering sacrifices and propitiating the gods in order that fame and gain, power and glory, wealth and children, comfort and welfare, can be secured. But even the gods have to receive their fulfilment from others sacrifices.

We do, however, find an idea of development in the Vedas, but it is a natural process arising out of the *tapas* of Prajapati, rather than the consequence of human efforts to develop the world. Though we do not find the word *vikasa* used for the process, the *brahmanda* or the cosmic egg has to 'hatch'. The *brahmanda* concept seems to be later in rising than the more intriguing concept of *hiranyagarbha* (Rg. X : 121) or the 'golden womb', from which all powers and existences proceed and come forth. The effective source of development here is not human plans, programmes and actions, but the fertile and creative womb of reality itself.

The other notion of development in our ancient tradition is found in the Sankhya concept of *Purusha* whose very proximity creates new agitations and development in *Prakrti*. But this is not again a notion of human beings acting corporately on *Prakrti* to develop it. It seems more likely that *purusha* represents the cosmic consciousness rather than the individual agent. *Purusha* is not subject-object consciousness, which comes from *buddhi*, which is part of *prakrti; purusha* itself is non-agent, non-enjoyer. *Purusha* in the Sankhya does not do or act. Especially in the Purushasukta of the Rgveda (X.90), *Purusha*, the thousand-headed, thousand-eyed Man is the whole of manifest reality, the All. He is not a worker or developer in our sense of the word, but the primordial man whom the gods sacrificed in order to produce everything. It is sacrifice, not technology, that creates development as unfolding, for humans as for gods.

The point is simply this, that the very concept of *vikas* as the result of human impact and operation on prakrti is not a traditional Indian notion, but comes directly from the European civilisation of the Industrial Revolution and the eighteenth century rationalist enlightenment.

Even when we come to the *Arthasastra*, the four *purusharthas* should not be confused with the goals of modern development. We often forget that the first *artha* is *Dharma* and the last is *Moksha*. The other two *arthas*, namely material gain or commodity production (*artha* proper), and *kama* or pleasure and physical, cultural and other satisfactions, are interposed between *dharma* and *moksha*. (The word *Artha* is here used in two senses : for the four goals in general and for the particular goal of material gain or commodity production).

The four are inseparable : it is not possible to pursue in isolation the goals of *artha* and *kama*, unless such pursuit is based on *dharma*, and has as its ultimate goal liberation or *mukti*.

As the Mahabharata puts it :

"With uplifted arms I cry, none heeds : from dharma, *artha* and *kama* flow; then why is not *dharma* pursued ? Neither for the sake of pleasure, nor out of fear or avarice, no, not even for the sake of one's life should one give up *dharma*; *dharma* alone stands for all time : Pleasure and pain come and go."

In Rgveda 5.63.7 we are told :

> "You, Mitra and Varuna, through the creative powers of the gods, protect the ceremonial discipline (vrata) with actions which uphold the world (*dharma*). Through the cosmic order (*rta*) you rule over the whole universe. You placed the Sun in the heavens, like a shining chariot."

It is easy to smile at the naivete of our ancient forbears who did not think the way we do. But they actually believed that the cosmic order or *rta* was the dynamic reality that kept the world going. They also knew that gods and humans could disrupt this cosmic order by their evil actions which introduced *antra* or disorder into this cosmic order. They lacked that sanguineness which characterises modern secular man with his vision of the world in which humanity and the world stood to each other as agent and lord on the one hand and on the other a world composed of energy and resources to be manipulated at will.

Mahatma Gandhi was one of the few who based his life on the assumption that the foundation of reality was *satya,* which in fact is synonymous with *rta. Satya* or *Rta* as reality is the fundamental meaning of *dharma,* that spiritual order which undergirds reality, to violate which is to invite ruin. *Dharma* not only holds things up it holds them together. In fact *dharma* seems to be a word synonymous with *rta* and to have replaced the latter in the Indian tradition. Buddhist, Jain and Hindu. Just a few sample quotations :

Mahabharata : 12.110.10-11. "In order to promote strength and efficacy among beings the *dharma* is declared. Dharma means what is accompanied by ahimsa. Such is the tradition which cannot be moved, *Dharma* is known by that name because it can hold the world up. It is by *dharma* that people too are sustained in their various vocations."

Manusmrti : 8.15. "*Dharma*, when violated, verily destroys; *dharma* when maintained, maintains. So never violate *dharma*; such violation will destroy us."

Taittiriya Aranyaka : 10.79. "Dharma is the foundation of the whole universe. In our world people go for advice and guidance to one best versed in *dharma*. By *dharma* one drives away evil. Upon *dharma* everything is founded. Therefore *dharma* is called the highest good."

In our tradition, *rta, satya* and *dharma* are practically synonymous; everything, including development as we conceive it, depends on *rta-satya-dharma* as the enabling framework. This framework is both metaphysical or ontological, and morally significant, but should not be confused with the various religions (wrongly called *dharmas*) or moral laws, often wrongly used as the equivalent of *dharma*. Morality, as a set of rules or as a corpus of values, would not be *dharma*. When we talk about value education and promotion of moral values in our society we have already deserted from our authentic tradition.

The problem is with our formative, fundamental understanding of the nature of reality itself. The western notion of development comes from a vision of reality where reality is one that is consciously or unconsciously held by the vast majority of our educated elite, since it is an integral and basic aspect of modern western-style education. My own questioning of the notion of development comes out of this perception that there is something wrong with the world view inculcated in me through many years of western-style education.

The secularism which many people preach today as anti-dote to communalism and as the way to keep out nation together, comes out of this western world-view, which holds that human beings and the rest of 'nature' are the only two realities which exist, and that the former can shape themselves and the surrounding reality by simply finding out the laws of nature's functioning (science) and the tools for manipulating it (technology), and then going into planning to achieve targets and goals.

These assumptions are based on false premises and go counter to our own tradition, which wants to keep the four goals in one integral framework. In fact the western liberal notion of development stands on extremely flimsy philosophical ground, though it has many achievements to its credit. Even secularism, if it is the ideology that undergirds the western liberal notion of development, has been very unsatisfactorily set forth as a philosophical system with some consistency and ground reliability.

The Marxist notion of development is more consistent and better philosophically grounded than western liberalism. Marxists see Development as a law-governed process in nature itself; human developmental activity is secondary and ancillary to the larger process : "Development occurs in the form of a spiral, in the unity and conflict of opposites, as transition of quantity into quality and vice versa. Each separate process of development (organic, economic, cultural etc.,) has stages, those of preparation of the premises for its formation. ... emergence, Development proper, death, decay of the process. (Dictionary of Philosophy, Moscow, Progress, 1984, sub voce 'Development', p. 105)

The Marxist vision, which few Marxists seem to have grasped, is close to the Indian tradition, in that it recognises a *rta* inherent in the universe, and sees human activity as co-ordinated with it or violating it. I am not suggesting that in actual practice Marxist governments and parties have acted on the original theoretical basis of Marxism. But the theoretical vision of Development in Marxism is certainly closer to our own authentic tradition (which also has often, in our history, been ignored or set aside by ruling groups and individuals). One can question the Hegelian understanding of the cosmic order which Marxism followed, but the fact of a cosmic order within which alone development is possible should interest us, and not be discarded as fantasy or superstition.

Secularism, as interpreted by Western liberalism, is incapable of doing justice to any notion of a cosmic order beyond the 'natural laws' of modern science; while the same secularism as interpreted in Marxist thought, does recognise such a cosmic order, not as transcendent but as immanent dialectical laws of development inherent in both nature and history. This should give us pause in our own reflection in India on the Development paradigm which we must develop in the context of our present situation.

This is the fundamental cleavage in paradigms of development. Once you embrace the western secular framework of reality, it becomes possible to conceive the human subject as primarily knower and agent, and thus to assume that development is a matter of applying science/technology to our surrounding reality. The assumption is that by science one knows and by technology one acts. By promoting science and technology, modern man believes, one naturally promotes development. This seems to have been Nehru's view as well.

It is necessary for us to have some grasp of how this western notion arose with the industrial epoch. Hegel was perhaps the first to tell us in recent times that reality was basically the absolute idea in process of dialectical development. The notion of development is central to Hegel's vision of totality. What we experience as world history, according to Hegel, is the working out of the Absolute Idea from potentiality into actuality, the undeveloped or unmanifest growing to become more developed and thus more manifest, until it generates its opposite and enters into dialectical interaction with it.

Both in his lectures on the philosophy of history and in his lectures on the History of philosophy, he explains his understanding of *Entwicklung* of Development as reality in process. He himself asks the question : "What is it that develops ?" (Was *antwickelt* sich ? *Gesch. Phil. I* : 42) and answers development has no content, that it is a formal reality (*Entwicklung ist formelle Taetigkeit, ohne Inhalt*). The content or subject of Development is reality itself as idea. As Hegel puts it in the Encyclopaedia (*Enzyklopaedie der philosophischen Wissenschaften-I.161 Zusatz*) Development is the forward movement of the idea as it struggles from potentiality to actuality through dialectical development.

But even in Hegel, it is history as process that is the main actor, not human beings organised as state or society. We make three big mistakes on our contemporary understanding of Development :

One, in thinking that development is fundamentally a human activity, initiated and run through by humans, without regard to categories like justice, peace, human dignity, identity and creativity, the unity of humanity etc. and not as a process controlled from elsewhere on a *dharmic* basis, in which human beings can be only privileged partners; two, in assuming that the principal agent in that human activity is the State which does all the planning, funding and execution; and three, in choosing the most vulgar criteria like growth in volume of commodities produced, increase or decrease of GNP, trade and foreign currency balances, rather than growth in the quality of life and of human relations, in justice and integrity, in promoting freedom, dignity and community, for assessing development.

An adequate paradigm for development for our time will have to take into account patterns which we do hastily reject, as for example, the Gandhian design. We need not merely criticise our present paradigms of development in terms of the three mistakes listed above, but also begin the process of creating new designs for development which from the beginning seek to eliminate the above three errors. For that too, we should not wait for the State to take the initiative.

RE-THINKING DEVELOPMENT

Kamal A. Mitra Chenoy

POLITICAL AND SOCIAL ASPECTS OF DEVELOPMENT

Arun Ghosh

While agreeing with much of what Kamal Chenoy has stated in his paper "Rethinking Development", I would like to focus on the objective situation in India, and dwell on the issues that face us in the context of the present debate.

There is no doubt that unfortunately, in India, the outlay on development planning has been high-jacked, particularly in the past two decades, by the affluent sections of the population. In fact, it is a combination of the landed gentry, the rising class of traders and industrial entrepreneurs (and the politicians who depend on their financing for getting elected), and of late the senior bureaucrats—who by and large come from the classes indicated above—that has managed the affairs of the nation over the past decades in a manner which, over the years, has aggravated the inequalities in income and wealth which we had inherited from the days of British rule.

A major pre-condition of the success of a "market economy"

is a reasonably equitable distribution of income. When we talk of the "market" in India, what is the market ? What is the size of the market ? And what are the forces dominating market demand? In fact, if we are facing a crisis of unprecedented proportions today, both in terms of imbalance between domestic demand and supply and of imbalance between imports and exports, it is essentially because : (a) Government revenue collection, particularly by way of direct taxes, has lagged seriously behind Government expenditure; (b) much of the Government expenditure has gone to increase the unequal distribution of income; and (c) Government trade and industrial policies have reinforced the same trends. In the decade of the eighties particularly, the pattern of industrial growth in the country was import intensive, and patterned to meet the growing demand for elitist consumer goods of some 10 to 15 per cent of the population.

The reasons for this pattern of development are threefold. First, we never had a proper land reform (except in Kerala and West Bengal); and while economic experts both abroad and at home urge us to follow the example of Japan, South Korea, Taiwan, they forget that all these countries started with land reform, and, therefore, with a reasonably egalitarian distribution of income. Secondly, all these countries also started with a primary focus on education, on raising the awareness and skills of the population. We in India have paid lip service to compulsory primary education for all children; indeed, even as of February 1991, fully 48 per cent of the population above the age of seven was totally illiterate. The incidence of illiteracy among women, particularly in rural areas and more particularly among those belonging to the scheduled castes and scheduled tribes, is appalling; lack of education and of skills has, therefore, been a major factor behind India's continued under-development, low productivity, and a high rate of population growth.

Finally, there is a third ominous development in India which is essentially political: the increasing centralisation of all authority and financial powers, with the result that over the years, the States have been rendered vassals (with begging bowls) to the power centre at Delhi. The centralisation process has in fact led to the Constitution being subverted, with the Centre assuming powers over subjects clearly earmarked as State subjects under the Constitution. It is unnecessary here to go into details of how this centralisation has been actually achieved and how this process has led to a paralysis of decision making by people (at local levels), and to a parody of the "market friendly" approach preached by the exponents of World Bank, IMF thinking.

In questioning the extant pattern of development being pursued in India, one needs to ask the following questions :

(a) Is the present pattern of development "sustainable" either politically or socially or even economically? Kamal Chenoy has rightly queried the sustainability of the present development pattern in the world as a whole. I would like to focus on the question of "sustainability" of the present pattern of development in India. Even from the limited point of view of economic viability, can we sustain a demand for oil products exceeding 100 million tonnes by the turn of the century ? This, when we have not been able to supply even the limited fuel requirements of vast numbers of rural people ?

(b) More importantly, can we ignore the increasing social tensions arising from the present pattern of development? The diverse "separatist" tendencies that we witness today are a direct result of wrong economic and political policies adopted in the past, and of the process of centralisation. Do we want a "market friendly" approach where "Special Protection Guards" have to accompany every individual who holds (or has held) political office of any kind, and their families ?

The answer to India's problems, therefore, lies in a restructuring of our political and social fabric. If we are to remain a democratic state, we must decentralise. And, this decentralisation process must start from the Centre, which should devolve authority and finances to the States, which should in turn devolve more authority and finances to locally elected panchayats and municipal bodies. The Panchayati Raj and Nagar Palika Bills can have meaning only if the Centre starts by shedding much of its power and authority.

The tragedy of life is that nobody want to shed power. It has to be wrested. If the political authorities are sensible, they would see the writing on the wall, and elect for a smooth transition, by "devolution" of power. That is the first need of the day, and that in itself can set off a wholly different, and indigenous pattern of development (through local area planning by the people themselves).

It is only when we empower the people that the process of deindustrialisation of the country, let loose recently, can be reversed. The two essential pre-requisites of such a reversal are: (a) employment (and a reasonable income) for all, and (b) a pattern of development based on mass demand.

There are many other elements to this broad pattern, which are in the domain of economic (and fiscal) policies. But these would follow somewhat automatically, provided the socio-political framework is right.

There is nothing wrong in a "market friendly" approach as long as the market is broad based, and as long as distortions by way of monopolistic control over production (or over marketed supplies) by a few does not exist.

As far back as January 1981, in a Conference on Poverty convened under the initiative of Tarlok Singh by the Indian Association of Social Science Institutions, Dr. B.K. Joshi (now Director of the Giri Institute of Development Studies at Lucknow) had stated that "poverty and under development cannot be understood except in the context of the social, political and economic structures and relations in which they are rooted. These structures and relations in most of the presently under developed societies, including India, have been shaped by their colonial past .... Further, to the extent the social, political and economic structures and relations characteristic of imperialist persist today, their impact on poverty and underdevelopment has also to be taken into account ... The explanation for poverty, and therefore its solution, lies .... (in) a radical shift in the distribution of power in Indian society ...." (See Tarlok Singh (Ed.) "Socio Science Research and

Problem of Poverty", Concept Publishing House, New Delhi, 1990). Alas, even though there is no overt imperialism today, covert imperialism is very much in evidence operated through international institutions set up and dominated by developed countries; and the only way we can avoid getting deeper into the quagmire of poverty and debt is by a *socio-political transformation* of the country.

What we need, therefore, is an understanding of the socio-political imperatives for India in the coming years. What we need is to release the energies of the entire population, and not give a monopoly of power and privileges to around 10 per cent of the population, who have thus far high-jacked all the benefits of development planning.

RE-THINKING DEVELOPMENT

Kamal A. Mitra Chenoy

A CRITIQUE

J. S. Bali

Prof. Chenoy's finding is that the current theories of market economy are nothing but resurrection of old notions, four centuries ago, of economic growth, free market and modernisation i.e. the magic of the market place, as if market has all the recipes to all economic problems.

I have not been able to understand his comment that the successes of Ronald Reagan and his successor, and of Margaret Thatcher and her successor have been short lived in nature. To me it seems that their achievements are continuing, though possibly at a lower pace, which could be attributed to several economic factors operating world-wide and not to the fragility of the principle of market economy which has been followed.

There can be no quarrel with the precept that the State should not take on the role of the trader or of commercial houses; therefore, the less the State intervenes in manufacture and trading activities like STC, steel and coal, etc. the better. The role of the State, should be to manage macro-economic policies, lay down priorities and be a watch dog.

The legitimacy of the public sector in our country was :

(a) Investment of the order of Rs. 250 crores in a steel mill in 1950s was just not forthcoming from the private sector.

(b) There was some angle of social benefits in PSUs.

(c) Undoubtedly, one of the main purpose of establishing a massive public sector and giving it commanding heights was that the public sector would be able to generate revenue surpluses which could support Government objectives and plans. Nothing of that sort has happened in 40 years though there has been mushroom growth of PSUs which are now perhaps nearly 300.

I am unable to comprehend the concept that the dynamics of current international economic order is based upon international capitalist imperialism. If there is some kind of imperialism it is because we, the Third World, have allowed it to happen. The Third World with its uncontrolled population expansion and growing crisis of commodity prices, a world in which several countries cannot even meet their food requirements cannot blame the West or G 7 or the World Bank for their performance. Even God helps those who help themselves. The Indian philosophy is also that one has to lift one's self with one's own efforts.

The pattern of mixed economy was the cause of our economic downfall. It resulted in massive corruption which is unabated. The political system has not only adjusted itself to this mixed economy but has fostered it. The largest single source of corruption is the electoral process.

Socialism is not dead and will never die, though communism may be dead. Mixed socialism practised by India has not delivered any results but pure socialism which is Communism practised by the Soviet Union and China has yielded results. I have no doubt in my mind that it is only socialism, if practised properly, which can bring about the basic developments of the human being in the field of education, employment, nutrition, housing, drinking water, etc. To achieve all these on massive scale as in India where population is nearly 90 crores, requires hard decisions. A soft state cannot deliver this. Once the basic needs have been universally met, the country and the society is on a firm footing to take off. At this stage, it is equally clear that the element of 'market', elements of competitiveness and efficiency will have to play their role in determining the levels of production and efficiency and prices. What I am pleading, therefore, is that there will always be scope for co-existence of socialistic pattern with market oriented economy, but Third World countries must not aim at the living standards or per capita income of the first world, nor make their high levels of consumerism and spending as the final aims of human beings.

We have achieved a great deal in the past 40 years despite conflicting ideologies. But the time has come now to take hard decisions. Undoubtedly we must firmly reject the imitative and derivative culture to copy the west without either having the means for it or the capacity. On saving the environment, i.e. environmental policy of the globe, my submission simply put is that unless population explosion is controlled, degradation of the land and desertification of the forest and damage to environment is bound to continue. I would have liked Prof. Chenoy to suggest new indices of development and growth. However, I am of the view that whereas indices such as per capita income, GNP, labour productivity etc. are required, indices like life expectancy, nutritional standards, foodgrains consumption per capita, infant mortality rate, education and literacy rates, availability of drinking water, rural sanitation etc. should also be included amongst the basic indices.

In the end I am not inclined to throw away the concept of 'market' provided we can use the market for giving us proper signals and directions to manage our economic growth. We have to learn to cut our coat according to available cloth, improve our quality of goods and manufacture and decrease costs by higher efficiency and competitiveness.

RE-THINKING DEVELOPMENT

Kamal A. Mitra Chenoy

A CRITIQUE

N. K. Seth

I am afraid I find the basic paper of Dr. Chenoy on 'Re-thinking Development' somewhat disappointing and confusing. It is full of vague statements and generalisations and its message is, unfortunately not very clear. He criticises the latest World Development Report for its 'neo-conservative ideas' and its conclusion that "A consensus is gradually forming in favour of a 'market friendly' approach to development", but he has no alternative to offer. He makes fun of Ronald Reagan as "the old hero of the American Westerns" and of Margaret Thatcher "as the Iron lady, heroine of the Falkland War."

Very few who have gone through the latest World Development Report will fully agree either with its analysis of the causes of economic stagnation in the developing countries, or with its prescription for the cure of economic malaise. But few will dare maintain that growth strategy based on centralised planning his succeeded, especially after the collapse of economies of Soviet Union and East European countries. If these countries which were until recently wedded to socialist model of growth have now consciously opted for free market economy, there must be valid reasons to do so. Market economy may not be a satisfactory answer for all the problems of developing countries but we must give it a try, especially when the "non-capitalist path of development" has failed and has infact aggravated the problems of poverty, unemployment and income disparities, which it sought to remove.

It is no good saying that socialism has not failed as the real true socialism was never practised. The world will have to go by the experience of the Soviet Union, where Communism or Socialism was actually practised. If the Stalinist version of Communism has collapsed the world has a right to conclude that the entire experiment in Communism/Socialism has failed as the world knew only one version of socialism i.e. the Stalinist version. It would, therefore, be extremely risky to try any modified socialist model of growth at this stage as it may prove more disastrous than the earlier one.

I am afraid Mr. Namboodiripad is completely out of step with the new world. I agree that land reforms are necessary but they are not a panacea for the economic ills of our country. I wonder which countries he has in mind who may be prepared to provide assistance to us on acceptable terms on the basis of a policy of self-reliance. Certainly no country of the erstwhile Communist World, including China, is in a position to help us. And we are in desperate need of funds in foreign exchange.

Mr. Dutt in his scholarly critique has tried to explain the rationale of having a planned economy in order to have control over production in a poor country in preference to allowing free play of market forces. The explanation is plausible, but he has to take note of the fact that inspite of all the controls, all the regulations and centralised planning, all these years, commodities of mass consumption have never been available to the poor at cheap prices. So what is the good of controls and centralised planning ?

RE-THINKING DEVELOPMENT

Kamal A. Mitra Chenoy

A CRITIQUE

A. K. Dasgupta

In the world today two trends are visible. The socialist systems, built on vigorous state intervention, are rapidly disappearing. This is one trend. The other trend is that the international bodies have started pressing vigorously the adoption of a market friendly approach to development in all countries which depend on aid and assistance from the developed countries. Shri Kamal Chenoy has made an examination of these two approaches—socialistic and market friendly—the focus of his paper. The paper leads generally to the conclusion that development in all societies in recent years should be traced to State intervention, and that, where development did not occur, notwithstanding strong State intervention, one should not relate the situation to failure of socialistic system but to uses of growth models involving parameters like per capita income, labour productivity, GNP etc., which are intrinsic to capitalistic theoretical frame. The conclusion is disarming to a large extent. Nevertheless, few issues might be raised from an altogether different angle.

India has used democracy to impose a very rigorous socialistic framework. Every part of our life is under public control. Central Planning touches on every aspect of socio-economic life. The Central Government determines what will be produced, how much will be produced, where these will be produced, what technology will be used, who will sell the products, how these will be sold and all related matters. Similarly the Government decides who will study in the schools and colleges, what they will study, how teaching will be organised and all related matters. The Central Government further decides what type of public health facilities will be provided, who will provide the facilities, how the facilities will be provided, who will avail the facilities and all related matters. It also decides the structure of social welfare programmes, public utilities, infrastructural facilities, the related technology and mode of delivery. It decides what to import and export, the agencies which will be involved, the methodology, the uses of imports and all related matters. It has also entered into civil affairs, civil laws, social relations and all such related matters.

The controls have been real, imposed through varieties of laws and regulations, and implemented by regular Government organisations, especially set up for the purpose. The parameters like per capita income, GNP, labour productivity, etc., mentioned in Shri Chenoy's paper have, at the most, been used for measuring the extent of success of the programmes; these were not relevant for formulation of different rules and regulations used for exercising controls.

Besides, the controls and plans, the degree of direct involvement of the Government in socio-economic affairs has also increased steadily over the years. In the areas of non-agricultural production, the share of the public sector is enormous. Majority of the schools and colleges, hospitals and establishments for social welfare are public bodies. In effect the socio-economic system that has resulted through controls and interventions by the Government is very very nearly the same as that which operated in fully socialist countries.

Internationally, it has also been a closed economy, with Government determining what should be imported, how much and for use of which establishments. Exports have been similarly regulated with all controls and interventions.

For the last 45 years, which is not a small period, this country has been one of the poorest in the world, regardless and of the indicators used for measurement of poverty, methodology used for determining the per cent of population below the poverty line etc. It is a very illiterate society; a very large proportion of the children die before attaining 5 years of age; a large proportion of the people, suffer and die from diseases like dysentry, gastric disorder, malaria and such other diseases which have disappeared from developed countries due to appropriate health care facilities; proportion of population in the slums of the urban areas, with beastly living conditions, is rising phenomally due to utter distress in the rural areas; proportion of the population working as daily casual workers, with very low wage, uncertain employment prospects, migratory living and consequent difficulties of family life, is increasing steadily; and most important of all is that one finds all around mostly ill fed, ill clad, emaciated, and sickly population, with dissatisfaction and un-happiness, written all over. The public services are deplorable; utilities in most part of the country are non-existent; elementary needs like drinking water, hygienic living conditions, reasonable educational facilities, are not fully met. The social and political relations are severely strained.

Thus, withcut regard to the theoretical justifications for this or that system of public organisations, a change is necessary, which might relate to the form of the organization or the approach or both.

Shri Chenoy might be right in suggesting that a socialistic system and a capitalistic system, both using similar parameters, might not be really different from each other. In fact, in terms of models used for describing the behaviour of the economics, the two systems of thought—capitalistic and socialistic are almost similar.

But there is one crucial area of distinction which is rarely emphasised. The subject of knowledge that might be called capitalistic economics, developed within the philosophical framework of individualism. Under this, individuals in Europe, distinguished from the kings and lords and barons and counts, for the first time received a social recognition and acquired a status; their rights and privileges were recognized; and most importantly, it was appreciated that only with total absence of interference by others, the finest human qualities and potentials in men could be expected to find realization. In Europe, this spirit of individualism overwhelmed all other institutions and the result was an unprecedented upsurge of development in all creative areas like arts, literature, science and technology. The structure of government and legal framework were also changed, in particular, the organisations under the government were focused to safeguarding the freedom of the individuals.

Market based economic ideas were also expressions of the same spirit of individualism in the economic sphere. Thus, the efficiency of the model of the economic system developed during this period was judged from the welfare side, taking account of the losses and benefits of the individuals participating in the process of production, distribution and exchange. The logic and the ideas employed in this evaluation and the results of the evaluation might be suspect, but not the framework of evaluation which was centered on individualism.

Suggestion of a competitive economy, as a framework within which economic activities might be conducted, followed from the same spirit of individualism. The belief was that should every one take economic decisions on the basis of his objective function and his constraints, the resultant could be most satisfactory for all. Ideas were developed which crystallized in the form of the body of capitalistic economic theories, proving the above belief. Again, one might suspect the logic, concepts and the parameters, but not the spirit which remained wholly individualistic.

The contrast of the above belief is the belief that the resultant of the free actions of all individuals is never satisfactory for all, and that a satisfactory resultant is only possible when a handful of persons plan the actions for all, and the individuals follow the dictates of this handful of persons, surrendering their rights of free action. The institution is feudalism, with the only change that the new generation of feudal lords could be expected to look after the interest of the serfs in a better way, with knowledge of socialist laws of history and economics, than the earlier generation of feudal lords, who were only self-servers.

I would like the issues raised by Mr. Chenoy judged within the above framework of the contrasting ideology presented above, and nothing else. I also think that the facts of history, rather than the laws of history, should be used as criteria for making the judgement.

Condition of life in India, with 45 years of guidance by a handful of people, has been noted earlier. One should not hold such a situation out as a justification for support of a belief that a system under guidance could deliver better results than a system governed by free action of individuals. It is, however, true that the modern generation of feudal lords do not legally own the properties as the earlier generation of feudal lords. But this legal aspect did not prevent this generation of lords acquire the benefits of over-lordship. In Soviet Russia the party bureaucrats and technocrats were one and the same, and the Community appropriated the most benefit in the society. In India, the ruling party, the bureaucrats and the technocrats and the professionals joined hands, and were the biggest beneficiaries of whatever development that occurred in the country.

It is true that sacrifice is the basis of growth so that if the current generation of feudal lords could not be expected to make sacrifices, others, i.e. serfs called people these days, must do so for the growth of the society. Some of our freedom fighters gave their lives. Those who survived the freedom struggle, died afterwards, with only a copper plate in return for their sacrifice. A generation of common people that followed the generation of freedom fighters, also died in abject poverty, making all the sacrifices for a better future. The prospects for the present generation are equally bleak, if similar guidance as in the past keeps on prevailing in the society.

With this evidence of history, therefore, one should prefer to rely on ones own capabilities and judgement, and insist correspondingly on a system of governance that might only make exercises of individual faculty, in whichever way it is sought, without violating similar claims by others, feasible and possible. It should be irrelevant whether the system is called capitalistic or individualistic or self-reliant, so long as the above condition is met.

Self-reliance is a term also used by interventionist governments, including India, and plans are made for making the economy self-reliant. It has only meant so far development of capacities for production of all kinds of goods within the country, and reduction of needs for import. It did not mean, on the other hand, development of human capabilities in the society in the best possible manner so that the society could be self-reliant, and all needs for knowledge and production capabilities could be met by the domestic population.

In a significant way, the above mentioned two interpretations of the term of self-reliance distinguish the two ideological frames—socialism and individualism. What has been observed historically is that the self-reliance of the latter sort is developed under systems built around individualism. It is also evident from Indian history that plans for developing self-reliance of the former sort increased the dependence of the country on other countries; as reflected in the huge external debt burden and needs for additional loans for servicing the debts.

An open competitive economy is a corollary of a system built around individualism. It is said that only the fit can survive in a competition. There should be no harm in such a system, so long as opportunities to become fit are open to all persons equally. Individualism with minimum state control, and maximum state support for infrastructure required for developing human capabilities, has succeeded in bringing about steady improvement in the quality of population in the countries, which in effect sustained the steady development of the economy and its competitive capability.

Mr. Chenoy seems to believe that planning and control, directed to achieve other ends than GNP related objectives, could be expected to produce miracles and relieve this country from the mess to which it has been subjected due to wrong choice of objectives. What he might have failed to realize is that it is not a part of the instinct of man, as a member of the animal group, to put the interest of others over his own. Thus everywhere, and at all times, men in authority, have used authority to help themselves primarily, and others incidentally. Things have not been different even in socialist states, and there could be no reason why it should be with men to guide the affairs.

Allowing individuals to run their own affairs, with only their interest in mind, is submission to law of nature with the hope of establishment of a parallel of ecological balance in human complex. In the animal world, notwithstanding the predatory behaviour of the animals, a proportional distribution of the animal species does emerge with growth of numbers, which is the measure of biological progress. In human society also a proportionality could be the most expected norm under natural conditions. In a way such is also realized. For example we find that in the market-based economies the share of wages in the national product has a tendency to remain constant, under conditions of vigorous economic growth, leading, in the process, to general rise of living standards.

RE-THINKING DEVELOPMENT

Kamal A. Mitra Chenoy

POLITICAL AND SOCIAL ASPECTS OF DEVELOPMENT : A SUPPLEMENTARY NOTE

Iqbal Narain

I have carefully gone through the paper entitled "Re-thinking Development" by Kamal A. Mitra Chenoy of Jawaharlal Nehru University, New Delhi. I have liked the paper and am inclined to agree with his major formulations. He has correctly argued, "In sum, therefore, a truly humane, sustainable model of development will have to be based on totally different indices and premises. It is surely high time that the task was more comprehensively attempted in this country." It, however, remains a fact that no alternative model has been developed now has the political and social aspects of development been discussed. There is still enough in this paper to show why the so called American model of development does not suit the countries of the Third World and in that lies the importance of the paper.

I may point out at the outset that the model prescribed by the World Bank, IMF, etc. is, in fact, Euro-centric, inclusive of the

USA. It is for this reason that Herb Addo talks of *Beyond Euro-Centricity Transformation and Transformational Responsibility* (1). Since the USA is, more or less, having the monopoly over the propagation of the model in the Third World today, it is correct to pin the model to USA in particular, and to western experience in general. It, however, remains a fact that the model cannot (in fact, should not) be replicated by the countries of the Third World. That the Third World can catch on the 'first' or the `second' world is the basic fallacy of the model which we should guard against in our pursuit of development. It is true that Japan and South Korea have done so but it does not necessarily follow that we would also succeed in copying the model. We should, therefore, think about development on an indigenous plane in the context of our own needs, though it is quite a tall order to execute.

We are specifically talking about India here though our musings may have some relevance for the Third World *per se*. To my way of thinking, Jawaharlal Nehru's vision, in spite of all its limitations, particularly in practice, is still relevant. It is unfortunate that the deviations of the vision began in the times of Indira Gandhi and Rajiv Gandhi. The process thus began is being completed now under Manmohan Singh. One may mention here in particular Jawaharlal Nehru's faith in self-reliance, which seems to be particularly in jeopardy today. Of course, he failed in land reforms, as EMS Namboodiripad has pointed out in his comments on Chenoy's paper. He also could not develop a work culture, specifically in public undertakings, as a result of which, they are in dock today. One may also like to attribute the fact of the rich becoming richer to Nehru's policies. He would still not like external exploitation of the country, and its resources, which is being forgotten completely today. Perhaps, Nehru's vision of development should incorporate Gandhi's views on limitations of human wants. In the words of Mahatma Gandhi, "our civilization, our culture, our swaraj depend not upon multiplying our wants—self-indulgence, but upon restricting our wants—self-denial"(2). It is a fact that Jawaharlal Nehru was influenced in good measure by the Russian experience which is being given up by Russia itself. We can, however, still retain in our country whatever we find relevant, though learning at the same time by the mistakes of the USSR. Though Nehru can best be described as a reluctant socialist[3], perhaps his model of mixed economy, as conceived broadly, is still relevant. Of course, we cannot compensate for the Russian might which was an anti-dote to the power and influence of USA and thereby provided an umbrella to the Third World countries. In short, I would thus urge upon the learned audience to correct—even supplement—wherever Jawaharlal Nehru was wrong instead of giving up his vision altogether.

Development is not merely an end value but also a means value. It is common knowledge that development is an important facet of a nation's life and this is more than clear from the fact that the extent of development is basic to the nomenclature of a country. We describe a country as either developed or developing or under-developed on this basis. But it should not be forgotten, particularly in the context of the countries of the Third World, that there is an over-arching consideration for which development is being viewed as the means. In the Indian context, for example, the Preamble to the Constitution mentions that justice, political, social and economic is the supreme end, and to this, development is to serve as the means. It is, therefore, necessary to find out whether the present view of development as pursued by our ruling elite is conducive to the concept of justice as postulated by the makers of our Constitution. If the answer is in the negative, there shall be a reason for having a second thought on the means and end relationship envisaged here, otherwise not.

As far as political dimensions of justice are concerned—and these, in fact, are to be viewed as political aspects of development also—a few can be mentioned here. The first and foremost among them all is the principle of universal adult franchise which means one vote being enjoyed by every adult in India, and this one vote carrying the same political weight. Secondly, it also means political participation, particularly in elections to the national legislature, State legislatures and local bodies. Thirdly, and it is a disputed point among the scholars—it also implies participation in the decision-making process in a vertical manner at all the levels, as already mentioned. Horizontally speaking, it means a share in planning, distribution of benefits, equal enjoyment of opportunities, equal pay for equal work, etc., if not having a right to work which would entitle the people to have comfortable living conditions. Of course, there is also the implication that people would enjoy fundamental rights, better known as human rights these days, inclusive of the rule of law. All these have been conferred on the citizens by the Constitution of India, and are more or less being enjoyed by them. These privileges will continue to be enjoyed by citizens in India so long as we have democracy in the country.

There is also the question of the regime which is most conducive to political dimensions of justice/development. It is becoming more and more obvious if we have a look at the experience of Yugoslavia and the Soviet Union that it is not enough to have the so-called cultural federation without an economic and political federation. One can perhaps propound here a theory of stages of growth following in the foot-steps of Rostow, and combining the experience of India, on the one hand, and that of the Soviet Union, Eastern Europe, on the other. We may begin immediately after liberation with a centralised federation and planning which gives predominance to the Centre. This may be possible if the country has a leadership of the national movement days, as we had in India, to begin with. This should, however, be followed by a second stage which should be there as soon as necessary. We should have by way of second stage a loose federation with enough autonomy to the States. This alone would preserve unity in diversity which has been the ideal in India since the days of Jawaharlal Nehru as the first Prime Minister of the country. We are, however, still at the first stage, by and large.

There is also a controversy on the issue whether there should be a presidential form of government or a parliamentary government under whose auspices the development of the country should take place. Whether we like it or not, in both these forms of government, elite would continue to dominate. It may, however be suggested that from the point of view of diffusion of participation even among elites and to a lesser extent among the common people, a parliamentary form of government is better than a presidential one because here people would participate politically to a much larger extent than perhaps it would be possible under a presidential form of government. They would be doing so either as ministers or as members of Parliament and State legislatures

This continues to be the view of most of the ruling elite today in the country.

Another facet of the political dimension relates to decentralisation of powers and authority, particularly to local bodies. It is a healthy sign that both Rajiv Gandhi and V.P. Singh thought of rejuvenating the urban and rural local bodies together and giving them both constitutional status and greater measure of powers. Rajiv Gandhi, however, adopted a bureaucratic approach and tried to reach the local bodies directly through the Chief Secretary, the Collector and his subordinates. V. P. Singh, however, followed the federal approach. He approached the State governments for rejuvenating local urban and rural institutions. A Bill is again on the anvil in the days of the present Narsimha Rao Government. It may be pointed out, however, that the political and bureaucratic elites have so far ensured that the local bodies do not have any substantial share of powers. It is, therefore, not a question whether the local bodies have failed. It could perhaps be argued that they have not been tried with faith and vigour, for the State governments are reluctant to decentralise powers further below them. There has thus to be a two-way decentralisation, one from the Central Government to the States, and the other from the State Governments to the local bodies. Unless this happens, decentralisation would remain just a ritual. It may also be pointed out that decentralisation should not be merely political-cum-administrative; it should also be financial and economic. Unless the local bodies enjoy powers of decentralised planning, with fiscal autonomy, decentralisation would remain unreal. This aspect of justice/development is still in the womb of the future.

As far as the social aspects of justice are concerned, which, again, may be taken as social aspects of development as well several questions arise in the Indian context. First, there is the issue of subsidies or reservations. It is an open question whether in a concept of development, which is marked by the market as the guiding force, it will be possible for the State to have enough elbow-room to provide for them. If the withdrawal of subsidies on fertilizers is an indication, the answer may be in the negative. We are too near to the issue of reservations and as such it may be difficult to opine on this in a dispassionate way. It, however, remains a fact that unless the scheduled castes and non-scheduled tribes enjoy equality of status and opportunity, they would not get prestige in the eyes of common men. Of course, it is also a fact that there are poor people even among the non-scheduled castes and scheduled tribes people and they should also get the benefit of concessions, if possible. The present Congress Government at the Centre is, therefore, combining the two.

Finally, we come to the economic aspects of justice/development. It is not enough to have more of exports or promptness in servicing of external loans or rise in GNP. All these are necessary facets but, more importantly, we have to think in terms of not having a consumerist culture of the western variety alone but also to swear by the Gandhian ideal of limited wants which may be combined with the doctrine of mixed economy, self-reliance, scientific temper and secularism of Jawaharlal Nehru. That perhaps can be treated as the beginning of the context of a new concept of development which is akin to our culture and needs as well.

One may, therefore, end up this supplementary note with a quotation from Rajni Kothari, who has visualised the alternative strategy of development in these words; "The basic thrust of the new approach came from an alternative conception of development which gives due regard to political and cultural factors as well as to alternative attitudes and values. It was stressed, for instance, that there can be no real autonomy or self-reliance without a measure of self-control; and unless there is restraint on the degree of competition, acquisitiveness and greed accompanying development, societies will always be subject to external forces. Similarly, unless some notion of restraint and even sacrifice is built into the thinking on development, the objective of collective self-reliance among Third World countries that are at different vantage points in their command over resources and skills will never be realised."(4)

References

(1) *Development as Social Transformation : Reflections in the Global Problematique*, The United Nations University, 1985, pp. 12-40.

(2) Quoted by R.K. Prabhu and U.R. Rao in *The Mind of Mahatma Gandhi*, Oxford University Press, 1945, p. 118.

(3) For details, See Amiya Rao and B.G. Rao: *Six Thousand Days*, New Delhi, Sterling Publishers Pvt. Ltd., 1974, pp. 4-23.

(4) Rajni Kothari : *Re-thinking Development: In Search of Humane Alternative*; Ajanta Publications, Delhi : 1988, p. 153.

RE-THINKING DEVELOPMENT

Kamal A. Mitra Chenoy

REINING THE IDEOLOGICAL HORSE—BY THE WHIP OF UTILITARIANISM

P. R. Brahmananda

Economics has its own terminology. Development in economics is interpreted as innovation and/or structural change in the proportions among different economic magnitude super imposed upon a basically unchanging commodity and factor growth scenario. A process of development implies sequential breaks and structural alterations in the circular flow of growth.

One simple interpretation of economic development is to perceive it as sustained capital accumulation plus continuous and discontinuous bursts of productivity growth.

Economic development autonomously or when spurred by planning with appropriate institutional changes must result in improvement in the well-being of all persons, or of the mass of the community constituting the majority, who did not enjoy the required well-being prior to development.

In technical economics, the results of economic development can be appraised along the lines of Paretian (after Pareto), or of social utilitarian calculus. If everyone's state of well-being is getting improved absolutely, or if those of some are getting improved while others remain where they are, the Pareto criterion is satisfied. If the well-being of the majority goes up, and of others goes down, the utilitarian calculus is satisfied.

The most important indicator of well-being is the consumption satisfaction. To this some would add producer satisfaction. Each individual is a consumer and also a producer. The net consumer's and producer's surpluses with respect to each individual must be going up according to Pareto. A weaker criterion is for some people's net consumer's and producer's surpluses to go up with those of none going down.

If broadly (a) the per capita consumption of essential wage-goods and of collective merit goods is going up, in a climate of free consumer choice, (b) the ratio of workers to population is going up in a state of free producer's choice, (c) if the real wages and work conditions of workers are going up, and (d) the per capita supplies of collectively supplied goods like education, health services, medical care, drinking water and sanitation facilities, social insurance, social security benefits, availability of public overheads and required infrastructure facilities, are all going up, economic development would have resulted in meaningful benefits to the mass of the people. The Pareto test would require that the development process should hurt none. What this means is that those who are adversely affected should be compensated so that there is implicit unanimous support for the development process.

In the utilitarian calculus development process may benefit the majority but hurt a few. Treating all individuals as equal, this calculus will place a premium on the majority getting improved. The compensation for the adversely affected is not mandatory. Since the poor constitute the majority, improvement in the lot of the poor in terms of the indicators mentioned earlier, would suffice for the utilitarian calculus. Re-distribution from the better to do are permitted here. The development process under a democracy without proportional representation, and under conditions of mass and widespread absolute poverty, and of shortage of resources, would surely tend to place a premium on the utilitarian culture.

If the developmental process leads to a higher rate of progress in (a) poverty eradication, (b) employment expansion, (c) improvement in work conditions, and (d) supplies of essential private and collective goods accessible to the poor, that process would be more strongly utilitarian than had the autonomous market process of change prevailed. Distributional changes required for the above would be sanctioned in the utilitarian calculus. Gandhiji's *Antyodaya* where improvements are inversely hierarchical from the bottom upwards is a special case of the utilitarian test with the marginal utility of income progressively falling with improvements in income.

The distinguished philosopher Rawls has formulated in essence the requirement of minimum essential goods for all as a necessary condition of social functioning in terms of social justice pre-ordained by a hypothetical social contract. In this view other primary goods can be safeguarded with this condition. Most economists would accept the Rawlsian condition though they may not all support the Gandhian *Antyodaya* standpoint. In a dynamic economy with growth the Rawlsian condition may imply that some minimal gains should continuously accrue to all to make the process socially just.

The peril of perfect uncertainty which Rawls assumes before social contract may as well lead to the Gandhian requirement of *Antyodaya*. There is no reason why only the Rawlsian version of social justice should be acceptable to all the stipulated assumption. The Gandhian Rule states simply that both productive improvements and distribution reforms must lend to inversely progressive gains from the bottom upwards. This leaves open the quantum of gains, that have accrued in the above manner. My submission is that the Gandhian Rule or test of social utilitarianism can be reconciled with the more general Rawlsian Rule.

Social utilitarianism is definitely opposed to the pursuit of Capitalism or Socialism or a mixed economy as an end in and by itself. It provides a yardstick or touchstone by which the isms can and have to be evaluated in a democratic set-up with periodic elections. In India *Nehru's* advisers, Nehru's followers etc., seem to have taken the progressive socialisation of the economy as being itself the yardstick of improvement in the people's living standards. Otherwise we cannot explain heavy industry for heavy industry, impcrt substitution for import substitution, nationalisation for nationalisation, unionisation for unionisation, self-reliance for self-reliance, autoarchy for autoarchy and such slogans. These different, complimentary goals had to be weighed in terms of their contribution to poverty eradication, employment-expansion, improvement in per captia wage-goods and collective consumption goods supply, efficiency of the production apparatus etc.

Judged from the four decades of development experience in India, the per capita consumption of essentials like foodgrains has grown at a rate only slightly above the population growth rate. The employment growth rate has been less than the population growth rate. Triple employment is far away. The poverty proportion in rural areas on a comparative, the Minhas basis, has been reduced only from slightly above 50 per cent to about 45 per cent or so. The poverty proportion in the urban areas, however, has fallen at a faster rate. Implicitly some urban bias has worked. The income-disparity, the wage-disparity, the consumption-disparity have all risen. But the overall conditions of work for the majority of the people has not improved much. The supplies of necessary per capita goods or wage-goods, have also improved only moderately. On a strong or weak utilitarian calculus, the Indian developmental process does not adequately satisfy the utilitarian test. The paradox is that the political process is characterised by democracy and adult franchise.

What does this connote ? Whatever the ideological system that has been in vogue in India, underlying the developmental process so far, it has missed the yard-stick of the people's well being. For the same reasons probably, socialism seems to have been rejected in Europe. Does this mean that the leaders in whom the people placed their faith did not keep the ultimate interests of the people in their minds ? The political process seems to have interpreted democracy only in political terms. What the leaders and their advisors thought was good for the people was probably not what the people thought was good for them.

Let us look at the developmental process from the Paretian yardstick. Over the last four decades we seem to have been having an average annual inflation rate of 7-8 per cent. There are hardly three or four years when prices have come down. We have, however, inflation—indexing of incomes only for 20 per cent of the work-force. The majority in rural areas are suffering from an imposed reduction in their basket of purchasing power. By what criterion can we term this process as socially just and as having been required by the models of development we have adopted? We know that inflation accrues from the twin causes of inadequate growth of wage-goods and of employment, and excessive growth rate of money supply. Can any socialist or left economist lay his hand on his heart and deny that the Indian developmental models, under whatever the political regime, have consciously underplayed provision for the growth rate of wage-goods and specially foodgrains and consciously overplayed the role of deficit causing inflation money supply. Had these two Himalayan errors been removed from the developmental process, probably the utilitarian test could have been satisfied and the weak Pareto test may also have been fulfilled. The economic development primarily ought to have the goal of people's well being, and the means or instrumentalities are adequate production and growth in wage-goods, and a satisfactory distribution, both under non-inflationary conditions. Rethinking development involves working towards the above.

Social utilitarianism, as said earlier, can be applied under capitalism, socialism or a mixed economy. It is theoretically neutral. But the socialists who perceive socialism as an end, irrespective of the material sufferings of the masses, have always hated social utilitarianism. Had the passion for socialism of the ruling class and their elite advisers in India imbibed, even on the grounds of compassion to the masses, with an equally ardent zeal for subjecting socialism to the touchstone of social utilitarianism there would have been probably less need for rethinking on Indian development.

Political scientists, particularly ideologists among them, are apt to place emphasis on participatory process, democratic process, decentralisation process, socialist process, capitalistic process, centralisation process, etc. The key idea here is 'process'. But economists emphasise the concrete effects/results of the processes; and these are in terms of measurable magnitudes/commodities and/or their monetary equivalences. These quantities are sifted to find out effects/results on well-being states *from an economic angle.* All processes, however inspired, have to be tested with reference broadly measurable quantities, ratios among them, and the changes in the above. The utilitarian calculus selects the magnitudes and their quantities with respect to measures of satisfaction attained by the citizens, empirically the respective merits of process have to satisfy the above test. If they do not do so, the ideologies and processes initiated by them will have failed the people in their economic aspirations.

In India we are now shifting to the market process primarily because the past processes have failed the people. We gave the previous processes and ideologies plenty of chances; let us now give the safety-neted market process. We did not cry wolf then; why cry wolf now.

RE-THINKING DEVELOPMENT

Kamal A. Mitra Chenoy

COMMENTS

P. D. Hajela

Dr. Chenoy's emphasis on a model of development which is humane, equitous and free from environmental and cultural degradation is well taken.

The issue is : which is that model and how precisely does current Indian social reality fit into that model ? Dr. Chenoy will not deny that attempts at some such model began to be made from day one of the post-independence era. Nehru gave the model in which democracy, socialism and secularism were to be integral parts of the same whole model. Of course, since a lot of un-Marxian stuff was thrown in, the Left wanted to back out of it. And now the Communist are making a mess of its secularism. The only part of the whole model which different groups have continued to hang on to, for various reasons, is democracy whose net advantage seems to be that, if it is not operated with the kind of inferiority complex and excessive intellectual dependence on the West have been so much in evidence in the country recently, it could have enabled us to rehabilitate the Nehru model, change it radically or build up a new one. However, the essence of the new model must again be the same, namely, integration of democracy, socialism and secularism into a single whole unit. But somehow for this to happen a high degree of intellectual self-reliance is necessary. We obviously cannot blame the West if we are ourselves so infirmly rooted in our social reality that even the slightest media wind from the West blows us off towards South Korea, Taiwan, Hongkong, Singapore, and we certainly, cannot blame them for pushing our own seats of higher learning in the country towards disaster.

The problem with the Nehru model was that it had no neat assumptions and analysis like the Marxian or Keynesian model of the mixed economy. But it was the best we had for a social reality that the Marxists and the mixed economists had to admit was too complex to be fitted into their own types, the Marxist type excluding private property, castes and political democracy, and mixed economy type, making the 'invisible hand' allocation of resources as primary with the State merely correcting contra-cyclical distortions. The Nehru model, on the other hand, had made the State the principal allocator of resources, and had accepted private property, to be utilised for social purposes.

Another problem for the model was that when economic expertise falling into either of the two "scientific" categories began to be asked to work out economic policies for implementing it, the Marxists thought that ownership of, meant production by the State was enough, and the mixed economists thought that adaptation here and there of the Keynesian monetary-fiscal policy mix was all that was required. Banks were nationalised just as money supply was expanded, and disproportionately large indirect taxes imposed. And at every stage there was euphoria. Now, more or less, the same experts are telling us that we have blundered; in fact so miserably that the Nehru model should be thrown into the dustbin of history. In such a background should one dare to ask whether it was the model which was at fault or the expertise which was pressed into service to work out the model ? If the Nehru model was "unscientific" for social reality, so would be the Western mixed economy model or the Marxist model sans political democracy and private property. Of course our quest for a humane model would go on. But it seems clear that it may be difficult for the World Bank and IMF to have as good an understanding of our social reality as we ourselves can have. Perhaps Nehru and Gandhi were no experts in the sense in which the so-called experts are, but they had a much better perception of our situation than our advisers from abroad.

The Nehru model had begun well with attempts to change the composition of output in favour of capital goods and infrastructure through the mechanics of planning. It also did well by stepping up the general rate of investment in the Indian economy and pushing that rate than what it might have been had it been left to free forces of the market. But it needed to go further, namely to change the pattern of consumer goods production in favour of basic goods, including food, drinking water, common man's clothing and shelter and transport, health, nutrition, education plus a less degraded environment, and since all this could not be done except through a drastic rearrangement of national priorities, both in terms of control of production as well as demand management, the model should have been extended in these directions as well. Somehow the planning in the name of the model gave the impression that once the capital goods and infrastructure sectors were in place, basic goods also would automatically follow. This could not happen because the raising of the aggregate investment rate created its own illusions. In the typically Keynesian manner, the assumption was made that once investment was taken care of, resources would be no problem, when in actual fact a continually rising ratio of planned investment to income could not go on without a serious resource crunch, both internally as well as externally, and without a sincere effort to raise resources through a massive attack on waste and consumerism.

It is true that resources have to be interpreted not merely as natural resources, but also as man-made resources where technology plays a crucial part. For the latter type of resources, integrating ourselves with the technological upsurge of the kind taking place in the West can certainly be of much advantage, but the question is whether this would be all that beneficial after all.

If after getting the technological resources, we cannot change the mix in favour of the basic good and we increase unemployment and inflation in the economy, what will be the advantage to the masses of India from such an integration ? Jacob Viner, a noted economist, had once said that economic development does not mean a rise in the per capita income : it means a rise in the per captia income of a vast majority of people. How will that occur with rising unemployment ? Further, what is the point in gaining through technology and losing through waste of our human resources ? That is why during the period of the Nehru model while science and technology were considered important, their adaptation to our resource endowments were also emphasised.

Thus we had a model which could with various improvements produce a just and humane social order—only if we could have held on to our convictions more firmly than, it now appears, we have been able to do.

DISCUSSIONS

I

Chairman Rasheeduddin Khan

Initiating the discussions, Prof. Khan remarked that the subject under consideration was very comprehensive. He pointed out that a considerable amount of new learning had emerged in recent years on the subject of development. In fact, since 1989 the basic assumptions of social science have undergone changes which only dogmatic adherence to old assumptions or mental inertia would refuse to recognise. These assumptions have to be re-examined, but re-examination did not necessarily mean refutation. It can also mean affirmation, but the nuances of that affirmation has to distinguish between what can be accepted and what has to be rejected. Monolithic assumptions, Prof. Khan stated, were invalid now.

Prof. Khan felt that the problem of development should be viewed in the historical context, for though history, and philosophy too, were not regarded as social sciences by hard core social scientists, they could not be excluded if social phenomenon were to be understood and a holistic view taken of human life.

In the historical background, Prof. Khan pointed out, the world after 1945 was entirely different from the world that had existed from the dawn of history. The post-1945 world, according to Prof. Khan, was marked by four major transformations. The first was that, notionally at any rate, war as an instrument of policy became obsolete. Despite the accumulation of arms that continued no one seriously believed that wars could further policy objectives. There was indeed not only an element of hypocrisy but of tragedy also in the situation in which considerable amounts of human wealth, skill and intelligence were spent on preparations for war.

Secondly, the formal, administrative and political colonial system had collapsed. A part of it had collapsed after the First World War, e.g., the Austro-Hungarian and Czarist empires, but after the Second World War, the colonies of even the victorious countries were freed. This in turn led to the abolition of the indigenous feudal and tribal systems in the erstwhile colonies. The post-1945 world thus witnessed liberation of mankind, where the rights of men were asserted, if not always implemented.*

The third change was the desire on the part of the decolonised countries constituting the Third World to catch up with the advanced countries at a time when in terms of investments, resources and technology the latter countries had advanced very far. The political doors were indeed open, but the economic linkages made the task of catching up very difficult. A new phenomenon, neo-capitalism, emerged in this context in a surreptitious manner, penetrating larger areas of collective life, especially with the information revolution, computerisation, knowledge, industry and cultural imperialism. This penetration in fact made the collapse of formal imperialism irrelevant by taking its place in a new form.

Neo-colonialism, Prof. Khan said, has multiple aspects, but three aspects of it should be kept in mind. They are (i) the globalisation of the world economy as envisaged by the Bretton Woods-GATT regime which had an edge towards advanced countries. The World Bank and IMF set up by this regime are not just exploitative institutions. They are commercial institutions which maintains the hegemony of the advanced countries while doling out negotiated loans to the Third World countries partly to avoid sharpening of global conflicts and partly to appear altruistic. (ii) The World Bank/IMF have been enormously expanded by the private commercial, financial institutions. The growth of the tertiary sector which now employs about 60 to 70 per cent of the manpower in advanced countries is a new postwar phenomenon. (iii) The third aspect is the growth of trans-national corporations with their global reach. Their function is to siphon off resources from Third World countries. The manner in which they have done so is well illustrated by the experience of the African countries.

Finally, the fourth feature of post-1945 transformation is that 120 odd decolonised countries do not constitute a homogenous group. India, for instance, is not yet another Third World country. In view of its size, population and resource endowments, India, and China too, can aspire for self-reliant development. This is not possible in many other Third World countries.

In this context, the basic problem of India is how India with its 5000 years of chronic unequal society could be transformed into a more or less egalitarian society. Neither the Left nor the Right, Prof. Khan said, had been able to work out a cohesive strategy of industrialisation. The Left, in his opinion, has overstated the ideal, the priorities and the objectives, but has not been able to suggest how these could be translated into operational skills.

Referring to the Soviet Union, Prof. Khan explained that one of the reasons for its collapse was the disproportionate concentration on security at the expense of development. In fact it was a diabolical strategy of the United States to engage the Soviet Union in an unequal arms race and thus ruin it.

India is not a socialist country, Prof. Khan remarked. We have a mixed economy. India's planning does not follow entirely the Gosplan model. It has borrowed from France too. In the thirties the objective put forward was Westernisation. Later, it was modernisation. Later still, the development school emphasised growth as the major index of progress. Now it is a more comprehensive idea of socio-economic transformation which includes plurality of approaches and recognises indigenous roots. The problem is how we achieve transformation in this sense. In India democracy has taken roots, but a little less than half our population is below the poverty line. How do we change this ? No systematic strategy of development has been suggested for this purpose.

II

Kamal A. Mitra Chenoy

Presenting his theme paper in two parts Dr. Chenoy stated that the first part was a sharp critique of the increasingly dominant model of development, the conservative model, while the second part suggested an alternative path. This was not merely a scholastic exericse, Dr. Chenoy added, for in India the ruling Congress (I), which is our centrist "umbrella" party had succumbed to the new conservative model. There is indeed an irony in this situation as highlighted by the presentation of the South Commission Report to the Prime Minister by Dr. Nyerere. The irony is that the 'reform' in our economic policies is being carried out by Dr. Manmohan Singh, a principal author of the Report which had so cogently criticised the development model now being introduced.

It is, however, not in India alone that this situation has arisen. The values referred to by the Chairman were the main staples of development thinking till the early eighties. The collapse of socialism, as it is termed, in the Soviet Union and East Europe has brought about a change, and there is a tendency now to accept the logic of the 'market friendly' approach to development as propounded by the World Bank Development Report. This approach, therefore, needs to be examined, and not merely from the point of view of its sustainability.

In order to examine the relevance of this approach to a country such as India, it is necessary to see what has happened in the U.S., which is widely taken to be a "success story" of "market friendly" development.

The indices of development in the U.S.A. show that the top one per cent of the population had, in total personal net worth, 33.9 per cent of the country's wealth in 1922. It fell to 29.89 per cent during the New Deal period, and by 1983 had risen to 42 per cent. The indices also show that while the real income (corrected for inflation) of 80 per cent of the people showed a decline between 1977 and 1988, the average real income during the same period of the top 10 per cent increased by 16 per cent, of the top 5 per cent by 23 per cent, and the top one per cent by as much as 50 per cent. This type of development, even if it is suitable for the U.S., is totally unsuitable for India where the immediate task is to eradicate poverty which engulfs a little less than half the population.

Besides, such increases in income and wealth are based on the super profits made by the Trans-national Corporations especially from developing countries. Figures show that between 1975 and 1981, the trans-national corporations made an average annual profit of 13 per cent on their investments in developed countries, and of 23.6 per cent in developing countries. The "success stories" of the U.S. and other advanced capitalist countries are indeed based on exploitation through various mechanisms, including the multilateral institutions set up by them.

This model of development with its high rate of use of resources, and the damage it causes to the environment is not sustainable. The U.S. alone uses 26 per cent of the world energy, the production of which increased by 43 per cent during the decade 1977-87. The U.S. is also the major consumer of such metals as copper, aluminium et al.

The problem of the developing countries is that of exploitation by the advanced capitalist countries. Unequal terms of trade, lack of access to technology accentuated by the measures proposed regarding trade related intellectual property and investment measures (TRIPS and TRIMS), control over credit, and operations of the Trans-national corporations are some aspects of this exploitation. The recent devaluation of the rupee was followed by a fall in the price of tea in the London market, and has resulted in a fall of exports in dollar terms.

Another aspect of development which needs to be considered is its cost in social and political terms. Dr. Brahmanand in his paper has referred to Pareto optimality, but has overlooked the fact that Pareto, a founder of the elite theory moved on to be a supporter of Italian Fascism. The World Development Report 1991 has identified the countries which have gone in for the Western capitalist model. These countries, of which Mexico is an important instance, have also gone in for authoritarianism. This link between the economic model and authoritarianism is not fortuitous. The cost of restructuring involves dilution of social welfare, and control of labour. The resulting discontent is treated as a law and order problem. The coercive apparatus of the State is, therefore, strengthened, and this leads gradually to authoritarianism.

Still another aspect of the adoption of this model is domination in socio-economic decision-making, and in the cultural spheres too, of the capitalist countries who act as creditors. An instance of this in the current Indian situation is the debate on Exit Policy which is linked to the IMF conditionality. It was not entirely accidental that an important decision in this respect was announced by the Finance Minister, not in the Parliament in India, but at the Fund-Bank meeting in Bangkok. Increasingly, national priorities are not determined internally but imposed externally. Similarly, in the cultural sphere. The Euro-American type of consumerism is becoming popular, and even advertisement carry pictures of foreigners in foreign countries using or enjoying the products advertised.

This has two consequences. One is the attempt by the major indigenous tradition to dominate minor traditions as recently demonstrated by the attempted demolition of the temples of *Bajrangbali* and *Sankatmochan* in the name of Ram. Secondly, foreign culture is imposed on the dominant but antiquated local forms. There is a need, Dr. Chenoy pointed out, to demystify the current Indian debate on development and keep these features in mind.

Finally, Dr. Chenoy wished to emphasise the fact that the pattern of Indian development in the past could not be regarded as socialistic. The non-capitalist content of the Nehru model of development, he thought, had been over-emphasised. He referred in this connection to the findings of the Industrial Licensing Policy Inquiry Committee presided over by Subimal Dutt, and how the Industrial Policy Resolution of 1956 was eroded by the Industrial Licensing Policy decisions made by the Government outside Parliament in 1970 and 1973. The areas reserved for the public sector were thrown open by these bureaucratic decisions not only to Indian capitalists but also to foreign investors in the name of the core sector. In the circumstances, Dr. Chenoy concluded, it was wrong to argue that socialism had been tried and had failed in India.

The theme paper having been presented, the Chairman called upon the writers of Critical Notes and the participants who desired to speak, to intervene in the order as below. Among the writers of Critical Notes, Shri E.M.S. Namboodiripad, Father Paul Gregorios, Dr. Arun Ghosh and Prof. A. K. Dasgupta being absent, their notes were taken as read.

III

R. C. Dutt

Shri R. C. Dutt had compared in his Critical Note the present wave towards the capitalist model of development to a similar wave in the thirties when the Great Depression had been regarded as marking the collapse of capitalism. Such waves were ephemeral, he stated, and referred in this connection to Shri N. K. Seth's statement in his Note that there must be reason behind the current trend towards capitalism and it should, therefore, be tried. This amounted to saying, Shri Dutt thought, Follow the Fashion.

On the other hand, he pointed out, the basic contradictions remained unresolved. Dr. Chenoy had pointed out how the developed capitalist countries consumed resources disproportionate to their share of the world population. This would not be possible if the developing countries developed and demanded their share of the resources. The capitalist countries had, therefore, a vested interest in the continued poverty of the underdeveloped countries.

Market was not inconsistent with socialism, but the market in order to function with justice needed reasonable equality of income and wealth. In the Indian context the market meant nothing to the millions in acute want and poverty. State intervention was, therefore, necessary. This had been conceded by Keynes who was not a socialist, and by President Roosevelt in his New Deal, but we are now told, in the name of liberalisation, that the State should not interfere.

There was a need for planning, Shri Dutt continued, to take the place of the market in the major investment decisions. Profit need not be regarded as morally reprehensible, but it can be allowed only within the discipline of the Plan. He referred in this connection to the contradiction in Shri Bali's Note. Shri Bali wanted the State to keep away from trade and industry. At the same time, he had stated he believed in socialism. What kind of socialism was it ?

Father Gregorios in his Critical Note had advanced the thesis that the Indian intellectual tradition believed in a cosmic order within which the human will and endeavour functioned. The Western model of development, on the other hand, was based on man conquering Nature and bending Nature to human will. This, he thought, was against Indian tradition. Without questioning the factual basis of the thesis which Father Gregorios had supported by profuse quotations from ancient texts, Shri Dutt thought that such a tradition introduced an element of fatalism which was probably responsible for the material backwardness of the country. There were, therefore, good reasons to depart from this tradition.

Finally, Shri Dutt referred to the view expressed by Prof. A. K. Dasgupta in his Note that development should be within the framework of individualism, and pointed out that there was no contradiction between individualism and socialism. He quoted in this connection what Jawaharlal Nehru had written in a letter in 1939 that he was attracted to socialism because it would free innumerable individuals from economic and social bondage and thus give them the opportunity to develop their individualities. In this view that there was no contradiction between individualism and socialism.

IV

J. S. Bali

In presenting his note, Shri Bali said that he was unable to comprehend what Dr. Kamal A. Mitra Chenoy was aiming at. A solution must be found, he said. He agreed with Dr. Chenoy that new development indices were needed, but that did not mean that the present indices like GNP should be abandoned. There was scope for co-existence of different models, Shri Bali thought, provided they were based on reason.

Shri Bali stated that having failed with the earlier model of development there was no harm in trying in a new model. The new pattern had considerably expanded the middle class. May be, he thought, this process would be further emphasised by the new pattern of development. Shri Bali believed in flexible response to development patterns, and thought that democracy was the best form of government.

Shri Bali then referred to the threat of population explosion, and felt that this threat had not received the attention it deserved. There was need for hard decisions. The State should be a hard State, as distinct from a soft State, he asserted.

State control of the means of production was right in principle, Shri Bali said, but the undue security which State employees enjoyed deprived them, he thought, of all initiative and innovativeness.

Individualism should be kept to the minimum and our social system should be directed to "socialism", Shri Bali concluded.

V

Prof. Iqbal Narain

While presenting his paper, Prof. Narain read out portions from paragraphs 4, 5 and 6 of his Critical Note with which he wanted to supplement the view-point of the main speaker in the context of social and political aspects of development. He regarded development both as an end and as a means to attain the concept of justice as postulated in the preamble to our Constitution. He talked about the frame of social justice in the main, while examining the social aspects of development. Turning to political dimensions, he referred to such issues as stages of federalism, decentralisation, secularism, reservation, regionalism and subsidies, as also the relative merits of the presidential and the parliamentary forms of government. According to him, federalism was the main remedy in India to contain pluralism and regionalism, and for this he wanted the federation to be a loose confederation of the States.

VI

N. K. Seth

Shri Seth presented his Critical Note with the remark that in India there was a tendency to live in a world of make-belief. In the recent past, he pointed out, four unfortunate things had happened, namely :

(i) The Soviet Union, which had been a tower of strength to India, had collapsed.

(ii) The USA had emerged as the only super-power.

(iii) In the absence of cold war, non-aligned movement had become irrelevant, and

(iv) Market economy had emerged as the only visible system.

One might have valid reasons to disapprove of these developments, Shri Seth continued, but they could not be wished away. There was wisdom, he thought, in coming to terms with the new order.

The disclosures of the horrors of the Communist regime (under Stalin) by Gorbachev had disillusioned Shri Seth. There must be something very wrong with an economic philosophy, he said, which could lead to a collapse of the nature we have witnessed.

Even the Communist Party of India, Shri Seth continued, was now talking of "socially controlled market". Dr. Arun Ghosh has also said that there is nothing wrong with the market provided there was no great disparity of incomes. Even Jawaharlal Nehru, for whom he had the highest admiration, would have modified his economic philosophy had he lived in the new world of today, Shri Seth ventured to suggest.

According to him, market economy (i) will unleash individual initiative, (ii) reduce corruption with loosening of the stranglehold of the State, and (iii) release secular forces, for in pursuit of profit no distinction could be made on the basis of caste or religion.

Shri Seth concluded by quoting approvingly the statement in the World Bank report that the State should supplement, and not supplant the market.

VII

Prof. P. R. Brahmanand

Complimenting Dr. Kamal A. Mitra Chenoy on his theme paper, Prof. Brahmanand stated that while Dr. Chenoy had presented the anti-thesis, he (Dr. Brahmanand) would now present the thesis.

Dr. Chenoy had referred to Eurocentrism. This was indeed true, Dr. Brahmanand said, for many great ideas came from Europe. Nationalism, socialism and planning were all ideas that emanated from Europe.

One such idea, Dr. Brahmanand said, was that of Adam Smith who had pointed out that human beings were not idealistic when it came to exchange, production and distribution for private gain. Adam Smith had developed the idea of the market and had expressed the view that market had probably a greater potential for good than any other institution.

Another idea of Adam Smith was that an economy should be judged by what it did to the ordinary people—to the majority of them. It was this idea that gave rise to the *utilitarian* theory and to the Instrumental approach. The collapse of the Soviet Union has shown that socialism, as practised in that country, failed to pass this test.

The heart of economic democracy, Dr. Brahmanand asserted, was the market. Interventionist policies have to work through the market in a wider sense. The two cannot be separated, he thought.

Referring to the phenomenon of inflation in India, Dr. Brahmanand said that the Indian system was more unequal today than ever before. This has happened, he pointed out, because the agricultural sector. The world, according to Dr. Brahmanand, has rejected inflation. If India does not accept the objective of not having inflation above the World rate, which is about three per cent, it will go the Latin American way. If we do not link up with the world in this respect, he warned, we shall have an inflation rate that we shall not be able to control. This is the central reason, he said, for international homogenisation. With such homogenisation there will be international discipline. We must become internationally competitive.

The foreign exchange reserves have increased as a result of the new policies, Dr. Brahmanand continued, by a larger extent than the receipts from the loan we have got from the IMF.

There is logic in the liberalisation policy, he thought, in asking the foreign investors to bring machinery and equipment along with their capital. The monetised budget deficit has also been sought to be reduced by 50 per cent, Dr. Brahmanand pointed out. This is something which no other country has been able to do in such quick time.

Dr. Brahmanand referred to a speech delivered by Dr. Manmohan Singh at Bangalore before he became Finance Minister in which he had outlined the policy which is now being adopted, indicating thereby that the policy was his, and not that of the World Bank. If the World Bank provides a safety net for the workers there is no reason to object to it. The World Bank loans are soft. They only required some flexibility. Such flexibility is good for India, according to Dr. Brahmanand. With the new economic policy the central source of corruption has gone, Dr. Brahmanand thought. Controls had, on the other hand, built up the parallel economy. The IMF conditionalities were no more than tests of viability. They were necessary to ensure that the loans were recycled.

Dr. Brahmanand agreed that we should be on our guard to protect our cultural system, but that does not mean that competition should not be allowed. We cannot afford to fail in our performance, Dr. Brahmanand concluded. An "ism", as such is not good enough.

VIII

Tarlok Singh

Shri Singh initiated his comments by pointing out that society had the obligation to re-examine past experience on the basis of present realities. These realities in the present context would include the experiences of the Newly Industrialised Countries (NICs), and the break-down of the system in the Soviet Union and the East European countries. Every system, he observed, should be judged by its fruits, not by its intentions.

In India, whatever the intentions, Shri Tarlok Singh observed, the public sector had grown in the same manner as the private sector by enlarging disparities and strengthening certain trends towards corruption. This was a reality. There were indeed good reasons for introducing licensing, but it was a fact that the power so conferred gave those who exercised it the power to demand a price for it. This does not, however, mean that one should go to the other extreme, and demand a free economy, for free economy can also be so used as to breed corruption.

The present government, Shri Tarlok Singh continued, was faced with acute short-term problems. The foreign exchange reserves were low, there was a threat of default on foreign loans, and the credit-rating of the country was poor. Most of the actions of the Government could be explained by these short-term considerations. In India, however, whether one owed allegiance to the Left or the Right, one could not deviate from the middle path. There were various constraints, regional, ethnic and occupational which government could not ignore.

For the same reasons, the present policy of deregulation, Shri Tarlok Singh continued, should be regarded as a cleansing process rather than a fundamental policy.

Shri E.M.S. Namboodiripad had said in his Note that a basic flaw in our development process was the failure of land-reforms. He was right, Shri Tarlok Singh thought, but land reform was not an attack on the richer peasants, as Shri Namboodiripad had stated. It was only the first stage in transforming the existing system. Security of tenure, limitation of holdings, reasonable rents et. al., which were not ensured, were only to lead to the second step which was to bring in the concept that land was for the well-being of all, a concept which would move towards co-operative development, though not in a rigid sense. The real issue is that in Indian conditions land cannot be nationalised. Greater productivity, better use of water and such other necessary measures could only be ensured by community action.

Viewed as a value system from all angles, not merely that of planning, self-reliance is a limited concept. The value system must include the concept of work for all, the concept of high levels of productivity in agriculture and a deliberate choice so to order our development that the country is not dependent on foreign aid or on foreign resources.

Errors have been committed in the past, Shri Tarlok Singh said. It was committed when the country planned for heavy industry without deciding how industry and agriculture should be integrated. Again, in the eighties there was a move towards high technology without relating it to the basic needs and the skills available. These errors have to be corrected.

Shri Tarlok Singh referred to chapter 3 of the Third Five Year Plan which was extensively re-written by Jawaharlal Nehru himself, even after the Plan had been approved by the National Development Council. He commended this chapter to the attention of all, for it contained a statement of the main road for India's economic development. The condition of the economy, he pointed out, was heavily dependent on the political system. We could have a better grip of our economy today if we could deal with our political problems, he said.

Shri Tarlok Singh further stated that planning was being conceived in narrow national terms. Regional planning was being overlooked. There was also inadequate development of human resources, and bureaucratisation of the development process. Development initiatives should come from below, not imposed from above. The role of macro economic planning, he pointed out, was not merely to correct various imbalances and achieve an over-all balance, but to ensure development of all regions and all sections of the population. A long-term framework and a broader horizon for planning was required for this purpose.

India has the capacity, the resources and the human skills, Shri Tarlok Singh concluded, to move the economic structure along the path of growth with equity within and equity without.

IX

Balraj Mehta

Shri Mehta referred at the outset to the view being vociferously articulated that the "dogmas" of socialism, Marxism et al. have become obsolete. They are, however, sought to be replaced by still older doctrines, going back to the 17th and even the 14th century. Adam Smith is supposed to have said that man was greedy by nature, and that in commerce altruism did not pay. In saying so, however, he was not reckoning with the pre-capitalist modes of production, nor did he take account of the fact that a new order produced a new kind of man. Socialism did not obviously produce a new kind of man, but this does not mean that man, his morals and his values have been static for all times, and will remain so in future. Development cannot be discussed on this static view, and one set of dogmas said to be outdated replaced by another set, older and more obsolete still.

Secondly, panegyrics have been showered on the Foreign Minister because the foreign exchange reserves have gone up. The fact, however, is that the reserves have gone up by about two billion dollars because we have taken loans of more than two billions during this period. Further, Dr. Brahmanand had said that we had agreed to foreign direct investments only on the condition that the investments brought in foreign equipment. But it has already been announced, Shri Mehta pointed out, that such conditions would be removed. Indeed, the Finance Minister has publicly admitted that this is one of the IMF conditionalities.

Thirdly, Shri Mehta said that the Finance Minister announced the exit policy at Bangkok to win the confidence of the foreign institutions. Dr. Brahmanand had referred to Dr. Manmohan Singh's speech at Bangalore when he was not the Finance Minister to make the point that it was only this policy conceived independently by him that had been implemented by the Government when he became Finance Minister. It was, however, stretching credulity too far, Shri Mehta observed, to suggest that such an important policy pronouncement as devaluation in two phases was made in two days after Dr. Manmohan Singh took over as Finance Minister. It was followed in quick succession by the trade policy and the industrial policy. All this could not have been done without blue prints of such policies being prepared well ahead in the government.

Turning to the IMF loan, Shri Mehta said that as a member of the IMF India had a right to withdraw a part of the fund without conditions. There was, therefore, no objection to the first tranche, the second tranche and even the stand-by loan on soft conditions from the IMF. We are, however, now talking of a structural adjustment loan carrying time-bound conditions which extend even to the political sphere. We have indeed taken an advance loan on this basis out of the six billion dollars loan extended by the Aid-India consortium.

Shri Mehta explained that the presently dominant view accepts the fact that India's development effort has failed, and then proceeds to attribute the failure to the planning and the development pattern adopted. According to Shri Mehta, on the other hand, the real tragedy is that the Plan and the development effort have succeeded in achieving the purpose for which they were launched.

The issue has been wrongly posed as Market vs. State intervention. What has failed, Shri Mehta asked—Market or State intervention ? The Soviet experiment at State intervention is said to have failed. But the failure has been in the political sphere. The rulers have been overthrown. Napoleon was defeated at Waterloo, but the era of capitalism he initiated continued. The October revolution, according to Shri Mehta, was not a socialist revolution of an advanced type. It has succeeded in establishing that the market cannot succeed without State intervention. This is now admitted even in the World Bank report. This would not have been possible without the October revolution.

The further question is : who holds State power ? On whose behalf does State intervention take place ? In India power is in the hands of the middle class. The right to vote has expanded participation from 10 per cent to 20 or 30 per cent of the population. It has not reached the masses yet. The prospects of development, and in particular of removal of poverty are dim, but let us not for that reason deduce it to poverty of philosophy, as Marx used to say.

Finally, Shri Mehta emphasised the importance of the stages of development, and was of the view that stages could not be jumped. A reason for the failure of the October revolution was just this. In India too, we cannot jump from the colonial order to socialist transformation. In our context, therefore, independent capitalist development is not retrogressive. The present tragedy is that autonomous capitalist development with the help of planning is being replaced by retrogressive, dependent capitalism.

There is no need to take up defensive position, as Dr. Chenoy has done in his otherwise excellent paper. Some go back from Marx to Adam Smith. In India we go back to the Gita and the scripture, and sometimes to Gandhiji, not to his mobilising power, but to his idea of trusteeship. There is no need for all this. Our basic re-thinking. Shri Mehta concluded, should be based on two important factors :

(1) Sovereignty of democratic India, and following from this

(2) Autonomy of India's development.

These should be the key to the new thinking.

X

Dr. V. G. Bhatia

Dr. Bhatia was of the view that it was no use criticising the capitalist model, or the experience of the United States or of any other country. What is relevant to us is what has happened in India. We have followed a certain path, and this has resulted in a very high proportion of illiteracy, especially among women, high infant and child mortality, high growth-rate of the population, and above all, widespread poverty and unemployment. And yet, it is sometimes said that ours is a success story.

In Dr. Bhatia's opinion these deplorable results have followed from the strategy that India has followed. With the limited resources of an underdeveloped country, instead of concentrating on the development of human resources, India adopted the Nehru-Mahalanobis plan of developing heavy industries. Resources were thus frittered away on capital-intensive, power-hungry projects. The incremental capital-output ratio (ICOR) in such projects has been very high. This path is now being discarded, but four decades have been lost already. Poverty has been unnecessarily prolonged. Though the rate of savings has risen as high as 20 or 21 per cent and the rate of investment has been 24% of GDP, the productivity of investment has been dismally low and therefore the rate of growth of per capita income has been negligible resulting in perpetuation of poverty and unemployment. We have even failed to double our per capita income after 40 years of planning.

India's failure has been in-built in the model of development adopted. This model must be modified. There is no alternative but to scrap the Nehru model, Shri Bhatia concluded.

XI

P. D. Hajela

Prof. Hajela in his Critical Note, referred to the Chairman's introductory remarks about the hypocrisy in conceding the impractibility of war as an instrument of policy but going ahead with the arms race, the collapse of colonial rule and such other pertinent factors which should be taken into account. Prof. Hajela wished to draw attention to another pertinent factor, namely, how spurt in technology had made the talk on economic systems somewhat irrelevant.

Technology has altered our concept of the market and of market intervention, Prof. Hajela continued. While earlier, growth and development were thought of both by Marxists and non-

Marxists, in the context of surpluses, and of capital accumulation based on the supluses, a situation arose at the Great Depression when, for the first time, surpluses were much in excess of requirements. It was in this context that Keynes pointed out that unless the State intervened it would not be possible to make the system work. This idea of State intervention gave rise to the concept of mixed economy, but this mixed economy which Keynes sponsored was in the context of technologically developed countries, and had little applicability to India. It was helpful only in the situation where capital resources were being created in excess of the utilising capacity of the economy.

In the sixties, Keynesianism was put to test in the Western world, and it produced tremendous results. In the process a new dimension was added. Technological spurt along the whole spectrum of production functions was such that productivity increased fast. The Marxian concern that the limited surpluses, appropriated greedily by the capitalists, would result in exploitation of labour and inadequate capital accumulation became largely irrelevant. The surplus was sufficient to take care of these requirements. Communist parties in developed capitalist countries thus lost their importance.

However, in developed free market countries, a different problem, namely, one of stagnation, arose. Keynesianism gave rise to inflation, and more so, to expectation of inflation, and therefore to wage demands higher than productivity gains. There was talk of a national wage policy, but it was not effective. Unemployment followed, so much so that Milton Friedman, followed by some others, started talking of a natural rate of unemployment. In any case, the consequence was that the capacities built could not be utilised because unemployment could not be reduced beyond a certain point. It was in these circumstances that sights were turned to the international market, and it is in this context that countries like India are being asked to open up and integrate with the global system.

The integration proposed is between two sets of countries which are very unequal and have entirely different situations. The market system in developed countries has not only deepened and widened the production structure, but has created a tremendous urgency that whatever capacity has been created must be utilised. Hence the demand for integration not only from the United States but from Europe and Japan. On the other hand, in under-developed countries, technology is not so advanced and the capacity to develop technology is limited. Unemployment is rampant in these countries. In sum, the reasons why integration is proposed do not exist in the under-developed countries.

Turning to the question why technological changes occur, Prof. Hajela asserted that it was wrong to say that changes necessarily occurred as a result of competition. It was also wrong to say that if the economy was opened up competition would follow. Are the multi-nationals conducive to competition, he asked. In our own country, does competition in the classical sense exist in our sprawling small-scale sector ? On the other hand, the Centre for Monitoring Indian Economy has in a recent report came to the conclusion that since the mid-eighties, the most growth-intensive sectors in the economy have experienced a growth in the concentration-ratio.

Prof. Hajela further stated that the incentive to technological changes is often provided by higher wages eating into profits. In South Korea, Taiwan and Japan, it was only when agriculture absorbed the available labour and the wages showed a tendency to rise that there was a demand for technological change. The position is very different in India with widespread unemployment and poverty. This is not the time for India to integrate for another reason as well. Integration might have been beneficial when the World economy was buoyant, but with the current slump in the developed world, there is not much to be gained by integration.

Prof. Hajela then read out certain portions of his Critical Note, and stated that the Nehru model has been unfairly accused of being Marxian, which it was not. Nor was it a mixed economy model as legitimised by Keynes. Private sector was the main concern of Keynes while the Nehru model emphasised just the opposite—the public sector.

Finally, Prof. Hajela referred to the view which had almost become an obsession, he thought, that there should be a change in favour of wage goods. But how could there be such a change, he asked, unless the demand structure was also changed. Such a change was possible only if the State came down heavily on consumerism and had a consumption policy which could tax consumption of the rich and raise resources.

The Nehru approach to development, Prof. Hajela concluded, had given considerable elbow room for meaningful economic progress, but the opportunity was not properly utilised.

XII

P. R. Brahmanand

Prof. Brahmanand replying to the points raised, stated that the foreign exchange reserve in June 1991 was about Rs. 2000 crores. It has since increased to about Rs. 6200 crores. The cut in imports. he explained, had saved about Rs. 3000 crores of foreign exchange. There has also been a drop in bulk imports. Remittances from Indians abroad have increased, and so has the inflow from non-resident Indians (NRI). There has been no increase in commerical loans and in commercial borrowings.

Inflation has also been sought to be controlled by imports, he added. The recent decision to import edible oil was an instance in point.

Regarding the query raised as to whether the present requirement of equipment import would be relaxed as a condition of the IMF loan, Prof. Brahmanand pointed out that the structural adjustment loan from the IMF had not yet been taken. When it is, the conditionalities of the loan will be placed before Parliament. At present the old policy stands.

Proceeding further, Dr. Brahmanand stated that some of the worst features of economic mis-management took place between January and June 1991. The present crisis is largely a result of the monetary expansion of Rs. 10,000 crores during this period. Such expansion was indeed unprecedented.

As regards future prospects, Dr. Brahmanand pointed out that there has been no major net increase in Reserve Bank credit since July 1991. The Reserve Bank has also been asked not to extend individual private credit. Even if, however, prices did not rise further in the current fiscal year, the average rate of inflation over the previous year would be 10 per cent, Dr. Brahmanand pointed out. This, he thought, was not good enough. The annual inflation rate should be no more than 7 per cent.

On the export front, prospects were very grim. The growth of world trade was likely to be less than two per cent. The pressure on import control will, therefore, continue.

Looking to the potential political constraints there was no alternative to seeking IMF loans unless we could pursue harder measures, Dr. Brahmanand concluded. Without these loans India's credibility will suffer. He agreed with Prof. Hajela that the world economy was very tight, and that technology was available only from the multi-nationals.

XIII

Balraj Mehta

Shri Mehta intervened to make three points : First, that Dr. Manmohan Singh, before he became Finance Minister, was deeply involved in policy-making during the period which Prof. Brahmanand had referred to as one of disaster.

Secondly, during the recent visit of the Managing Director, IMF it was agreed to convert the Stand by Loan to a Structural Adjustment Loan (SAL). The conditionalities of SAL are under implementation.

Thirdly, inflation is piling up. The hope of the Finance Minister that prices would go down, as they generally do during October-December, materialised only for three weeks this year. If the rate of inflation is to be kept below 10 per cent massive deflation will be needed with a negative growth rate. This will create its own problems. Railways will suffer loss of freight, power generation will suffer and there will be widespread unemployment.

XIV

A. N. Pandeya

Prof. Pandeya said he would try to restore the perspective with which the Chairman had started the discussions. It was Karl Marx, he pointed out, who gave a sense of long-term duration of human history. It was a land-mark departure from the Western historiography, and it presented a secular picture of the transformation of human civilisation and society.

The problem which confronts us, Prof. Pandeya continued, namely, to find an alternative to the capitalist path, is not new. Capitalism reached its take off stage by the end of the 18th century when its career of globalisation became irreversible. But from the 18th century itself it raised a parallel agenda to find an alternative to it. All Utopias, down to the efforts of Gorbachev, represent attempts to find alternatives.

Dr. Chenoy has also suggested an alternative in Marxian language, but Karl Marx would have called it "poverty of "philosophy", as he had characterised Pierre Proudhan's book, Philosophy of Poverty." Marx thought that Proudhan had wanted to retain the fruits of capitalism, but not pay its costs. Such an alternative cannot provide a programme, Prof. Pandeya thought, from which policies can be drawn.

Critique of capitalism, Prof. Pandeya observed, required affluent material basis. This was denied to Karl Marx, but now with the emergence of a knowledge industry, such critiques are pouring out from the heartland of capitalism, that is the United States, in the name of humanising Marxism. The attempt is to have the best of both worlds, but a national programme cannot be operated on this basis. This was Prof. Pandeya's objection to Dr. Chenoy's exercise also.

There is validity in Marx's insight that the capitalist civilisation is inherently global. Capitalism now generates a penetrating global pressure which affects the style of living, culture, in fact everything. It is total. It is a phenomenon which has the iron necessity of natural history, where human will and conscious choices are over-ridden, and everything is reduced to the calculus of utilitarianism, of which Prof. Brahmanand has spoken.

Capitalism is indeed exploitative, but there was no social order, Prof. Pandeya asserted, which was not exploitative. There is no *homoequals* without *homo-hierarchial.*

There was no way of jumping out of the global pressure by adopting an Utopian form. France in West Europe and Japan in East Asia learnt the game, turned it to their relative advantage, and joined the mainstream. In India, our intelligentsia think that we have missed out in the last forty years. So we have indeed, but there is no short cut. Our thinking section has the obligation to think and act as watch dogs.

Marx had said that man made history, but there was no clean slate. In India we have the misfortune of having a long, continuing civilisation. The search for Utopia has been perennial, but the dream cannot be realised except by a long route.

Let us act with wisdom, caution and responsibility, Prof. Pandeya concluded. There is no short cut, but we can prevail.

XV

H. N. Ray

Shri H. N. Ray expected the discussions to be more pragmatic, and to offer concrete suggestions. There was inadequate realisation of hard realities, he thought, and no indication of the depth of the crisis.

The World Bank Report 1991, had been unfairly criticised, according to Shri Ray. The Report is pretty factual and has narrated the experiences of several countries. It does say that inequitable income distribution slows down development. It has pleaded for land reform, and attaches importance to education.

Dr. Chenoy had stated in his first paper that the Exit Policy contemplated dismissal of workers without benefits. This is not true, Shri Ray pointed out, as the Prime Minister and the Finance Minister had said, the workers interests would be safeguarded. The National Renewal Fund was meant to take care of the workers.

Dr. Arun Ghosh had emphasised decentralisation, Shri Ray continued, but had not mentioned the necessary safeguards. Few would argue that the State Governments functioned more efficiently than the Central Government, or that the municipalities are better than the State Governments. There was a danger, Shri Ray warned, that the rural elites would hijack the panchayats for their own benefits.

There was an important role for the State, Shri Ray continued, to mobilise resources and allocate them to sectors according to their priorities in the national interest. Annual budgets were not adequate for this purpose. Longer perspectives were needed. There are indeed some achievements that the State and Planning effort can claim, but over-regulation of trade and industry is harmful, as also interference in the management of the public sector.

There has been a perceptible fall in the efficiency of our institutions, Shri Ray thought. The foreign banks, for instance, functioned more efficiently than the Indian banks though the staff and the milieu were the same. To improve efficiency, there was need, according to Shri Ray, for administrative reforms, not for ambitious schemes. The law and order situation has to be improved, as also the judicial process. The tax machinery was in shambles. Job security was being over-emphasised to the detriment of efficiency. There should be no reservations in regard to promotions.

It is necessary to rethink our strategies, Shri Ray concluded. Exports should be promoted and have to be internationally competitive. The private sector has come of age, and should be given additional responsibilities so that the public sector might concentrate on the core sector.

XVI

P. G. Menon

Shri P. G. Menon invited the participants of the seminar to visit a certain rural development project, namely, the Project for the Eco-Regeneration of the Pushkar Lake Valley System (1,200 sq. k.m.) in Ajmer District, Rajasthan. There, the participants could, he claimed, see for themselves how several of the issues raised by them were being tackled; issues such as how to motivate the weaker sections into acting 'responsibly'. At Pushkar, the government and non-government organisations were working together to make eco-regeneration generate both self-employment and wage-employment activities. Indeed, it was the local people who were working for their own development, the outsiders functioning only as catalysts and helpers. In the project area, land prices had gone up five times, now just the doubling of land-prices which normal inflation would have accounted for. This was just one of many examples.

Shri Menon pointed out that no one at the seminar had referred to a major social problem which was emerging. This was the marked increase in the consumption of narcotics even in rural India, including Pushkar. According to U. N. figures, the international narcotics trade is now worth around one-and-a-half trillion U. S. dollars annually.

As for potable water, which the Chairman had referred to, Shri Menon felt that the following example would illustrate the increasing gravity of the rural situation : many seminar participants would recall that about 25 years ago, in the very vicinity of the IIC, many buildings were plagued by sub-soil water. This excess had disappeared, and the *water-table even in our capital* has in many areas dropped to below 50 feet.

XVII

Kartar Singh

Shri Kartar Singh emphasised Science and Technology (S & T) as an important factor for development apart from the four other factors mentioned by the Chairman. Recent experiences, especially the Gulf War, he said, had demonstrated the importance of S&T, and the pace at which technological changes were proceeding. India had undoubtedly a large number of scientists and technicians, but she considerably lagged behind in this sphere.

It is no use finding fault with what has happened in the past, Shri Kartar Singh continued. What we should address ourselves to is : where do we go from here ? We are indeed in a crisis, but we have a strong base, natural material and manpower. For the last forty years we have had capitalist development. The world is inter-dependent. No country can have full-fledged sovereignty. Dependence on other countries does not mean loss of sovereignty.

Developed countries will undoubtedly want to dictate to us. The extent we are able to meet it depends on what sacrifices we are prepared to make. None of the political parties, however, Left or Right, has had the courage to come out with a programme involving hard decisions.

One of the major handicaps India suffers from is illiteracy. There is a talk of privatisation of education, but there is little reference in this to primary education. It is only if all political parties get together, Shri Kartar Singh observed, that the Government can be forced to recognise the importance of primary education.

XVIII
Ashok Mathur

Shri Ashok Mathur stated there were two paths of development which were polar opposites—the market-friendly and the socialistic paths. The viable path in his opinion lay in between these two opposites.

Where does one start, Shri Mathur queried, and answered the query by saying that one should start with planning a model for development as both the Soviet Union and India had done. Certain infrastructures have to be provided for development, and they can be provided only by State intervention.

The Plans are said to have failed in India as in the Soviet Union. Why, Shri Mathur asked. First, the past experience should not be denigrated. There have undoubtedly been failures, but the achievements should not be overlooked. Infrastructural facilities, such as transport, and power have been substantially developed, though same bottlenecks do arise from time to time.

Secondly, a reason for the failures, according to Shri Mathur, was that a suitable incentive system had not been incorporated. The public sector management should be improved, he said, but there was no reason to throw out the baby with the bath water.

Thirdly, controls undoubtedly create problems but liberalisation does not mean that the controls should be abolished altogether. The police force is not wound up if crime increases.

Fourthly, there is the question of expenditure on Defence which diverts resources from development. This problem has interface with economic and political realities. There is no easy solution.

Fifthly, lack of democratisation led to failure of the Plan in Socialistic countries, as Shri R. C. Dutt has pointed out.

Finally, there is the question of population, China has been able to control it, but not India.

XIX

V. P. Gupta

Shri V. P. Gupta said that he would not like to go into the question of whether the Indian development model had been capitalistic or socialistic. According to him what was important was, how the model had worked.

In Shri Gupta's view the Indian model had been of growth but not of development; the rich had become richer, the middle class had grown in numbers, some benefits had trickled down to the poor but not to the extent desired or expected. After forty years too, the number of persons below the poverty line was very very large. It had, in fact, increased in numbers, though perhaps not in proportion to the population.

The problem in India is of employment and ensuring purchasing power at least to meet the basic human needs. Shri Gupta pointed out that poverty anywhere is a threat to prosperity everywhere. Any model has to take care of the unemployed. What is needed is a man-oriented development and not production-oriented or goods-oriented. The latter only encouraged consumerism and class hatred, Shri Gupta concluded.

XX

Saheb Singh

Shri Saheb Singh pointed out that the Finance Minister, Shri Manmohan Singh had talked of the Exit Policy in India, and had only repeated it at Bangkok. Unfortunately, the media highlighted what he said at Bangkok without referring to his statement in India.

Liberalisation measures have been announced by Government, Shri Saheb Singh continued. The ball was now in the court of the traders and industrialists, but they were asking for more and more. Will they play ball ? Shri Saheb Singh was very doubtful.

The National Renewal Fund concerned only a small proportion of the population. Seventy per cent of the population who lived in rural areas, on the other hand, were highly dissatisfied. If nothing was done for them, this discontent, Shri Saheb Singh thought, would rip aside the economic and the political system.

In regard to direct foreign investment, Shri Saheb Singh said, we were looking for not only machinery but also technology which included management skills, work environment and behavioural patterns. There will be an impact of such investments on our culture which cannot remain unaffected.

Proceeding further Shri Saheb Singh pointed out that even our Constitution had been framed by the elites of our society. The Constituent Assembly had not been elected by universal adult franchise, nor was the Constitution approved by a referendum.

Finally, Shri Saheb Singh referred to a view expressed in a speech by Prof. Brahmanand about seventeen years ago disagreeing that India was a rich country inhabited by poor people. Prof. Brahmanand, on the other hand, had thought that India was a poor country inhabited by poor people, and had pointed out that if population continued to grow at the present rate, even water would be scarce. If Prof. Brahmanand was of the same view now,

Shri Saheb Singh would like to ask him how he expected that foreigners would invest in a country of such poor resources.

XXI

N. S. Saxena

Shri Saxena was of the view that ideologies under discussion had some relevance till the mid-sixties but ceased to be important thereafter. Politicians continued to talk of ideology, but they had only one ideology, and that was to remain in power.

Shri Saxena quoted the case of a Chief Minister who entertained 40,000 guests at a wedding party and served them a meal which must have cost at least Rs. 50 per head.

The attitude towards the public sector was determined, Shri Saxena said, not by ideological considerations, but by the money that could be extracted from them. He knew of two public sector undertakings in U.P. which were exploited by politicians. If these undertakings did not exist there would be no deficit in the U.P. Budget.

Socialism was introduced in the Soviet Union, according to Shri Saxena, not by Lenin but by Peter the Great. It was Peter the Great who founded the public sector, brought technicians from West Europe on high salaries, and hanged all officials guilty of corruption.

The elites in the Soviet Union enjoyed a standard of living higher than what prevailed under the Czars. There was corruption and nepotism, and it was these that had led to the collapse of the Soviet Union, not Socialism.

Recounting his long experience of anti-corruption work in the police, Shri Saxena said that in 1952 they dealt with cases of embezzlement of a few thousand rupees, in 1969 about Rs. 50,000 to Rs. 60,000, but now the cases involved millions of rupees.

Shri Saxena would be happy to live under any system. Ideologies were important, but politicians had spoiled them by their demand for votes and notes, Shri Saxena concluded.

XXII

General Sudan

General Sudan wished to speak only on Defence expenditure, and the possibility of reduction of such expenditure. Nehru's model of self-reliance, General Sudan said, had been almost achieved in the Army. There is near self-sufficiency in the indigenous production of Defence equipment. This has to some extent been achieved with Soviet help. Now with the collapse of the Soviet Union spare parts would be difficult to procure, and even those available will be against hard currency payments. This might lead to cannibalisation of equipment, but the equipment so cannibalised will have to be replaced not only on payment of hard currency but at higher prices.

Besides, the Gulf War has shown that the Soviet equipment is not the best available. The Armed Forces would thus have to look for alternative sources of supply, but this again will mean payments in hard currency and at higher prices.

Continuing, General Sudan said that importing equipment from the West would involve a complete change in the weaponary pattern of the Defence Forces.

A cut in Defence expenditure was certainly desirable, but it depended on the security perception of the country. To cut Army expenditure would mean a reduction of manpower, but as long as the Army has to be deployed in various border areas on account of the present threat perception, such manpower reduction was hardly possible.

Much as General Sudan would like Defence expenditure to be cut, he concluded, he did not see this happening in the foreseeable future.

XXIII

Kamal A. Mitra Chenoy

Dr. Kamal A. Mitra Chenoy, replying to the criticisms advanced, stated that there was no one model of development which could be regarded as the alternative. His critique in the first part of his paper of the mainstream model was intended to show that it was no alternative at all. Moreover, he had clearly stated that there is no single alternative model, and had instead only provided a broad alternative framewok.

The World Bank/IMF model of development was not based on the actual experience of any developed country, not even of South Korea and Taiwan. The latter two countries were highly protectionist, and had a substantial amount of state intervention. There were no competitive markets, Dr. Chenoy continued, either internationally or internally in such countries. The international market was oligopolistic, not competitive. The internal markets in South Korea and Taiwan were also not competitive. They were highly oligopolistic.

The path indicated by World Bank/IMF was not feasible for India, considering the complexity of India's socio-political context. If we follow this path, grave social and political consequences will follow as has indeed happened in Latin American countries. Mexico, Brazil and even Egypt who had resource endowments and entrepreneural classes comparable to that of India, are not democratic, while India still is. Nor are those economies relatively free of external debt. No one today, talks of the "Brazilian miracle", that Simon Kuznets and others touted in the 1960s.

Shri M. S. Saxena had referred to widespread corruption in the country. This showed degeneration of politicians. Nehru's attempt to build up political institutions has weakened considerably.

The main thrust in an alternative model of development, Dr. Chenoy asserted, has to be on democratisation. Decentralisation, if it is to be only a transfer of power from national to regional elites, is no alternative. Nor is the Presidential system.

The alternative must be on a different terrain. It must deal with the problem of women who have for long been oppressed. It must deal with the problem of population by educating and providing welfare benefits to the poverty stricken masses, for development is the best contraceptive.

Voluntary movements with considerable resources, Dr. Chenoy concluded, are in evidence at the micro-economic and micro-political levels. They must turn their attention to the macro level and align sympathetic political forces at the national level to concentrate on the economic and political problems of the country. But these long-standing problems can only be solved by an approach radically different from that being adopted today.

Part II

APPLICATION OF TECHNOLOGY FOR DEVELOPMENT

APPLICATION OF TECHNOLOGY FOR DEVELOPMENT

Dr. A. Rahman

I. General Remarks

1. The area of choice for the generation of technology decides its application and the forms are conditioned by the socio-political goals of a country and the cultural ethos.

2. Looking at the historical aspects of the generation of technology in contemporary society, two features emerge very clearly :

(a) (i) Technology is generated to meet the needs of the military—

a primary need creates complementary and ancilliary needs; hence different packages of technologies are built, normally termed as systems, once the specific sets of technologies of the system are produced as prototypes. They are tested and produced on mass scale for use.

(ii) The time scale of development and use, depends upon technology, normally between 5-10 years.

(iii) The technologies thus available also become obsolete between 5-10 years; if not earlier, by subsequent developments.

(iv) Once they are obsolete and become redundant for the army, their possible use in civilian area explored and commercial production is undertaken. (aircraft, electronics, food processing, antibiotics, etc.).

(v) This relationship underwent a major change, to begin with, in two countries, Germany and Japan. They were defeated in World War II, and their major industries were destroyed. They had to start afresh. They concentrated on civilian industries, and generated necessary technologies for the purpose.

Technologies were generated keeping in view specific industries and to capture the market.

(vi) Some of these technologies, though developed essentially for civilian market, were useful and were used in developing military systems.

(b) (i) The second set of technologies were produced for consumer needs to meet the fashions and cultural ethos of countries.

(ii) The products themselves may or may not need new process, but major development in technologies in this area cover mass production processes and improvement of quality.

(iii) They cover high competitive areas, include marginal changes. The products have short life, due to quick fashion and taste changes.

(iv) The products are sold through high pressure salesmanship, the latter creating the demand.

(c) (i) Recently, some new areas have emerged, where technologies are being developed to meet specific purposes : to check environmental pollution, remove the deleterious effects of technology, reduce waste, promote use by-products, recycle materials, etc.

(ii) Another area which essentially covers new field is biotechnologies essentially for civilian use.

(iii) It is quite possible that some of the technologies developed may also be used, if and when needed, for purposes of war.

II. Developments in India

1. *Before Independence* :

A casual survey of areas of research would reveal :

(a) Research in frontier areas of science—physics, astrophysics, mathematics, (Raman, Saha, Bose and others).

(b) Research in the area of natural resources, fauna/flora, chemistry of natural products, (Siddiqui, Seshadri, Birbal Sahni, Bahal and others).

(c) Area of nutrition and food technology. (Kamla Bhagvat and others)

The work done established that Indian scientists were as good as best in the world, led to the creation of technologies for the use of natural resources, and to development of industries based on them. They also helped in upgrading some of the indigenous and traditional industries.

2. *After Independence* :

(a) For some reasons the above mentioned areas of research and motivation for them got disrupted.

A possible reason was that large number of scientists were sent to U.K. and USA, who on return worked in areas where they had worked in these countries.

(b) India evolved a scientific policy, but no technology policy. It developed infrastructure for research but :

(i) Did not link up research with industry, or imported areas of technology.

(ii) It depended on import of technology for industrial development. Even here it was guided by ideas evolved in Europe and USA that

Intermediate technology was appropriate technology, small was beautiful.

In the generation and application of technology—one notices many stages :

(a) Import substitution, export promotion,

(b) Self-reliance,

(c) Rural development and meeting people's needs,

(d) Development of sophisticated technology.

In all these areas, no attempt was made to generate technologies to meet specific purposes, but effort was made to use existing knowledge. In application of technologies no major impact was created.

III. Nature of Technologies

Technologies can be categorised as :

(i) Armament production and defence technologies.

They are high energy technologies and use non-renewable materials. They cover a system, i.e. a number of technologies, from different fields are integrated to produce a system.

They are science based and cover advancing area of science.

(ii) Consumer technologies. They cover :

(a) Entertainment industry, including sports,

(b) Convenience gadgets

(c) Food

(d) Pharmaceuticals and cosmetics

(e) Fashion industry.

These technologies aim at making new products as well as develop new processes for making products. They cover areas of advance research, as well as use already known knowledge.

(iii) Machinery, machine tools and instrument development technologies. They are key to industrial development and aim primarily at improving efficiency and productivity, through saving energy and materials, and improving the quality of product.

(iv) Remedy technologies. They Cover :

(a) Checking environmental degradation

(b) Checking pollution

(c) Waste utilisation

(d) Recycling of materials.

Each one of the above areas cover technologies to check deterioration of environment. They develop instruments for the purpose, develop technologies to use materials and also aim at developing alternative processes for the existing ones.

IV. This brief and indicative categorisation would reveal that researches of different fields of specialisation require to be put together to develop a system or solve a problem.

A break through in one area may lead to and necessitate the development in other areas to meet the requirement of a system or to find a solution.

Areas (i), (iii) and (iv) are those where technologies are developed for a defined purpose, and when developed it is expected that they would be utilised as and when they are completed and made available.

However, their application is subject to various factors. Some of these are :

(i) Product or process becomes obsolete before it is applied;

(ii) Economically it is not found competitive;

(iii) Existing process or product is well established. Industry may purchase the technology and may not use it, or suppress it so that others may not use it.

(iv) The impact of technology, when used, may affect other areas, e.g. employment. It may not suit culturally, or have other deleterious effect and hence not used.

(v) Other factors.

V. For effective development and use of technology in India, a national will and a policy backed by the necessary resources is required. India, not having a defined technology policy, covering both its development as well as its diffusion, has so far depended on ideas developed elsewhere.

Taking the complexity of her social structure and culture, and the complexity of technological requirements, on the one hand, and, on the other, globalisation of technological developments, and pressure on less developed countries to fall in line and environmental and other dimensions, India requires to develop a strategy. The latter should cover :

(a) Selection of a few areas, one or two, to make an international breakthrough.

(b) Use of existing knowledge to increase the efficiency of existing industries and increase their productivity and quality of products.

(c) Phasing out of environmentally bad and high pollution industries.

(d) Develop more effectivity maintenance and repair systems to increase the life of products.

(e) Instead of discarding the whole product, when a better system is available, change only those parts of the system which would upgrade the product.

(f) Make a major effort in the diffusion of technologies, particularly to artisan and craftsmen.

(g) Develop and use technologies of waste utilisation and recycling of materials.

(h) In the development of technologies, cultural and social

impacts and moral and ethical issues, besides those of environment and pollution, be taken into consideration.

VI. The possibilities of implementing such a strategy would depend upon :

(a) Creation of understanding of science and technology amongst people and promotion of scientific literacy and scientific and technological culture.

(b) Public debate on policies and programmes to develop national consensus.

ACQUISITION AND DEVELOPMENT OF TECHNOLOGY* (THE INDIAN EXPERIENCE)

Ashok Parthasarathi**

(Additional Secretary)
(Department of Scientific and Industrial Research)
Ministry of Science and Technology

The Impetus

Technology, in the sense of knowledge organised to do a task, has always played a major role in economic and social activity. Indeed the material levels of living, the character of social

---

* Originally given as a lecture at the National Defence College, New Delhi. Subsequently published in Economic and Political Weekly, Vol. XXII, No. 48, Bombay, November 28, 1987. Later published in a revised form in Development and South-South Cooperation, Journal of the Research Centre for Cooperation among Developing Countries, Ljubljana, Yugoslavia, Vol. III No. 5, December, 1987. Subsequently published in Interciencia, Vol. 13, No. (5) 1988: 241-251.

** The views expressed in this paper are those of the author and not necessarily those of the organisation to which the author belongs.

and cultural life, and the security of societies have always been closely related to the technologies they used. But the occurrence of the Industrial Revolution, first in Britain, its spread to other parts of Europe, and then to the USA, Japan and the USSR, led to technology coming to occupy the centre stage in the development of nations.

It was not surprising therefore that the technological backwardness, in which colonial rule had consciously kept what are today called the Developing countries, should have been a key concern, if not obsession, of the leaders of the independence movements of our countries. Whether it was Soekarno, Nehru or Mao, Nkrumah or Nasser, they all voiced their concern for rapid technological advancement of their countries as one of the corner stones of both the fight for freedom and of the nation-building task thereafter.

Underlying this view was the conviction, based to some extent on history, that what distinguished a poor country from a rich one, a strong country from a weak one, was "modern" technology. At the same time, there was the associated stream of historical analysis of how dominantly agrarian societies transformed themselves into industrial societies, from societies based on subsistence agriculture to high productivity economy, all of which led to the spotlight being put on industrialisaton. The combination of these two streams of appreciation led to focussing on industrial technology in the economic development of the newly independent, poor countries of the world. Consequently from the time they came to acquire political independence. (1940's for the first group, 1950's for the second and the 1960's for most of the rest) the poor countries of Asia and Africa set out to industrialise themselves drawing on industrial technologies from the highly industrialised and rich countries.

In India, this recognition of the role of technology in development, and the commitment to its acquisition, development and use, was first enunciated, and has since been enshrined, in the Scientific Policy Resolution (SPR) of 1958. The SPR, drafted by Nehru and approved by Parliament states in its opening paragraph :

"The key to national prosperity, apart from the spirit of the people, lies, in the modern age, in the effective combination of three factors—technology, raw materials and capital, of which the first is perhaps the most important, since the creation and adoption of new scientific techniques can, in fact, make up for deficiency in natural resources, and reduce the demands on capital".

More recently, in 1983, the Government has enunciated a Technology Policy Statement which deal with technology very comprehensively.

The Early Years

The international climate at the time *viz.*, the 1950s, when the first group of developing countries (Indonesia, India, China, Egypt), launched on "The Great Ascent" to improve the levels of living of their people, was one in which the highly industrialised countries started providing developing countries with what has since come to be called "economic aid" and "technical assistance". With economists calling for such "transfer of resources" from the rich to the poor, the process of acquisition of industrial technology also came to be called "transfer of technology". However, as we shall see later, this terminology was misleading if not actually incorrect.

With the developing countries having little or no industrial infrastructure, let alone industrial productive capacity, the first "transfer of technology" took the form of the supply of complete factories and industrial plants by a "Northern" country to a "Southern" Country. The actual actors involved in the process of "transfer " at the working level were commercial enterprises in highly industrialised countries and commercial enterprises in developing countries. Typically, a cement plant or a chemical plant was transferred by the supplier sending production equipment to the developing country, installing and commissioning it and then training technical personnel of the purchaser to operate and maintain the plant. The skill formation component was realised by supplying the requisite knowledge through technical documents (often called the know how) and through "hands-on" training, both at the supplier's own plant and at the purchaser's new plant (often called "show-how"). However, in some cases local skills to even operate and maintain the plant were not available, in either the requisite quantity or quality. In such cases, the supplier's technical personnel themselves operated and maintained the plant for quite some time, before local technical personnel were able to "take over" the plant. Such transfers came to be called "turn-key" transfers of technology, as the supposition was that all the purchaser had to do was to "turn the Key" and the plant would start and operate; he had very little to do himself except provide local logistical and infrastructural support. All the early Mining, Power, Steel and Chemical Plants in this country which came up during the late 50's and till the mid 60's were set up with "technology transfer" undertaken on this basis. The same was the case in other large developing countries like China, Indonesia or Egypt.

Growing Awareness of High Costs and of In-Built Dependence

As experience was gained with operating and maintaining industrial plants, as we built up our secondary and tertiary education systems and started producing personnel with knowledge of modern S & T, and getting those personnel trained in the plants of turn-key/near turn key plant suppliers (in both OECD and Comecon countries), as the netwerk of R & D laboratories and engineering design companies which we were fortunate to have set up through the vision of Jawaharlal Nehru came up, and, above all, as we built up our capital goods producing industries, we came to appreciate several technical and commercial realities of industrial technology.

On the one hand, we came to realise that, in the modern age, technologies were consciously generated through :

(a) Organised R & D and design engineering

(b) Innovations made in the course of the production process itself.

The first is often referred to as "Technology from Science", and the second "Technology from Technology". However, in either case the generation of the technology was undertaken largely, commercially, through the investment of economic resources by the technology supplying companies. Gradually, it also became clear that the governments of the technology supplying were also playing a large part in the technology generation and utilisation process through a number of mechanisms from direct financing of enterprises, to assured purchases of the final product, to protection from foreign competition etc. This appreciation led to the recognition that, technologies in general, and industrial technologies in particular, constituted commercial commodities and carrying them constituted *commercial transactions*. Hence one should really speak of "Technology Transactions" rather than of "Technology Transfers". There are no "free lunches" in the realm of technology any more than in any other area of commerce.

This in turn led to the recognition that there was an international market for technology as for any other transacted commodity, with its own dynamics of supply and demand. However, this market, the experience of many developing countries indicated, differed significantly from the market for say agricultural commodities, minerals, manufactured products, or capital goods, indeed it was unique in many ways.

First there were no "standard" prices for know-how packages unlike for, say cement or tractors. Therefore, it is a market in which prices depend much more heavily on the degree of competition that was available or could be generated by a buyer than in the case of goods *e.g.*, consumer goods or capital goods.

Secondly, that information of all types—on the number and quality of alternative suppliers, on their respective financial position at the time a technology purchase was being contemplated, of their track record of performance in similar technology transactions in other countries or with other buyers in the past—has a profound effect on the buyer's options, on his negotiating leverage and on the price and other terms of the final technology purchase, but such information was extremely hard to come by, indeed was kept as secret as possible by the technology seller.

Thirdly, that sellers tried to impose numerous restrictive conditions in the agreements governing technology transactions; restrictions relating to the buyer purchasing capital goods or components and parts only from/through the seller, which normally meant the seller charging much more than the open market price for these; restrictions on exports, restrictions by way of demanding a minimum quantum of payments irrespective of the volume of production by the buyer; restrictions on the buyer modifying or even improving the technology purchased. There were, in addition, many restrictive provisions relating to taxation, rights and obligations of the buyer, laws and adjudicatory bodies under which disputes between buyer and seller would be settled, etc.

Fourthly buyers also found that the seller often palmed off on them obsolete technologies which the seller himself was in the process of discontinuing in his own plant, because he had developed a newer, more efficient technology.This resulted in the cost, quality and other characteristics of the product produced by the buyer being worse than those of the seller, right from the time the technology was purchased. Apart from being deleterious to the domestic economy of the buyer, this obsolescence tended to build non-competitiveness in the international market into the production structure of the buyer right from the beginning, thereby affecting the export performance of developing countries.

All these factors, the developing country, governments and the enterprises found, were loaded against them, due to the "gap" in knowledge and practical industrial experience in allied technologies or areas of industry; "gap" in terms of experience in negotiating agreements for technology purchase and the "gap" between the economic and political power, not only of the technology selling enterprises, but of the governments of the countries to which those commercial sellers belonged, on the one hand, and those of the developing countries, on the other. This was true after supplying countries both of the OECD and the Comecon.

By around 1970, i.e. after about 15 years of experience of the process by developing countries, a major new dimension of technology transactions became increasingly apparent. This was the role of Trans National Corporations (TNCs) in these transactions. The setting up by TNCs of wholly owned subsidiaries in many developing countries, and joint ventures with local firms in other cases, injected the element of ownership by foreign entities of the plants in which the "transferred" technology was being put to use. What is more, increasingly those plants were being pulled into a global network of subsidiaries of the so-called "mother" company of the TNC headquartered in a highly industrialised country. As a result, the plant in the developing country began to be controlled "extra-territorially", bringing back all the exploitative relationships of foreign companies in colonial times. With this "globalisation" of industry, came the phenomenon of "transfer pricing" between constituent units of the same TNC whether these were wholly owned subsidiaries or joint ventures, thereby greatly increasing the costs of technology purchases to the developing countries.[3] This added yet another dimension to the critical issues of costs of technology purchase *viz.*, the dimension of developing country governments having to pay what are essentially "intra-firm" payments, without the legitimacy and appropriateness of those payments being assessable or testable against any competing prices.

Finally, there was the high cost of international technology transactions to the developing country buyers. Various studies undertaken by the United Nations Conference on Trade and Development (UNCTAD) indicated that over the last 15 years, the developing countries had made identifiable and measurable payments—and that too in precious foreign exchange—of $0.61 billion for their foreign technology purchases in 1970—a figure which has gone up to 2.62 billion per year by 1980[5] and was estimated to be around $9 billion in 1985. The 1980 figure constituted 5 per cent of the total export earnings of non-OPEC developing countries, while it had become 7 per cent in 1985. However, even these large amounts did not capture all forms of technology payments. For example, the data in regard to payments for components and parts, and primary and intermediate materials above their "fair" competitive market price, were known to be substantial, but data identification and collection limitations prevented their quantification.

As a result of realising—if slowly—these characteristics of international technology transactions, developing countries came to recognise that such transactions had varying degrees of "technological dependence" built into them. This realisation, in turn, led to a concern for acquiring at least some degree of "technological self reliance".

If one were to distil a set of aphorisms—may be they are slogans—on the issue of dependence *vs.* self reliance, they would look like this:

Point

Industrialised nations are an "S & T Supermarket" For Developing Nations

Counter-point

"Goods" (Technologies) in that "Supermarket" come with strings and at Exhorbitant prices

Point

Developing Countries have 'the Benefits of being Latecomers' in S & T

Counter-point

Learning from your own mistakes affords greater benefits

Point

Don't Re-invent the Wheel (Buy from the "Supermarket")

Counter-point

Learning by doing is essential for Locally Rooted Development

Unbundling the Technology Package*

But coming to practicalities, how does one acquire such technological self reliance? By the early 1970's studies and actual experience of the content of technology transferred revealed that industrial technology was not a "black box"; that it had a structure with a number of constituent elements, the most important of which were :

* This and the next three sections draw heavily on a paper by Ignacy Sachs, Economic and Political Weekly, Bombay, Vol. V, Nos. 29-31, Special Number, July 1970.

(a) Documented Knowledge (DK)

(b) Skills (S)

(c) Hardware / Machinery (H)

Experience showed that technology was partly disembodied (DK), partly embodies in hardware (H) *i.e.* machinery or capital goods, and partly embodies in human skills (S). While DK, often loosely termed "Know How" was regarded as the core of the technology, operationally it was meaningless to speak of "transfer of technology" without dealing with the other two main elements *viz.*, H and S. The relative contributions of these three components varied widely from technology to technology *i.e.*, from production process to production process. They also varied in the same production process over time, due both to the demands of the market and to the relative costs of labour and capital.

Dependence and Self Reliance

If we use the subscript *'d'* for domestic and *'i'* for imported / foreign, the matrix of the possible situations is the following one:

(a) $S_iDK_iH_i$: Foreign specialists apply a foreign invented technology and operate imported equipment (Turn Key Plant).

(b) $S_dDK_iD_i$: Local manpower works with foreign know how, using imported equipment.

(c) S_dDKd_i : Equipment has been imported for domestically developed know how put into operational use by local manpower.

(d) $S_dDK_iH_d$: Using foreign know how, local manpower undertakes production using locally produced equipment.

(e) $S_dDK_dH_d$: All three elements are local.

From the viewpoint of the degree of technological dependence, or contrary wise, self-reliance, involved in the particular technology transaction, Case (a) is obviously one of total technological dependence while Case (e) is one of total self-reliance, while the intervening cases reflect varying degrees and forms of technological dependence.

Such a matrix can be used to analyse the degree of technological dependence of a country in many ways and from different perspectives :

(i) as a "snap shot" of the state of technology in different sectors of industry at a given point of time.

(ii) as a "dynamic flow chart" of the way in which the technological level/status of the industrial economy as a whole has evolved over time—Case (a) being the point of departure at time t1 in the past and the subsequent cases the status at later points of time.

(iii) as a "dynamic flow chart" of a sector of the industrial economy evolving over time.

(iv) both a "snap shot" and a "dynamic flow chart" of a particular company or organisation.

The matrix does not imply, however, that reaching Sd DKd Hd in all sectors of the industrial economy and/ or in all enterprises in a particular sector, should necessarily be the goal of either technological development strategy or economic development strategy. The planner, whether at the national or macro level or the company or micro level, has considerable freedom of choice. In many lines of production, the planner might opt for Case (a), as a long term solution. But in others, he would feel the need or compulsion to opt for Case (e). In such cases, he would need to decide which of (b) (c) or (d) is the appropriate initial goal to strive for, which one would be the next goal and so on. In other words, what the exact route should be to go from state (a) to state (e) in that particular technology.

Need For Strategies for Technological Development—Not Mere "Transfers"

This analytical framework came to be increasingly elaborated in the early 1970s as a result of several studies by UNCTAD, and by radical economists and S & T policy analysts, particularly in Latin America, in this Country and in some S & T policy Research Institutes in the UK. As knowledge of it diffused through the developing countries, the United Nations System, and some of the more liberal industrialised countries, it became clear that "technology transactions of transfer" was only one component of the much larger issue of "Strategies and Policies for Technological Development of the Developing Countries". Such a strategy needed to spell out fairly precisely, priorities at the national, sectoral and enterprises levels—the paths or routes to be followed for the technological development process, the organisational and managerial structures needed to deal with S, DK and H, and most importantly to inter-link them, and the time scheduling of the operations. Of course, this task had to be undertaken taking into account the character and goals of the overall industrial strategy of the developing country concerned, on the one hand, and on the other, the capacity of the systems in the country responsible for generating or producing S, DK and H. These were :

For S : The educational system

DK : The R & D laboratory and engineering design bureau systems

and H: The industrial or more especially the machinery manufacturing or capital goods producing system.

Adaptation and Absorption

If technological dependence is to be minimised if not avoided as an integral objective of a strategy of technological development, and if self reliance is to be advanced, it is extremely important to recognise, that an imported DK may serve as an input, both for production and for R & D. Of course, in the former case it is immediately used in the production process, whereas in the latter case, it is used as a base for improved /new technology through scientific research in a laboratory of engineering research design bureau. If we keep in mind this double function of the DK acquired as part of imported technology, the transfer process can be made to take one of the following 4 forms, through conscious policy decisions and actions : (Figure-1)

1. Adaptive Transfer
2. Full Transfer
3. Full Adaptive Transfer
4. Pseudo-Transfer

If we recall the experience of most developing countries on international technology transactions discussed earlier, it will be seen that "Pseudo-Transfers" are likely to constitute the bulk of such transaction, if the transactions are left to enterprise to enterprise decisions and actions, without the intervention by a State which has a defined technology development and utilisation strategy. It is certainly the case with transactions between the principal of a TNC belonging to a highly industrialised country, and its subsidiary/affiliated company in a developing country. Under this type of transfer, an "echo principle" operates in regard to technology imports *i.e.*, every so many years, say 5 years or 8 years, it becomes necessary for the technology buyer in the developing country to purchase the up-dated or new version of the original technology in order to renovate or upgrade its own technology.

In the short run, pseudo transfers are the easiest to work out. They also create the comfortable feeling that one is getting access to "The latest technology" . But, they ignore the specific conditions of the importing developing country. Furthermore, they perpetuate a situation of complete technological dependence, not to speak of the burden which the payments for technology under such forms of transfer place on the country's foreign exchange resources.

Using the above categories, it is easy to construct a scale of preference for the modes of acquiring technologies and inducting them into production system.

Autonomous Effort/*i.e.*, Domestic Technology Generation

Full Adaptive Transfer

Full Transfer

Adaptive Transfer

Pseudo Transfer

However, in actual practice, no developing country is in a position even today to mount an R & D effort of such scale, quality and speed as to be able to generate all the technologies it needs even on a secondary *i.e.,* adaptive basis, let alone on a primary *i.e.,* autonomous basis. Nor, perhaps, would it be desirable, whether for the technological development of the country, for its industrial development or for its overall economic development. Therefore, all the 5 modes—including the pseudo transfer mode—will have to be employed. What is crucial is :

(i) to be aware of these different modes, not only at the national planning/policy making level, but at the sectoral level, at the enterprise level, and at the user level.

(ii) to recognise that there are different types and magnitude of costs and benefits in each of these modes—technical, financial and political.

(iii) to develop at the sectoral, enterprise and specific product levels—criteria of choice between these modes for "feeding" a particular production mission with the technology it needs.

If we were to take this analysis one stage further in terms of operationalisation, the central issues, of policy making for designing an integrated strategy for self-reliant technological development, would be :

(a) What criteria to apply to decide which technology should be imported and which should be generated at home.

(b) How to build up the 4 systems, *viz.,* educational, R & D, design engineering and capital goods production and inter-connect them in such manner that the technologies (involving all 3 elements S, DK and H) chosen to be generated at home, are, in fact, so generated, in defined time frames, and with high probabilities of technical and economic success.

(c) In those cases where it is decided to import the technology, how to integrate that imported technology into the domestic S & T system, so that the domestic technological capacity is strengthened, and not only subsequent import of similar technology is obviated, but locally generated equivalents, if not superiors, generated and utilised. However, there is also the 8-fold path of the Buddha, which has proven its efficacy in the case of many of the industrially more advanced developing countries like ours. The core ingredients of the recipe are 6.

(i) Setting up a policy-making and implementing agency which should, on the one hand, frame a strategy appropriate to the country/sector concerned; on the other hand, control the actual purchases of foreign technology, including the screening of large projects, from the viewpoint of the choice of technology, source of purchase and negotiating support, and on the third hand, develop through planned funding, indigenous know-how generation, and the linking of that know-how to the S and H elements, promote the putting together of the indigenous technology package, and get it into commercial production, all with the close involvement of the customer or user.

(ii) Building up, under the auspices of such an agency, a strong industrial information system, able to provide public and private companies in the production system of the economy, with independent knowledge on sources of DK and H—and in some case also S, both abroad and within the country, thus strengthening the bargaining power of the technology purchasers.

(iii) Setting up engineering design and consultancy organisations, particularly in sectors like steel, petroleum, chemicals which are process based industries, which organisations can help to define the plant and equipment design and engineering elements of the total technology package, and use that definition to (a) "unpackage" foreign technology packages, and (b) "package" domestic laboratory scale process know-how into complete industrial projects.

(iv) R & D laboratories performing a 4- fold function providing specialised advanced training to S & T personnel coming out of the higher education system.

Doing applied research, oriented at developing laboratory scale know-how.

Assisting the policy making agency and the enterprises in identifying, selecting and negotiating with foreign technology suppliers to effect the purchase in the most "unpackaged" form possible and thereafter, participating, with the technology importing enterprises, in the absorption, adaptation and further development of the imported DKG—documented know-how.

Domestic Technology Generation and Commercialisation

I would now like to turn to consider, in some depth, the process of domestic generation of technology and its commercialisation. As touched upon earlier, the commitment of Jawaharlal Nehru to science and scientific thinking led to the building up, from the very early years after Independence, of a capacity for what was termed over the period 1947-1967, "scientific and technical research". This "capacity" took the form of setting up a number of research laboratories under the Council of Scientific and Industrial Research (CSIR) as far as the general economy, particularly the industrial sector of the economy was concerned. These laboratories were organised on the basis of scientific disciplines *e.g.*, the NPL (for physics) or the NCL (for chemistry), on the basis of sectors of industry *e.g.*, drugs, electronics or aeronautics, and on the basis of addressing the needs of a particular region *e.g.*, the Regional Research Laboratories, at Hyderabad, Jammu and Jorhat. This thrust was paralleled with the build up of a similar institutional infrastructure under the Defence R & D Organisation (DRDO) i.e. a set of discipline/sector based laboratories. However a rather different structure was set up in the area of atomic energy *viz.*, one major R & D Centre, but encompassing practically all the areas of science and engineering needed for that atomic energy programme—from biology to physical science and metallurgical engineering to electronic engineering. I refer, of course, to what is now known as the Bhabha Atomic Research Centre (BARC), Bombay.

The research laboratories of the CSIR and to a lesser extent of the DRDO were originally set up on the premise that the mere assemblage of scientists in laboratories and "letting them loose" to do research on scientific problems of their interest and choice would "automatically" result in contributing to the industrialisation of the country, or to its defence preparedness. Reference was often made in this connection to the statement in the Scientific Policy Resolution (SPR) of 1958 of how "new scientific techniques" could make up for deficiencies in natural resources and reduce the demand for capital—an objective of particular importance in a country like ours which was short of capital. However, hardly any attention was focussed on quoting the SPR fully and correctly in this important respect. What the SPR (now almost 30 years old) had stated was :

> "the creation AND ADOPTION of new scientific techniques can, in fact, make up for a deficiency in natural resources, and reduce the demands on capital".

The critical importance of ensuring adoption of the results of R & D was given hardly any intellectual attention, let alone governmental action. As a result, the building up of the industrial capacity of the country proceeded in the period 1955-1970 almost totally on the basis of imported technology, while the "scientific research" capacity was built up largely independently of the nation's industrialisation effort *i.e.*, the Pseudo Transfers discussed earlier. What is more, since the laboratories of the CSIR and the DRDO were staffed at their inception from the only pool of scientific manpower available *viz.*, the universities, the laboratories tended to have far closer interactions with the universities than with industry.

Between 1950 and 1970, the nation had invested some Rs. 150 crores* in the CSIR laboratories and between 1959 and 1970 some Rs. 60 crores had been invested in the DRDO laboratories and questions were rightly being raised as to what tangible economic returns the nation had secured from this investment. Incidentally, investment in CSIR Labs over 1970-1985 has been a further Rs. 1000 crores and in DRDO, a further Rs. 1300 crores. The ensuing debate shifted the focus for the first time from "science" and "scientific research" to "Technology and Technological Innovation" as the key issue, even as far as the domestic R & D system was concerned.

Technological innovation may be described as the process by which knowledge on how to produce a product not available in a given market, or how to improve the performance of an existing product, reduce its cost, or market and distribute the product more efficiently, is made a reality. The process of technological innovation can be visualised conceptually in terms of "a chain made up of a number of links". This is shown in Figure 2.8.

Features of the Model

If we examine this model closely we will see that it has been so structured as to enable each activity in the chain to be associated with (a) the kinds of manpower needed to undertake it, (b) the goals such manpower is expected to work towards, and (c) the institutional setting which the work is to be carried out.

Part A covers basic research, undertaken usually in academic institutions and, to some extent, in government laboratories, by scientific staff who are leaders in some specialised field, and aimed, not at making any particular invention, but at the advancement of basic scientific knowledge. Part B spans the gap between basic research and engineering design, which we often call Development in the R & D sense . The kind of personnel

---

* 1 crore of rupees (Rs.) is 10 million rupees. At the prevailing official exchange rate, this amount has been equivalent to : US $2.5 million over 1947-66 to US $1.5 million over 1967-1979, to US $1 million over 1980-85 to US $0.75 million today.

required here are largely those with scientific backgrounds acquired from participating in A. However, and this is important, it also includes some engineers. The activity undertaken is often as complex as that tackled in Part A but is more directed at producing a new product or processes in a defined time frame. Part C is a stage manned almost completely by engineers whose sole aim is to get products and processes ready for production. The final part D deals with the (supposedly) well understood activity of industrial production, marketing, sales and after-sales service.

Implications for policy making

We can draw several important deductions from such an "innovation chain", relevant to policy making :

1. Innovation is inextricably concerned with interfaces—technical interfaces, economic interfaces, institutional and behavioural interfaces—and it is on the identification of such interfaces and on ensuring smooth and effective flow of information and action across each of them that successful innovation largely depends. (See Figure-3)
2. The fact that administrative control over each section in the chain frequently lies in the hands of different organisations, makes such interfaces often noman's lands. This requires that, at least in the early stages of the development of an industry, the innovation process as a whole must be conceived, planned, promoted, coordinated by a single over-riding managerial authority.
3. The activities in the chain are, by and large, sequential in occurrence. But, and this is an important proviso, the activities also overlap considerably on all the counts mentioned earlier. They also overlap in terms of time. This provides some scope for undertaking activities in parallel, thereby shortening the total "innovation lead time".
4. Each activity will take a certain minimum amount of

time, no matter how large an investment in men and money is made on it. Therefore, the time-phasing of the various activities in the chain plays a crucial role in ensuring that the innovation is successful.

5. There is a resource threshold, in terms of annual outlay on men, equipment and material for each segment of the chain, which must be crossed if the project is to move to the next segment in any finite time interval.

6. The magnitude of such critical or threshold level of resources required to complete each activity is far from uniform across the chain. However, in general it increases as one moves towards the final stages of the chain.

7. While the ratio between resource requirements for various stages in the chain will vary from product to product, studies have shown that in a majority of cases the distribution of costs across the chain is typically as in Figure 4.9.

8. The kinds of skills and aptitudes which the manpower deployed in each of these stages need to have, vary considerable, particularly in regard to specialisation. The development of manpower must therefore be undertaken keeping in mind the nature of the activity which each type of professional is to be deployed on.

Cause of our failure

Once the concept of "the innovation chain" came to be accepted in the early 70s its inherent characteristics were recognised, and the implications for technology policy perceived, it became relatively easy to see why the efforts of most CSIR and DRDO laboratories over the previous decade, on an activity loosely called "R & D", were not producing "results" in terms of industrial technology and production, anywhere near those realised using imported technology.

First, while the innovation chain as a concept was known to policy makers in a theoretical way, no attempt had been made to use it in real life decision-making up till then. Moreover, at the operational level—of managers in industry and project leaders in R & D laboratories—there was lack of awareness of even the existence of such a chain. As a consequence, the fact that interface problems are bound to come up at some stage in the development of what starts off as an R & D project in a laboratory, came time and again, to be recognised only when the laboratory claimed it had "completed" its task, but no manufacturing unit was willing to undertake commercial production, or the customer/user denied that his needs had been met.

Secondly, the features of the institutional structure available to us at that time for bringing about technological innovation, viz. organisational and managerial separation of the different institutions responsible for various stages in the chain, lack of the most rudimentary information system on needs, production programmes underway, development projects in progress, etc. militated strongly against the essential prerequisites for successful innovation.

Thirdly, much of the success of technological innovation and, more narrowly, of goal-directed RD, depends critically on our having the ability to make demand forecasts with increasing accuracy. What is more, such demand assessments have to be reduced to product specific terms if successful technological innovation is to be achieved. Such demand forecasting is difficult, and calls for the use of sophisticated techniques. But the fact that, for a large part of the capital goods sector at least, the government or government companies were—and still are—the major buyer, should make things much easier. But equally important as having such a forecast at all, is its availability sufficiently far in advance of the time when the product is first needed, to enable not merely R & D but also the remaining stages in the chain to be undertaken in time. In-short, the need is for planning.

Fourthly, most industrial units, and almost all R & D laboratories, were extremely weak in production engineering capacity, and indeed persons trained in the design, development and engineering of production machinery, jigs, tools and fixtures were woefully small in number. This proved to be a major bottleneck in ensuring that process know-how or product design, once proven on the laboratory scale i.e. brought upto stage 6 in the innovation chain, was carried forward to the next two stages viz. engineering of production prototypes and designing and fabricating of equipment enabling volume production.

Fifthly, the very fact that the overwhelming bulk of our industrial production in 1970 was based on imported technology prevented manufacturers from having to face the difficulties of true technological innovation.

As we saw earlier, under a foreign licence or technology import agreement, the licensor usually provides the following inputs :

(a) the complement of production equipment needed for the production process.

(b) detailed plant layout, and either written instructions or its own personnel for installing and commissioning production machinery.

(c) details of production process with blue-prints, production drawings, testing and approving procedures.

(d) bill of materials for the products covered by the licence.

(e) training at their plant of our staff who are to supervise production, and the testing and control of quality, volume, etc.

(f) training of workers for various operations through the deputation of one of their plant supervisors or equivalent production operatives to this country; and

(g) consultancy services to overcome testing troubles.

These inputs correspond only to those related to stages 8,9 and 11 of the innovation chain. However, this does not mean, of course, that the licensor did not himself go through the earlier stages in the chain, particularly from 4 onwards. But that experience is never communicated in the transfer process, even implicitly. Consequently, when presented with domestic "know-how", which has only come as far as stage 5 or 6, the local manufacturer is reluctant to commit the men, money and intellectual and managerial effort needed for him to learn how these stages are performed. This is particularly so when he is sure that he can continue to rely on packaged technology from abroad on a continuing basis *i.e.* through what has earlier been called "pseudo transfers".

Over the last 15 years *i.e.* since 1970, awareness and understanding of these realities of the "innovation chain" have been steadily diffusing more and more extensively into most of our R & D agencies, our manufacturing companies and among major customer groups including user agencies in government.

Those who have had any involvement in India's defence production and defence R & D over this period, will, I am sure, agree that DRDO today is very different indeed from what is was in 1970 in terms of planning for and realising successful technology transfer and commercialisation of a range of military systems and equipment.

From my experience in the Department of Electronics (DOE) over the same period, I can say that this has certainly been so across a wide front in professional electronics. The Department of Space has built such thinking, planning and action into its R & D Centres right from the inception of the Department in 1972. This is also the case with the Department of Atomic Energy and its domestic technology generation and commercialisation or utilisation activities, and with several CSIR laboratories.

To cite a few specific examples of successful domestic technological innovation :

As for DRDO, I would cite the Mountain Gun, the Special Anti-Tank Ammunition, Low Level Radars, the Advanced Panoramic Sonar, as examples of major technologies which have been successfully developed, put through the innovation chain and in various stages of regular production already, or in the next 2-3 years, at levels ranging from several tens of crores to several hundreds of crores worth per year. What is more, the whole project or programme in these cases have been undertaken with considerable professionalism and confidence, though not without many agonising moments.

Electronics as an example

Apart from the low level radars and the advanced panoramic sonars already mentioned, there are at least some 40 major professional systems/products in the area of defence, telecommunication, TV and radio broadcasting, civil aviation, industrial electronics and control systems and computer-based real time systems, which are now in regular commercial production, based on domestic technology development, either financed by, and/or promoted, coordinated and pushed through by the DOE over the last 5-6 years. If one were to cite just two instances there would be the massive increase in national TV coverage from 30 per cent to 70 per cent brought about in a span of 18 months in 1983 and 1984 under the Special TV Expansion Plan, and the Pulse Code Modulation (PCM) Multiplex Equipments.

The former involved around Rs. 50 crores worth of TV transmitters, and the direct-from-satellite TV receiver terminals associated with them, direct reception community TV sets, studio equipments etc. All this equipment was designed, developed, prototyped, field tested, mass manufactured, installed and commissioned, in 18 months from go. The Pulse Code Modulation Multiplex is an advanced digital electronic equipment, which forms the backbone of the 10 year plan of converting our entire telecommunication network into a completely digital system. Prototype developed by the Telecommunication Research Centre of the Department of Telecommunications in 1981, the PCM Multiplex was successfully industrially engineered, batch produced, field tested and put into commercial production by 1984-85. It is now in volume production by 5 public sector companies, to meet the large requirement of around 10,000 nos. needed over the Seventh Plan (1985-90) and around 20,000 nos. over the Eighth Plan (1990-94). This production of a single product valued at around Rs. 100 crores over the Seventh Plan alone, constitutes the largest production of any single indigenously designed telecommunication equipment over 1985-90.

Many more such examples can be given. A representative list of indigenously developed and successfully commercialised hi-tech electronic systems and equipment, is given in Annexure

I. These are all the results of RTD and engineering done over the period 1978-1984 and launched into commercial production over the last 3-5 years. The indigenous technology development and commercialisation task has been conceived, planned, in many case financed and in all cases promoted, monitored and launched to free flow commercial production, by Department of Electronics working closely with the customer (s)[1] user agency (s) concerned. As a result, out of the approx. Rs. 1250 crores of professional electronics production in calendar 1985, around Rs. 250-300 crores worth consisted of products based on domestically developed technology *i.e.* around 20-22 per cent. The corresponding figures for 1986 are tentatively estimated to be Rs. 1,800 crores and Rs. 450 crores, or about 25 per cent.

Similar examples could be given in the case of Space and Atomic Energy and the laboratories of the CSIR. There are, in addition, many successful technological innovations in several more conventional areas of industry e.g. machine tools, petroleum exploration and refining, chemicals and petrochemicals etc. which also shall not be recounted here for the same reason.

What I think one can say with confidence, however, is that in many sectors of industry, including those involving sophisticated technology, we now know what it takes to bring about successful generation and commercialisation of indigenously developed technology. Perhaps more importantly, I believe that, at least in a number of areas, we also know why failures occur, to the point where we can forecast with reasonable accuracy that an incorrectly structured and managed technology development project - particularly one which violates the principles of the "Innovation Chain" is almost certain to fail. In short, that there is a "Technology" of Technology Transfer, calling for specialised analytical , managerial, and behavioural skills on the part of planners and policy makers and technology generators and utilisers.

Self Reliance

The identification and analysis of the key issues focused on here also enables one to arrive to an operational formulation of the concept of self-reliance in technology.

This formulation encompasses a number of levels. The first level is that of decision-making. Self reliance means that we are in a position to define our own goals—goals which are appropriate to the development strategy and development pattern which the country has chosen. Next, that we are able to define the types of technologies we need to realise those goals, and the modes through which such technologies are to be acquired or generated. The second level is that of undertaking, MAKE or BUY choices at the sectoral and enterprise levels, in relation to the specific set of technologies needed for the development of the sector or enterprise concerned. Third, how to identify and select from the foreign technologies available for those products for which the second stage exercise has shown that technology purchase is necessary. Fourth, self-reliance in being able to negotiate effectively to acquire those foreign technologies on the most favourable terms to the buyer. Fifth, self-reliance in building up S & T expertise in all key areas of national importance, and in increasing that competence and capacity to the "critical levels" needed for generating technology domestically in the core areas.

Self-reliance does not mean building a wall around oneself, it does not mean autarchy, even less, isolationism. But it does mean being "maximally in command" of the whole technological strategy at the national, sectoral and company or agency levels.

As our the late Prime Minister Smt. Indira Gandhi, who did so much to enhance our self-reliance in general and in S & T in particular, put it :

"Self Reliance means the assertion of our right to formulate our policies, programmes or institutional mechanisms. We have to make our own choices, taking account of world developments in science and technology but without being swayed by fashions within science, or the S & T foreign policies followed by advanced countries".

References

1. Scientific Policy Resolution, Government of India, New Delhi, March 1958.
2. Technology Policy Statement, Department of Science and Technology, Government of India, New Delhi, January 1983.
3. UN ESCAP/UN CTC, Costs and Conditions of Technology Transfer through Transnational Corporations, New York, 1984.
4. United Nations Conference on Trade and Development (UNCTAD), Major Issues arising from the Transfer of Technology to Developing Countries. Report by the UNCTAD Secretariat, UN Publication Sales No. E. 75. IID. 2, 1975.
5. Cited in Emil Hebolzheimer and Habit Quaene, "Transfer of Technology Transactions", UNCTAD Trade and Development Review, No. 5, 1984, pp. 201-213.
6. See my paper "An Apex Body for Electronics", Paper presented at the National Conference on Electronics, Bombay, March, 1970, later published under the same title in Commerce, Bombay, August 1, 1970.
7. Scientific Policy Resolution, *op. cit.*
8. See my Paper "Development Strategy for the Electronics Industry" presented at the National Conference on Electronics, Bombay, March 1970, and later published in Economic and Political Weekly, Bombay, Vol. V, No. 48, November 28, 1970.

   For a slight variant see "The Process of Innovation" in "The structure and functioning of Technology Systems in Developing countries" (1D/WG:301/2) quoted in UNIDO, the Technological Self Reliance of Developing Countries : Towards Operational Strategies, New York.
9. *Ibid.*
10. See for instance, "Focus: Television The Great Leap Forward", Business India, Bombay, June 18-July 1, 1984.
11. Indira Gandhi, "Science for Social Change", Special Lecture at the Science Policy Foundation, London, March 26, 1982.

Figure - 1

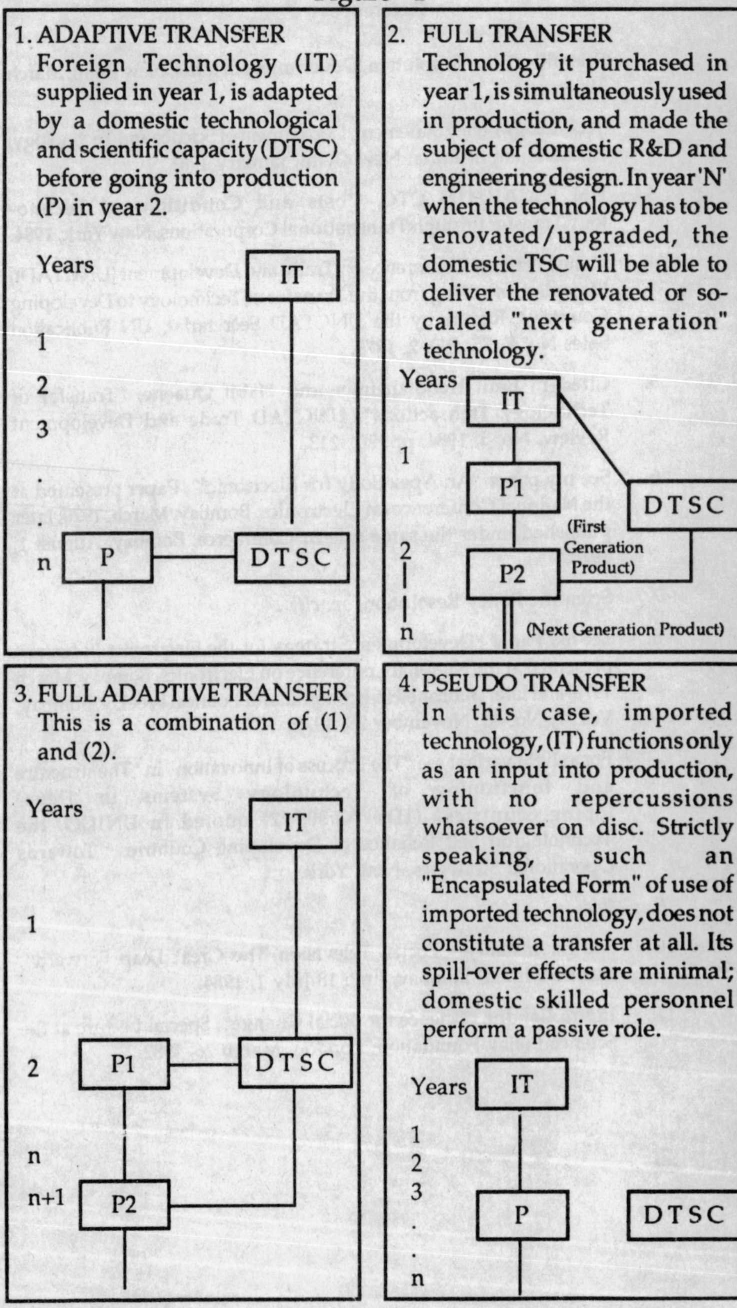
1. ADAPTIVE TRANSFER
Foreign Technology (IT) supplied in year 1, is adapted by a domestic technological and scientific capacity (DTSC) before going into production (P) in year 2.
Years
IT
1
2
3
.
.
n
P
DTSC
2. FULL TRANSFER
Technology it purchased in year 1, is simultaneously used in production, and made the subject of domestic R&D and engineering design. In year 'N' when the technology has to be renovated/upgraded, the domestic TSC will be able to deliver the renovated or so-called "next generation" technology.
Years
IT
1
P1
DTSC
(First Generation Product)
2
P2
n
(Next Generation Product)
3. FULL ADAPTIVE TRANSFER
This is a combination of (1) and (2).
Years
IT
1
2
P1
DTSC
n
n+1
P2
4. PSEUDO TRANSFER
In this case, imported technology, (IT) functions only as an input into production, with no repercussions whatsoever on disc. Strictly speaking, such an "Encapsulated Form" of use of imported technology, does not constitute a transfer at all. Its spill-over effects are minimal; domestic skilled personnel perform a passive role.
Years
IT
1
2
3
.
.
n
P
DTSC

Figure - 2

THE INNOVATION CHAIN

Research Through Development of Use		Phase	Description of		Nature of activity
		1	Activity Scientific principle, invention or discovery of a new phenomenon	A	Pure research without industrial motive
		2	Preliminary measurement and analysis		
		3	Basic research necessary to get an understanding of the phenomenon	B	Applied research where scientific staff trained in A are required
This is the area where close attention by policy management first appears	improvements and modifications	4	Construction of workable model with application in mind		
		5	Development of prototype for demonstration		
		6	Demonstration and evaluation to assess value for production		
		7	Engineering design of production models	C	Development by engineers with production in mind
		8	Tooling and manufacture		
		9	Inspection, quality control and testing	D	Manufacture, marketing and use
		10	Marketing and acceptance by the public buyer.		

Figure - 3

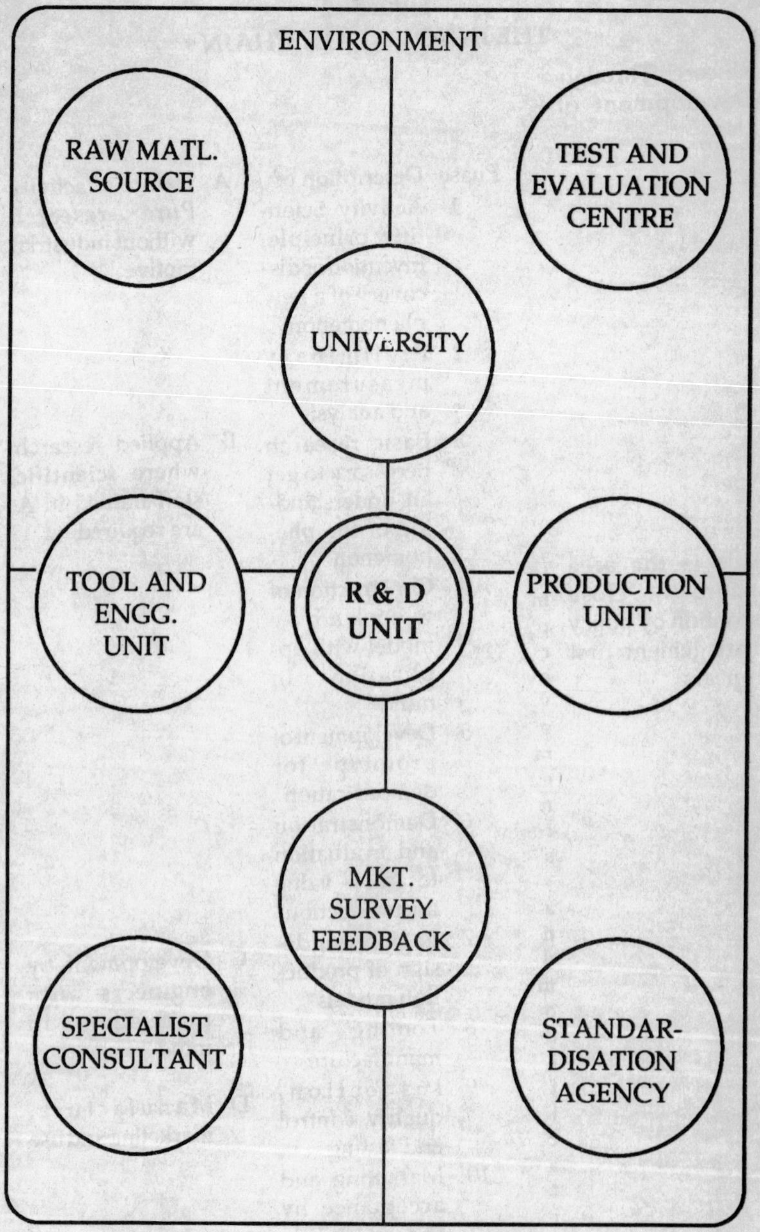

LINKAGES NEEDED FOR R & D UNIT

Figure - 4
TYPICAL DISTRIBUTION OF COSTS IN SUCCESSFUL PRODUCT INNOVATIONS

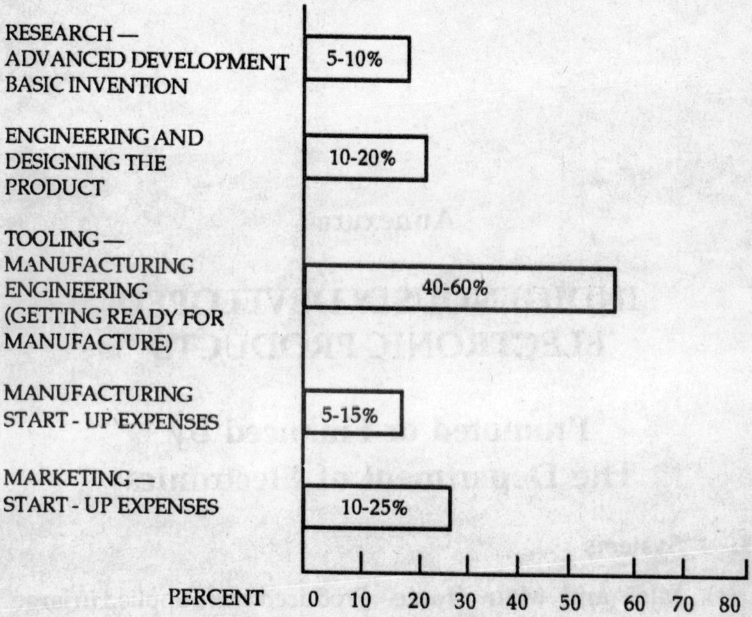

Annexure I

INDIGENOUSLY DEVELOPED ELECTRONIC PRODUCTS

Promoted or Financed by The Department of Electronics

1. Systems

(1)	Mini and Main frame Computers (TDC-312, 316 and 332) ECIL, Hyderabad.	Produced and Supplied in large nos. Tech. being upgraded with imported know-how.
(2)	Mobile and Static Automatic Computerised Data Handling Systems (ADHS) for the Air Defence Network ECIL, Hyderabad Jointly with TIFR, Hyderabad	Systems field proven and large volume production by ECIL.
(3)	Autonomous Display Consoles for ADHS ECIL, Hyderabad.	System developed and tested and commercial orders being placed by Air force.

(4)	Systems Integration of INTEGRA Series Computers CMC, Bombay.	Indigenous capability in system engineering of computer systems for supply and support of larger computers, developed and being used.
(5)	Mobile Digital Electronic Exchanges for Army Tactical Communication Network, ITI jointly with TIFR and BEL jointly with LRDE.	Know-how transferred to designated production company after successful field trials and large volume production underway.
(6)	UHF Radio Relay Communication Systems for DOT, Railways etc. GCEL, Baroda with SAC, A bad	Know-how developed, commercialised and supplies made.
(7)	Computerised Message Switching Systems for Defence Services ECIL, Hyderabad.	In regular commercial production.
(8)	Computerised Message Switching Systems for Civil Aviation Deptt. CMC, Bombay.	Supply (meeting ICAO Standards) completed.
(9)	Computerised Message Retransmission systems for overseas Commn. Service ECIL, Hyderabad.	Supplies already made to OCS.
(10)	Computerised Railway Passenger Reservation Systems, CMC Bombay.	Delhi system operational Around Rs. 40 crores worth of orders for other 3 metropolitan cities in hand.

(11)	PCM Digital Multiplex GCEL Equipment, Baroda and ITI, Bangalore jointly with TRC, New Delhi.	Rs. 5 crores worth supplied by GCEL. Around Rs. 100 crores worth of supplies to be made over remainder of Seventh Plan by 5 public sector companies.
(12)	Air Route Surveillance Radar (ARSR), HAL, Hyderabad.	Development of this major system successfully completed and 4 systems worth Rs. 20 crores supplied/committed for supply.
(13)	Precision Approach Radar (PAR), HAL, Hyderabad.	Development of this major system successfully completed and 5 systems worth Rs. 3 crores supplied to Civil Aviation Department.
(14)	Wind finding and Weather Analysis Radar, BEL, Bangalore.	Equipment successfully developed and 8 radars worth Rs. 3 crores supplied/committed for supply.
(15)	Very High Frequency Omni Rangc (VOR) Air Route Navigation Equipment.	Equipment successfully developed and 19 VORs worth Rs. 1.7 crores supplied to Civil Aviation Department.
(16)	X-band Radar Beacons, SAMEER Bombay and Marine & Communications Electronics (MACE), Vishakapatnam.	Equipment has successively undergone user evaluation by Director General of Light Houses and Lightships. Know-how transferred to MACE, for manufacturing.
(17)	Distance Measuring Equipment, BEL, Bangalore.	Development and Field evaluation successfully completed by CAD and ready for production. National Airports Authority planning to order 5 units.

(18)	Common Antenna Direction Finder (CADF) Equipment GCEL, Baroda jointly with LRDE, Bangalore.	Around Rs. 3.5 crores worth supplied/committed for supply, till end 1987-88.
(19)	Hydro-Meteorological Monitoring System (involving communication, telemetry and computerised data handling and handling display GCEL, Baroda.	Around Rs. 3.5 crores worth supplied/committed for supply till end 1987-88.
(20)	Meteorological/Data Collection Storage and Transmission Systems (DCSTS) via. INSAT.	Around Rs. 3.5 crores worth supplied/committed for supply till end 1987-88.
(21)	Disaster Warning Receiver Systems (DWRS) using INSAT ECIL Hyderabad jointly with SAC, A'bad.	In volume commercial production.
(22)	Oceanographic Monitoring Systems. ECIL, Hyderabad.	In volume commercial production.
(23)	Video Teaching/Training Systems. GCEL, Baroda.	Around Rs. 3.5 Crores worth committed for supply by end 1987-88.

2. Equipment and Instruments

(1)	Aircraft Cockpit Voice Records. ECIL, Hyderabad.	Under production and continuous supply to Indian Airlines and Air Force.

(2)	Radio Theodolites for Meteorology SAMEER, Bombay.	Developed and 5 Nos. batch produced and supplied to IMD.
(3)	Groundwater Exploration Logging Equipment ONGC, Dehra Dun and UPTRON, Lucknow.	Know-how taken from ONGC, Dehra Dun, prototypes engineered field tested, cleared and commercial supplies made.
(4)	Microwave Distance Measuring Equipment ECIL, Hyderabad.	Successfully developed and supplied in quantity to Survey Agencies.
(5)	Sequence Event Recorders UPTRON and KELTRON.	Successfully developed and supplied to Power Plants.
(6)	Microprocessor Based Automatic Built-In Test Equipment for Radar and Communication Systems BEL, Bangalore.	Know-how used in various Major systems.
(7)	Electronic Axle Counters for Railway Wagons III, Delhi and CEL, Sahibabad.	Field Trials completed successfully, technology transferred for productionisation and in regular commercial production and supply to Railways.
(8)	Thyristor-Controlled Equipment for EOT Cranes University College of Technology, Calcutta.	Successfully undergone field trials and transferred for productionisation.
(9)	AC and DC Drives for Process Industries KELTRON, Trivandrum.	Techniques for DC-DC power conversion and speed control of large induction motors using thyristors developed and successfully gone through field tri-

	als in actual industrial situations; orders placed and further exploitation underway.
(10) Programmable Logic Controllers for Process Industries, ECIL, Hyderabad.	Successfully developed and supplied to Steel, Cement and Power Plants.
(11) Input/Output Printers for Computers. DELTRON, Trivandrum.	Prototype model developed and fabricated for multi-lingual printing in Indian Languages. To go into commercial production soon.
(12) Bosignal Processing Techniques and Hardware, Indian Institute of Science, Bangalore.	Both hardware and software capability for Arrthythmis monitor developed. Know-how transferred to industry and productionised.
(13) 100 KW Mediumwave Radio Transmitters BEL, Bangalore.	Around Rs. 37 crores worth supplied/committed for supply till end 1987-88.
(14) 10KW and 1KW TV Transmitters BEL, Bangalore.	Around Rs. 35 crores worth supplied/committed for supply till end 1987-88.
(15) 100 Watt Low Power TV Transmitters GCEL, Baroda and BEL, Bangalore.	Around Rs. 16 crores worth supplied/committed for supply till end 1987-88.
(16) 10 Watt Very Low Power (Unattended Model) TV Transmitters.	Around Rs. 5 crores worth supplied in 1986-87 committed for supply in 1987-88.

(17)	Direct-From-INSAT TV Receive Only Satellite Ground Terminals (both attended & unattended) ECIL, Hyderabad and BEL, Bangalore.	Around Rs. 9 crores worth supplied/committed for supply up to end 1987-88.
(18)	Radio Studio to Transmitter Communication Links AIR R & D Centre jointly with MELTRON, Bombay.	Around Rs. 5 crores worth supplied/committed for supply up to end 1987-88.
(19)	Radio Transmission Net Working Terminals using INSAT SAC, Ahmedabad jointly with KELTRON. Trivandrum.	Around Rs. 3 crores worth supplied/committed for supply up to end 1987-88.

3. Strategic and other Components

(1)	TR Cells in different frequency bands, PIN and schotty barrier diodes, and other critical microwave components, TIFR, Bombay.	Being batch produced by SAMEER and supplied regularly to the Defence services and other users.
(2)	Vacuum Contact Switch BEL, Bangalore.	Productionised to specifications of BHEL which is main customer.
(3)	Microwave tubes, CEERI, Pilani and CEL, Sahibabad.	Know-how generated, technology developed for various techniques used in the fabrication of the tubes and tubes produced supplied to the Defence Services.

(4)	Rectilinear Trimpots and Tantalum Capacitors ECIL, Hyderabad.	Production established around the technology developed with production investment from ECIL.
(5)	Miniature Servo Components, ECIL, Hyderabad.	Synchros and Servo motors meeting Defence Grade Specifications developed and successfully batch produced for strategic end uses.

COMMENTS ON DR. A. RAHMAN'S PAPER

Kamal A. Mitra Chenoy

My comments on Dr. Rahman's stimulating and informative paper on "Application of Technology for Development ," in the main, addresses issues not addressed in the paper.

The paper does not explicitly deal with the North's control of technology and India's lack of access to modern technologies. Surprisingly, there is no reference to the widely discussed TRIPs (trade related intellectual property rights) issue, where North-oriented patent laws are being sought to be forced down the South's throat. This is especially serious matter as India, largely because of its own default, is somewhat isolated in the GATT over this issue. If the new patent laws, as incorporated in the Dunkel Draft Text (DDT), become part of GATT, then the application of technology for development in India, will be subject to stringent controls, and very substantial royalties extracted by the TNCs which have cornered most patents.

Important changes in Patent law laid down in the DDT involve the expansion of patents to include: (a) product patents, as well as process patents, so that the product itself becomes patented, not only the process by which it is made; (b) natural processes such as bio-technology can be patented—thereby privatising the most promising frontier areas of current scientific research; (c) patents will be valid for 20 years, and not 5/14 as at present under the Indian Patents Act, 1970; and (d) the burden of proof will not be on the plaintiff, as is the normal principle of law, but on the defendant. In effect the accused will have to reveal the process to the accuser in court, thereby losing the secrecy of the process.

Any discussion on technology and development should therefore begin with an expose of the DDT and The TRIPs issue. The proposed changes in India's patent regime will irrevocably hamstring all efforts at technological self-reliance, as even intermediate technologies, will be restrictively patented for 20 years, *i.e.* until they become wholly obsolete. Moreover the TNC holding the patent cannot be directed to produce the product in India, and may choose to import it *in toto*. Given the declining value of the rupee, it is likely that Indian producers will be constrained to import technologies wholly and pay for them in scarce foreign exchange.

Apart from this current threat, the problem of technological dominance remains. Third World countries are normally denied access to the most modern technologies by the North. Technologies imported are usually not the newest 'sunrise' processes, but obsolescent 'sunset' ones. The quantum of R & D required to develop the necessary technologies is staggering and beyond the individual capacity even of a country like India with its reserves of scientific and technological personnel.

In this area there is an imperative need for South-South Co-operation. Any plan for technological self-reliance must factor in such co-operation, given the bleak reality of the unequal international economic order. Any discussion on such a topic should therefore, deal, at least in passing, with strategies for maximising India's bargaining position vis-a-vis the North in the matter of technology.

It is also necessary to highlight the problem of the repetitive import of technology. For instance, in the two wheeler industry, India has gone in for a number of collaboration agreements, all for 100 c.c. two-stroke engines. This is in stark contrast to the policy adopted by the Japanese through MITI, where this ministry ensured that the most modern technology was imported at the most advantageous terms and given to the most efficient producers. Here also, there will have to be at least some regulation, to ensure that there is no repetitive import of technology, much less import of obsolete technologies.

The relationship between technology and the specific development model will have to be addressed. The coming Earth Summit is sure to declare, the present model of development is just not sustainable. Therefore, the choice of technology will have to be based on the preferred model of development. High-energy intensive development will have to be displaced by environmentally-friendly strategies. This will shape the choice of technologies and their development pattern.

Environment is an area where the North-South divide also operates. It appears that conditionalities witnessed in GATT deliberations will also be sought to be imposed in relation to the Earth Summit. Thus, while the North will insist on bio-diversity (especially in tropial eco-systems) being a common heritage, it will simultaneously insist on "privatising" bio-diversity in the shape of the bio-technology involved in the primary process by patenting it.

It is surely now necessary for emphasis to be laid on the importance of an educational system which accelerates our technological development and maximises technological training. The problem of 'brain drain' or the reverse transfer of technology will have to be tackled. At least 70 per cent of our III- trained graduates migrate, at substantial cost to the country. It would only be equitous to mandate that these highly-subsidised engineers pay back the exchequer the cost of their education, or alternatively to rule that they work in select priority areas for at least five years before being allowed to migrate.

In view of the importance of the need to understand the dynamics of internal and external realities : social, political, economic, ecological, psychological and cultural in any viable effort to build and sustain an alternative development and technology strategy the relevance of the social sciences and the humanities will have to be recognised.

Very often, these are the areas which are officially designated as "superfluous" and "irrelevant" to employment oriented education.

Technologies are not "socially neutral". Many modern technologies are labour-displacing, a major problem in societies such as ours. A technology policy would have to take the employment issue, as indeed the vexatious issue of equity into account. Unless the development and technology patterns are equitous, there can be nothing approaching a "national consensus".

In fact a national consensus on such major issues will be problematic. Beneficiaries of the old regime, and sectors of society sympathetic to old models, or to foreign power blocks, will almost invariably resist equitous and sustainable packages. Moreover, the proviso for a national consensus is prone to be used by forces inimical to change, who insist upon an agreement with the ruling elite as a pre-condition.

While an informed public debate on policies and programmes is necessary, this again raises the question of the appropriate agencies. Can the private media which is business - controlled perform such a role? Of course, the question of agency is not the focus of Dr. Rahman's paper, but it is perhaps of enough importance to be mentioned as worthy of notice.

It would perhaps bear repetition to aver that the possibilities of such a strategy would only be possible if a democratic international political and economic order is established. A technology policy can only be viable if it is part of an overall effort to achieve this elusive but irreplaceable goal.

COMMENTS ON DR. A. RAHMAN'S PAPER

'APPLICATION OF TECHNOLOGY FOR DEVELOPMENT'

P.D. Hajela

A mere look at Dr. Rahman's brief but concise paper suggests that both the taxonomy to technology and also the diverse directions it can take are bewildering.

For a layman like me, the issue is how a country having no militarist designs, a colonial past which distorted its pre-capitalist industrial and agricultural growth, and a per capita income amongst the lowest in the world, can indulge in technological leap frogging. If it is a matter of free market conditions, the issue will have to reckon with labour abundance, entrepreneurial inertia, excess demand conditions and a higher education environment which breathes all-round frustration and adversely affects the growth of the scientific paradigm which Dr. Rahman rightly regards as a necessary concomitant of the technological paradigm which we need to create in the context of the country's economic development.

Both surplus labour and excess demand conditions make for high profits and therefore, lead to the emergence of entrepreneurial inertia. Why should one innovate if profits can be high without innovation? That labour surplus exists, tending to prevent any particular rise in real wage rate, is inferred from the unemployment situation in India. As for excess demand, that is due to the compulsions of investment planning in the interests of growth with social justice.

The advantage of low real wage rates in respect of attractions to foreign investment and technological leap-frogging therefrom is no longer a substantial as it could have been earlier because of the newly emerging techno-economic paradigms in which foreigners have started looking for a new set of inter-related technological phenomena and ethos for pushing forward with their products. Witness the manner the Japanese car makers have penetrated U.S. market inspite of high real wage rates in that country.

Competition as an influence on cost-consciousness and technological upgradation could be important but in the small - scale sector, even in agriculture where the producers are numerous, the latter just cannot have resources or risk capabilities to research and innovate. The green revolution was essentially the consequence of government intervention not competition.

In the organised private sector such evidence as we have, would suggest that the liberalisation of mid-eighties strengthened oligopolistic tendencies and increased the concentration ratio in some of the most growth intensive sectors of Indian industry. Oligopolies are known to innovate but Indian oligopolies enjoying the protection of excess demand conditions in the economy have preferred to use price manipulation as a means of profit maximisation more than cost reduction product improvement. Look at the case of the tyre or synthetic industry.

In such a background, foreign participants could help but how much is the real question. Why will not the foreigner like to enjoy the inertia of his counterpart if it can be possible for him to avoid being on his 'competitive' toes all the time in our internal market? If the foreigner comes to produce for markets abroad, the case will be different but the big question is: why can't he sell abroad from his own native land?

In view of such questions, it is more likely that foreign

investors may try less direct investments and more licensing of their technology. Foreign investments could come more for capturing the internal market rather than for exports and foreign technology could come more in the shape of licensed patents than in the shape of foreign investments. The Dunkel proposals and the pressure of Super 301 alongwith the IMF/World Bank restructuring are all part of a scheme to make things easier for the foreign investor and foreign technology. The question is how precisely will all this make things easier for us? Will labour surplus be absorbed? Will savings rise so fast that excess investment leading to excess demand conditions will be corrected? Will our own entrepreneurial inertia born out of excess demand conditions disappear as a result of foreign investment pressure?

Technological spurts can occur in all sorts of ways. Incremental technology could even be a regular and frequent affair, but radical technology or change in technological paradigm or techno-economic systems could take place in jumps at irregular intervals only. Indian's concern for a jump is understandable. But it cannot occur irrespective of the objective economic and social reality in the country. First of all, we should have fast employment intensive growth in which infrastructure, agriculture, essential consumer goods, housing, health and education have all a major part to play. At the same time, economic policy must firmly come down on waste and luxury consumption in both the public and private sectors and raise taxes mainly from the gainers of the development process. There has to be, so to say, a system approach to waste and resource mobilisation so that excess demand can be controlled. The sooner we can change our objective economic situation in this manner, the better will it be for our attempts at technological leap-frogging.

A POLICY FOR RELEVANT TECHNOLOGY

P.R. Brahmananda

Dr. A. Rahman in his classificatory paper has dealt with technology from the angle of general development, also with reference to defence. I want to discuss the issue of technology from the angle of relevant development under Indian and similar conditions. Relevant development, also termed *basic* development refers to production of goods and services of primary/core significance in productive policies and programmes to eradicate poverty and obtain full year, full employment for all, on a normative, socially acceptable, real wage-rate. From the developmental angle the real wage-rate will have to be moving up after triple full-employment has been obtained taking into account population growth.

The initial situation in India is characterised by mass poverty and substantial underemployment and unemployment. The population size is large and will continue to grow over several decades ahead. The constraints/limitations arising are on the score of high exploitation—cost of natural resources, limited per capita, inadequacy of overall capital and absence of relevant technology.

Given the initial situation and the constraints, the *commodity* aspect, over several years ahead, will have to be dominated by first order or necessary wage-goods, and production inputs for the same and of exportable commodities in which India has a dynamic advantage. Since imports reduce costs and overcome domestic constraints of non-available resources and help in efficient development of domestic resources, the goal of trade is to augment domestic supplies of productivity in wage-goods and in export-worthy sectors.

Not all available technology is relevant from the above angle. That portion of technology which is directly or indirectly related to wage-goods and exports in alone the relevant technology, apart from defence. The products referred to above are basic. The technology relevant for the above is basic.

As the system develops the second order wage-goods will all become important. The concept of basicness and relevance is related to the stage of development as typified by the relevant major social goals. Development of science to the extent it is related to basic technology is important; but other science, to the extent it helps in exports, is also important. Here also we have to distinguish between basic and non-basic science.

Certainly, scientific subjects as well as technologies in the development of which we have a comparative advantage are basic. If we can export physicists, bioscientists, statisticians, economists, doctors, artists, business managers, mathematicians, writers, journalists, engineers, craftsmen and so on, and their services, these lines should be deemed as having comparative advantage and they will become basic.

Note that we have two criteria for basicness :

(a) Direct and indirect involvement in wage goods production including inputs for the same etc., related to the above are products and processes in basic needs.

(b) Direct and indirect involvement in export of goods and services which have a comparative advantage, statically and dynamically.

I submit that technologies must be sifted with respect to the above two criteria. Most developed countries are reaching stationary populations. Their requirements of first and second order wage-goods have been satisfied. The technologies most relevant to them are for the further order of consumption goods and the inputs etc., for the same. These countries are not interested in *our* basic technology. They will not be spending much R and D outlays on this. The developing countries have to fashion out their own technologies for products and processes relevant to the well-being of their people. It is here that a social commitment by the scientists and technologists in the developing countries become important. The technology policy also has to aim at the development of the commitment as above. It is not easy to achieve this. All the pull is the other way round.

Past experience shows that general imitativeness and conformity is the rule. To be like the western societies means that more and more non-relevant development engulfs the economy. The absence of a commitment *even against* odds as referred above on the part of scientists and technologists is a weakness of our society. There is no binding national ethos with respect to relevant development and technology. The multiplier effects on the economy of relevant development in science and technology with reference to products are immense. They help in speedier eradication of poverty and early attainment of triple full employment. In the absence of a basic-non-basic classificating scheme as above and socially committed 'supported wills and' quests, it is only randomly that progress in science and technology helps the poor, the under unemployed, and the needed export lines in which we have comparative advantage.

The issues raised above are very important in the present context of the aims of international homogeneisation of our economy. Underlying the above is the quest for cultural and elite homogeneisation particularly reflected in the styles of living and the social costs demanded for achievement-motivated endeavours. Unfortunately the vast masses of the poor may be either left out, or their interests sought to be fulfilled as a trickle-down result of the growing affluence of the top and the top-middle. Technology without getting sifted is like the camel in the Arab's tent. It may be the masses of the poor and the unemployed who may be edged out in a vissionless, priority-less, process of indiscriminate technology entry just for the sake of international homogeneisation of markets. Let us beware. In the past we suffered from defining basicness with respect to the heavy industry complex, we may now suffer from treating *all* consumption goods and their input requirements and *all* technology relevant to the above as basic.

Granted the impeccable logic of the above propositions, what follows?

First, the industrial policy must discriminate in licensing for basics and against the other lines.

Second, the Foreign Investment Board must also do as above.

Third, plan priorities must also do as above.

Fourth, fiscal policies, trade policies, tough policies should also practice discrimination as above.

What will be discriminated against are all types of luxury goods and input industries for the above, also technologies for the above.

Secondly, all types of heavy and related industries developed on a faulty concept of basicness so far need discrimination against.

Thirdly, potentially comparative advantaged justified export lines as also import-substitution lines need favourable discrimination.

APPLICATION OF TECHNOLOGY FOR DEVELOPMENT

NEED FOR A NEW PARADIGM

P.G. Menon

I fully agree with Dr. Rahman' s theme paper, as far as it goes. I believe that it needs an additional dimension. This I now briefly delineate:—

Technology should be as much for Man-the-Worker as for Man-the-Consumer. This is because millions of people spend much of their waking time at work. Technologies generally tend to subordinate the worker to the machine. This is anti-human.

The very roots of term "technology" ("techno" "logos") hints that the concept is meant to be 'machine-friendly', not 'worker-friendly'. A typical instance: the technological work-process is generally so designed as to effectively put the worker 'in solitary confinement'. This denies his social needs. And as Tawney remarks, "Since even quite common men have souls, no increase in material wealth can compensate them for arrangements which insult their self-respect and impair their freedom... unless industry is to be paralysed by recurrent revolts on the part of outraged human nature, it must satisfy criteria which are not purely economic" and — I would add — technological.

"The craftsman himself can always, if allowed to, draw the delicate distinction between machine and the tool. The carpet loom is a tool, a contrivance for holding warp threads at a stretch for the pile to be woven around them by the craftsman's fingers; but a power-loom is a machine, and its significance is that it does the essentially human part of the work." (Ananda Coomaraswamy).

Science was equally indifferent to the manual worker, and perhaps more contemptuous. Aristotle considered him an 'animate machine', hence akin to an animal, and hence akin to a slave. He stated that in the ideal city, no artisan would be a citizen. Archimedes, who so effectively harnessed science and technology to produce defence equipment during the siege of his city, refused to publish his engineering works. Plutarch writes that the soul of Archimedes was so elevated that he repudiated the entire science of inventing and building machines, and generally any art which serves some economic use, and turned his mind to writing about things whose beauty and subtlety were in no way linked to necessity.

Question : How many topnotch scientists of each succeeding generation can you name who consciously set out to improve the means of production used by the common people to feed, clothe and house themselves ? (Plato is believed to have invented a hydraulic alarm-clock.)

It was the Industrial Revolution which established technology "in the driver's seat". The work-world was turned topsy-turvy. The machine became the expensive worker, the fixed resource, the output of which had to be maximised. The "willing hands" that industry hired were adjuncts to the machines; and they were disposable, because the enclosure of the commons had produced so many of them. So the worker had to subordinate his pace, and everything else, to the machine. Even recently (1987), when the Pope said publically, in Canada, that : "At times, technology cannot decide the full measure of its own allegiance: whether it is for humanity or against it", the response of the President of the Canadian Chamber of Commerce was : "It is a message we regret having to hear because it means, really that the economic realities have not penetrated to the people who wrote the text for the Pope."

Work according to the Protestant Ethic, was a 'disutility', hence the question of making it interesting, or even less unpleasant, did not arise. (But a *'job'* was different. Said J.P. Morgan : "My job is more *fun* than being king, Pope or Prime Minister, for no-one can turn me out of it, and I don't have to make any compromise with principle").

The Employer's perception of "Worker" was thus expressed by 'the father of modern scientific management', Taylor : "The employee is (1) a constant in the production equation, (2) an inert adjunct of the machine, prone to inefficiency and waste unless properly programmed, (3) by nature lazy, (4) and his main concern is self-interest. He must therefore be tightly controlled and externally motivated in order to avoid his natural desire to avoid work ..." This paradigm became self-fulfilling, for it created an industrial system and technology-designs which denied human nature meaningful expression in the work-place. The alienation encourages indifference, inattention, boredom, carelessness; this invites accidents, reduces productivity. At the worst, suppressed human nature turns hostile, and workers use their faculties to sabotage the system.

The conventional response of the technologist has been to make the machine more 'fool-proof', or even less dependent on the worker, through automation, etc. The focus on increased technological specialisation (assembly-lines, special-purpose machine-tools ....), the increase in the size and complexity of the work-place, all helped to marginalise what was once known as 'Homo Faber': (Remember Charlie Chaplin in "Modern Times"?)

The irresponsible attitude displayed by Labour (which at home behaves as responsible adult men) was then posited by 'Management' and by a surprising number of Industrial Psychologists as being the true nature of the lumpen proletariat. Consequently, the inventors and designers of new technology still strive, generally, to reduce the labour-intensity of techno-systems of production via capital-intensity; and those promoting India's 'development' laud this approach even if it means beggaring India and turning it into an abject (and 'bonded'?) debtor.

In India, "Taylorian' paradigms continue to colour advances in technology and technology-use, such as Terotechnology, Group Technology, Reliability-Maintainability concepts, safety-systems. The proof ? The advice of the operator or mechanic is not routinely sought by designers and financiers before decisions are finalised regarding these matters. And although "workers participation in Management" has been talked about, not so "Workers participation in technology - design", despite there being enough Indian case-experiences, from Quality Circles etc. to show that workers do have the ability both to understand and apply the techniques required for such 'humanistic' technology re-design, techniques such as Ergonomics ("the laws of work") and Value-Engineering.

The Japanese indigenised their industrial revolution/ development, and modified western technology to make the Japanese factory a work-place congenial to the Japanese worker, so that his/her potential could be evoked, socialised and directed for constructive use.

In India, studies of machine-tools, and of earth-moving equipment showed that at least 30% of them were so designed as to be unsuitable for even the Indian male operator. As for women, and the left-handed......

The Taylorian paradigm has infected much of technological development. It results in the typical worker becoming a typical nuisance to the typical Management; and vice versa. Hence the adversarial approach to the Exit Policy now on the anvil. Should it go through, I am convinced, with reason, that it will recoil upon its advocates, and actually reduce, to lower than what it is, the already low productivity from our technological assets. This is aptly illustrated by the ongoing conflict over the Tehri Dam Project. The attempt to force an Exit Policy on its Project - affected persons has caused an ongoing *dharna* alleged already to have cost the Project an additional Rs. 100 crores, reducing the profitability of this modern technology-driven development project.

The contempt that learned professions often display towards the laity was thoroughly discussed in this room by Eric Ericcson some years ago. Apparently, the Tehri Project, over-all, is technically sound, but its engineers have never felt it necessary to 'reason together', or to explain unemotionally; they merely 'argued at ......

An Exit Policy approach to Development is not sustainable, in the absence of social security, etc. The advocates of modern science & technology (including us here), would do better to focus on a meaningful Entry Policy for the un-employed, the under-employed, and even for the wrongly employed (i.e, the 'over-staffing' which, too, an impoverished country cannot really afford), an Entry Policy to create personally and otherwise gainful things for them to do *instead*. "There must be a better way. Find it." (Edison).

A question to Dr. Rahman: "Do not our scientists and technologists have the knowledge to devise technologies appropriate for use by India's "weaker sections", technologies that are intensive not of fiscal capital but of resources such as labour (in Coomaraswamy's sense), sunshine, microbes, photo-synthesis and other free gifts of nature ?" Such technologies would need to be based upon a symbiotic relationship between Technology, Management, Labour/Worker Nature ? This is possible. So believes the Consortium of Indian Scientists for Sustainable Development.

Having heard, and read, Dr. Rahman over decades, I do believe that he would agree that technologists too, and not merely technology, should subordinate themselves to the 'gens' and their quirks, and not vice versa. If this belief is indeed covered in his basic theme paper (perhaps under Item (f)), then it needs to be uncovered, and so presented as to help us in developing a technological paradigm-cum-strategy for a participatory democracy which is poor in money but with a super-abundance of people and various other natural resources.

I end by re-asserting that the prevailing model will not do, if after over 40 years of it in a free India, "A survey of the agricultural poor and landless labour in a leading State" recently finds that 50 per cent of the adult women have only one sari, and 95 per cent of adult women have no petticoat; and 70 per cent of the adult males have only one dhoti.

COMMENTS ON DR. ASHOK PARTHASARATHI'S PAPER

P. D. Hajela

Amongst the many important points Dr. Ashok Parthasarathi raises in his paper entitled 'Acquisition and Development of Technology : The Indian Experience', the one relating to the chain of factors essential for technological growth is worth taking special note of. In this chain, there is reference to a proper assessment of market demand. A little later, Dr. Parthasarathi refers also to the fact of CSIR 'innovations' not moving out of the shelves to the market, creating the impression that some important links in the chain were not being observed. It is not off hand clear whether it was improper assessment of market demand which created the situation, or the fact that the cost implications of the CSIR innovation were not fully worked out, or it was the 'foreign' technology complex which came in the way. Further, it is not mentioned if the CSIR efforts were more relevant to the capital goods sector which we first wanted to build in our plan strategy, or the consumer goods sector which the market was tending to push forward in all manner of directions often with the help of foreign technology.

It may be worthwhile bearing in mind that the planning and market in India have not necessarily coordinated their efforts, particularly in respect of the composition of output. There has somehow been the assumption in most people's mind that once capital goods have been taken care of, infrastructure and consumer goods sector would so manage themselves that all capital goods will be automatically in demand.

This assumption could be valid for the defence sector because it is by and large a 'captive' sector. If, therefore, there have been impressive achievements in the Rand field, and expectations in respect of technological developments have been fulfilled in this sector, it is because the demanders of technology and its suppliers could have good coordination. The same cannot be said about the rest of the economy where planning and market do not move in the same direction and where the consumer goods sector is not 'captive' at all, even if the infrastructure sector was. In fact, even the infrastructure sector could go out of hand because of the difficulties of managing the macro-economy. The annual rates of investments in railways and energy sectors have fluctuated widely because of 'resource crunch', which is in a way symbolic of the kind of problems we face in our macro-economy policy. Even the uncoordinated behaviour of the consumer goods sector is a consequence of the inability of our fiscal policy to link capital goods capacity to more essential consumer goods that we really wanted; on the other hand, the durable consumer goods sector that eventually grew out of proportion (the 'demand' factor to which technological development could be finally linked) to the national product was not the target of the plans we were formulating every five years. It was unavoidable in such circumstances that technological developments that did occur in the non-defence sector got seriously handicapped due to lack of coordination between planning and market in the country. The planning authority was unclear — so were the research institutes — about what demand to size up, the one relating to consumer goods, that were not the first priority anyway, or that other, which was such a priority but would not grow because of our inability to order macro-consumption behaviour firmly and appropriately. This not only threw technological efforts in disarray, it led to a mismatch between structure of demand for output, on the one side, and the composition of output on the other. Our own capital goods developed idle capacity while 'pseudo technology transfers' partly encouraged by the craze for foreign capital goods began to get the upper hand all over.

There is obviously a difference between technological development induced by market compulsions, including both demand and competition, and that in which market itself is to be conditioned by societal imperatives as conceived by democratic economic planning.

This makes integration of technological change with appropriate macro-economic policies a necessary condition for its growth and viability. Demand will still be important but it will have to be so tempered with fiscal policy, political will and moral suasion that technological development, planning and market can all subserve the common good rather than the good of only a small minority in the country.

TECHNOLOGY AND DEVELOPMENT : ON THE TWO NOTES AND BEYOND

Prof. Iqbal Narain*

I

Dr. Rahman talks about application of technology for development. He has also made some observations in the specific context of India, besides dealing with the theoretical dimensions of technology. As far as his note is concerned, the following points deserve our consideration :

(a) It is worthwhile to remember that technology would become obsolete between five to ten years.

(b) India evolved a scientific policy but not technology policy. In fact, he makes a plea for evolving a technology policy. I agree that this should be done before long so that India knows what it is to have today, and what it should avoid in its pursuit of the economic policy of liberalization.

* Senior Fellow, Institute of Development Studies, Jaipur.

The following comments are offered to Dr. Rahman's paper.

(a) Dr. Rahman recognises lack of linkages between industry and research in India. But he does not tell us how this can be achieved. Is there need to leave R and D to the private sector in this respect ? If not, how is public sector R and D are to be made effective on this score ?

(b) It has been argued that formal R and D in agriculture is oblivious of the experiments and innovations being done at the ground level by artisans and farmers. The scientists do not even try to understand them. The same probably holds good for public sector R and D in the industrial sector. Will it be correct to say that R and D institutions need to reach out to learn and contribute in these local experiments which go on continuously ?

(c) Dr. Rahman has argued that existing knowledge should be used to increase the efficiency of industries both qualitatively and quantitatively. It can, again, be asked here : how is this to be done ?

(d) Dr. Rahman completely ignores the issue of intellectual property rights and the role of market and non-market forces in technology development and diffusion. These issues are being debated all over and are, particularly, relevant in the context of the liberal economic policies introduced by the Indian Government.

In sum, the impact of liberalization, planning and other market oriented economic policies, an indigenous R and D and technology development needs to be discussed thoroughly. Unplanned opening up, when other countries in the world are closing down, and unrestricted play of the so-called market forces can lead to disaster. Selective liberalization can perhaps be the key.

II

The following further observations are made not only on Dr. Rahman's paper but on that of Dr. Ashok Parthasarathy :

(i) It is true that the days of colonialism are over but it has to be noted that neo-colonialism still persists. The advanced countries of the world even today depend on cheap labour of developing countries for their continuous economic growth. They are happy if they can get even raw-materials for their use. At the same time they spare no pains to dominate the developing countries, both economically and politically, particularly in their foreign economic relations. In fact, the neo-colonialism of today is as dangerous, if not more, than colonialism of the past because of its subtle nuances in working.

(ii) The advanced countries of the world would also like to stick to protectionism as far as their own economies are concerned so that their own economic growth is not interfered with by what they consider to be foreign influx.

(iii) It is also useful to remember that earlier we differentiated between science and technology but now this distinction tends to be forgotten. Thanks to various break throughs in technology. In this connection it is well to remember what Rajni Kothari has observed :

In the beginning, science and technology flowed in independent streams — one close to natural philosophy and the other to practical craftsmanship. Gradually as technological break throughs began to tantalise everyone, a myth was created that science and technology were parts of the same enterprise, 'modern' and 'rational', which promised perpetual 'progress' for mankind.

III

Political Implications

It is relevant to ask how the import of technology affects our economic independence which is an inalienable part of political independence. It is feared that it would limit, if not interfere, with our economic independence. That we would become captives in our decision-making processes and in our choice of technology. It would, further, interfere, with our political independence because all that happens in the sphere of economic freedom has its repercussions in the field of politics too.

Social Implications

From the economic point of view the following questions arise. Can India afford the cost of technology, particularly of the latest variety. Also, what repercussions does it have on the employment problem of the country, if not on ecology.

Turning to sociological implications, the basic question is of preparedness for the use of technology in general and high technology in particular. Is the country prepared to handle the latest drives of technology ? Alternatively, does India's culture ordain slow movement on the part of the people and should we have that type of technology which can go along with them ?

Secondly, the issue of social justice is also relevant. In India, we have not merely to provide for the poor against the rich. Even among the poor, there are Scheduled Castes, Scheduled Tribes, women, minorities and others, for quite a few of whom there are proposals for reservations and quotas. Free economy in general and technology in particular would admit only of merit and efficiency. It is an open question how to reconcile the competing claims of free economy and technology, on the one hand, and social justice, on the other.

COMMENT ON PAPERS BY DR. RAHMAN AND DR. PARTHASARATHI

A.K. Dasgupta

In both these papers issues of policy related to technological development in the country have been raised. In India, there has been a concern for technological development for a long time. Many policies have been adopted in this context. Instruments and agencies have also been established for bringing about rapid technological development in the country.

There is no doubt that India has acquired extensive capacities for production of a wide variety of goods and services during the last 40 years. In many of these areas very advanced technologies have been adopted for producing the goods and services. Nevertheless, notwithstanding the diversification of our productive capacities it has not been possible to obtain a modest degree of self-reliance in the matter of technology development. The analysis of this feature has been the basic core of both these papers.

Dr. Rahman feels that we should adopt a separate technology policy instead of one S and T policy as we have today. Dr. Parthasarathi has suggested a programme of action which could be expected to lead to indigenous technological development and self-reliance. He has also cited cases where good results have been obtained by following programmes of action in a meaningful manner.

My feeling is that the approach is narrow, and that policies and programmes could be meaningful only in the context of given areas of activities, and not in a general way, for they might not lead to a general environment of progress which alone could be relevant in the context of the country. I give below the reason for the above statement.

Historians, both liberal and Marxian, have used the artefacts discovered in the process of archaeological researches, as evidences for supporting the ideas relating to cultural progress implicit in their ideology. The artefacts are products of men, and bear out in normal inspection, the technical and material input involved in the production of specific items. A chronological ordering of the artefacts discovered in these researches should also bring out the progress achieved in the productive capacities by men over the ages, and also the inputs for such progress. Such an exercise has not been carried out. There is nevertheless no doubt that starting from the technical level associated with the stone age civilization to the level associated with the modern days, the progress in the technical area has been enormous and continuous.

A simple measure of this progress is the variety, in count, of the manipulative techniques used by men in different periods of time. This number has steadily increased. Presumably, in some periods it increased very fast; in some of other periods rather slowly.

It was this steady growth in the technical level which has been used as the evidence for building up ideas about natural evolutionary process of social development by archaeologists and historians. Implicit in this order of belief has been the appreciation of the autonomous character of technical development. It should be noted, however, that the growth occurred in the count of variety at any instant of time. Thus possibilities of some varieties going out of use, after being in operation for a period of time, are open, as also the possibility of variation in the rates of growth at different periods, and as between different areas.

Appreciation of the natural growth propensity of the magnitude referred above is crucial for all discussions relating to aspects of technological development. Since the magnitude has a natural tendency to grow one should also be able to identify forces inducing the growth. As it is in the pervasiveness and the persistence of the forces that the tendency to grow is dependent, one should also be able to analyse the structure of the forces operating in a region for finding out why the rate of technical development has been prevailed, and how the matters might be corrected, should that become necessary.

The fact that technical progress has been a natural process is being stressed for evident reasons. It allows drawing lessons from analogous natural systems; for example, the river, which has also a natural flow. The actual course of a river depends on the terrain and topography of the region through which the river flows. Depending on these features the river charts out its own course, and continues to flow along the course. The course of development of technology in each region could also be seen as established on analogous basis. In the case of river, the flow is sustained by evaporation and precipitation; regarding varieties in work-techinque, by other factors.

The most important in this generation of flow has been the reproductibility of a technique and the associated probability of changes (in the products and the processes forming the technology) while being reproduced. The variations evident in the forms of animal and other power driven carriages over time and over regions bear testimony to the above features. Another factor has been the exploitation of opportunities which one or more known techniques, processes and materials offered. Thus every increase of the current count of variety, as accumulations of previous developments, also increased the possibility of creation of additional varieties. In effect, it opened up the possibility of expanding the varieties as time passed.

This process of technical development could be self-feeding, and as a matter of fact has been like this in the past. The course of progress in each country has, however, been determined by the environmental features. In America, abundant varieties of natural resources were available, while manpower supply was limited. Thus technological progress was weighted in the direction of labour-saving. Germany, on the other hand, has not been favoured with abundant varieties of natural resources, and thus the technical progress in this region has focussed on process development for creating varieties which nature denied.

Creation of variety in the area of techniques is primarily the result of what has been called adaptation and innovation; the latter covering the developments consequent on the opportunities offered by past developments. Both these activities are professional skill and knowledge-intensive, and with these inputs of professional skill and knowledge the reproduction of a technique could be expected to differ from mere copying to embodying additional capabilities, leading on to creation of a new variety. In a way, this feature could be parallel of the process of differential reproduction and selection among the animals, leading to the evolution in the animal world. Incidentally, evolution in the animal world has also led to continuous growth of animal species variety.

The process of differential reproduction and selection has found no scope in India due to a variety of reasons, with the result that the natural tendency for technical progress has been arrested. A very specific reason has been that we depended almost wholly on import of packaged technology for continuous modernization of technology. Under this system, very little work related to adaptation and innovation is involved, with the result that no new variety is generated within the country, stopping further technological progress, and increasing the dependence of the country on imported technology.

The above has been particularly true in respect of those areas of activities, products of which are sold in the market, which may be capital, including intermediate products, or consumption goods. On the other hand, it is this area which, due to the size in terms of number of units and of associated technical varieties, has to be the cradle for sustaining technical progress at the national plane.

The number of varieties that can be created at any point of time is proportional to the size of varieties currently in operation in the country. The imported technology, therefore, in so far as it adds to the variety in operation, has a positive role in the creation of additional varieties. Thus one finds that all countries which have made vigorous technical progress has also been large importers of technology. Japan and South Korea have made commendable technological progress in recent years, and both countries have been large importers of technology. Japan has also become a large exporter of technology, and evidently this could be possible as Japan also began to add varieties of its own.

Initially, Japan imported total technology, but soon concentrated on import of raw technology, which required extensive work in the areas of adaptation and innovation before output could be produced. Thus R/D work became a necessary complement of the technology import, and its intensity increased in proportion to increase of import of technology, with the result that the technology on field in Japan in most cases became indigenous, and under pressure of competition, some times more developed than the technology at the exporting end.

The Japanese case brings out clearly how natural could be technological progress. Contributions of policies were a largely related to creation of environment, where in creative faculties of the people could flourish. Japan had two laws dealing with foreign investment and technology import—The foreign Investment Law and Foreign Exchange Control Law. These related to screening the proposals, for which formal and informal guidelines were used, with a general understanding that technical assistance contibuted to the development of the economy and, therefore, was desirable.

India has also been a large importer of technology and yet the natural technological progress has remained nearly arrested. This could be possible not for lack of policies for inducing technological progress, but for existence of definite hurdles and hindrances on the path of progress. It should call, therefore, for removal of the hurdles. The current liberalization should make things somewhat simpler, in so far as there might occur some relaxation in the protection offered to the Indian industrialists. On the other hand, the present liberalization, without removal of the projection, might increase the degree of technological dependence of the country.

The above are the issues which should form an integral part of our discussion on technology and development.

INDUSTRY, TECHNOLOGY AND MULTI-NATIONALS

J. D. Sethi

Those who are pillorying the Rao-Manmohan's economic policies should stop to address themselves three questions. First, what is new in the New Economic Policy ? On serious reflection, it would be found that the current policy is an accentuation and a logical outcome of the policies of the last four decades. The new elements have been introduced rather dramatically in a short span of time and would not have provoked criticism had there time-spread been longer. After all, liberalisation and globalisation began more than 11 years ago.

Second, almost the whole of large scale Indian Industry has been tied to foreign multinationals and technological regimes. India has less than 10,000 large manufacturing units and the number of collaborations signed are more than 15,000. It is difficult to pinpoint a single new major industrial unit to have come up with entirely Indian money, management and technology. The foreign brand consumer goods produced in India dominated the Indian market. The FERA laws have been the most useful instrument in the hands of the multinationals.

Third, India's science and technology policies have been so poorly organised, made so dependent on external knowledge and so much divorced from linkage with industry that except for selected areas, there is hardly any worthwhile R & D. Out of 5,500 crores of rupees spent on R & D, nearly 5,000 crores go for nuclear, space and defence research. There was no reason or motivation for the foreign collaborators to participate in genuine technological effort. The science laboratories and establishments are producing junk. Despite a very heavy scientific and technological establishments, the two remain distinct.

There has been massive confusion and dependence in Indian policy in respect of import of technology and domestic R & D. Even on paper, Nehru had a science policy but no corresponding technology framework. Indira Gandhi had announced a technology policy without a science policy. Rajiv Gandhi had neither. There is not much point to speak about others. The critical point is that the foreign aid to which the Indian industrialisation was tied as well as the continuation of the colonial structure thwarted the growth of indigenous science and technology. Both in theory and practice, we put too much emphasis on science and too little on technology, getting the worst of both. By contrast, over the last 41/2 decades, Japan put all its eggs in the technology basket. After having acquired technological supremacy, she is now moving towards big science.

The continuous import of the same old technology, its heavy consumer bias, stiffling conditions of collaboration agreements etc. are crippling our industry. The only effective defence against technological colonialism, namely, the development of our own science and scientists, technology and technologists etc., has become a victim of this colonialism. Our scientists got recognition in their own land only after they were given recognition abroad. The entire atmosphere and organisation of research in India was designed to dovetail it to scientific developments elsewhere and had little relevance to the development of those technologies and such adaptation of imported one as would have been both commensurate with our own factor proportions and change in these proportions in desired directions.

Technology may be said to recognise national boundaries. There is as yet no such thing as its international application, except what the multinationals decide. Nominally each nation alone uses and develops technology by its own conscious deliberate action, but not in reality. Technical change is one thing but a choice of a particular technique is quite another.

No wonder, that the multinationals have been making consistent inroads into Indian economy and the Indian policy responses have been so enimical to indigenous development that it seems the Government of India and the multinationals have converged to deny India the opportunity to exploit its technical manpower. Besides, there has been total confusion in science and technology policies.

More than capital and other resources, natural and manmade, it is the growing technological gap between the rich and the poor that lies at the source of great world disorder. The new order threatens to make the situation explosive and condemn the poor countries to new economic and intellectual domination. Three distinct trends are noticeable. First, technological development in the Advanced Developed Countries (ADCs) has given rise to the power of collossal corporations. And it is these corporations which with their technological, financial and communication power have become both the makers of the goods and the makers of the desire for them.

Second, although high degree of specialisation, complexity of decision-making, risk and financial backing make technological development take the organisational form of big corporations, beyond a certain limit these corporations break through national barriers to become multinationals. The present vechicle of economic domination by the North of the South is the multinational corporation. Over 4,000 of these exist today, most with headquarters in the USA but a growing number of others with headquarters in Europe and Japan.

Third, these corporations squeeze out small competing firms in the LDCs, evade local taxes through numerous devices, send large profits back to ADCs, utilise capital-intensive technology that was once used in the industrialised countries, and successfully dump them in the LDCs.

The analysts of the multi-nationals, be they of dependency and inter-dependence theory, accept the fact that "The power of the global cooperation derives from its unique capacity to use finance, technology and advanced marketing skills to integrate production on worldwide scale and thus to realize the ancient capitalist dream of one Great Market."[1] However, one of the important features of these companies is their "overwhelmingly oligopolistic character that is, they dominate in markets effectively controlled by a few buyers or sellers".[2] Their large size, control of technological and product innovation and differentiation, brands and patents, power over investment location, research programme, transfer prices etc. give multinationals, political power to determine the range of oligopolistic global strategy and a common global control.

Earlier in search for markets and profits MNCs drove into LDCs, but later their main interests pushed them towards those areas which were trade oriented. The ADCs constituted the trade dominated area. The LDCs both welcomed as well as repelled them, depending upon their own evaluation. Those who welcomed them without safeguards came to grief because of the economic control exercised by the MNCs. Those who tried to repel them, but also failed to develop their own science annd technology, have also came to grief because they lost the trade leverage and ultimately forced to reverse their negative attitude.

Multi-national trading regimes may be in private hands as in the West, semi-public enterprises, again in the West, or fully owned and controlled by the State as in the communist countries. Now, these multi-nationals take recourse and finally work for countries which have reached a certain stage of development, not necessarily for the country of their origin. For countries below that critical level of development, these multi-national corporations may not work and are not known to have worked for. Instead, scales are reversed in order to control these countries. The restrictions they impose with respect to technological diffusion, export markets, domestic competition etc. make them barriers to development because they create enclaves and impose a new dualism on an existing dualistic economy.

Even with most favourable MNC package, the LDCs are not allowed to determine the appropriateness of commodity production and technological use. The net result is the prepetuation of domestic dualism of the colonial era and this ensures profits for the MNC. MNCs determine the share of trade for the LDCs as prompted by their global strategies as well as the aforementioned dualism. Since the trend is towards greater trade integration among the ADCs for a variety of reasons, trade of the LDCs loses its autonomous character. Thus the MNCs, with their control over resources, their oligopolistic power and their focus on ADCs economic development etc. ultimately marginalise and darwinises the LDCs, first on trade and then through trade in the economic development of many of the LDCs, ironically by operating within the LDCs official policies.

We know "75 per cent of the Western World's production comes from between one and two thousand firms. In the United States 60 per cent of the national capital is in the hands of just two hundred firms. In France, where integration is considerably less advanced, 0.4 per cent of business enterprises, that is to say 800 firms, are responsible for 47 per cent of total production. Similarly, international investments are the prerogative of a restricted number of firms in Britain : just 165 Biritsh firms are responsible for 80 per cent of overseas investments. In Germany 82 firms provide 70 per cent of foreign investments: three-quarters of United States external investment comes from 190 firms".[3] The general trend is that rise of few oligopolistic firms control anywhere between one-half to two-thirds of the total production.

Another impact of the technological gap is the shift from turning old colonies as sources of raw material and market for the goods of the metropolitan power, into a new instrument of control by the multi-nationals of the combined resources and markets of the many countries. But more significantly, it is the transfer of light industries into areas of cheap labour that marks the new phase. Goods requiring sophisticated technologies are kept at industrial centres and those requiring old, and new but limited technologies, are spread out.

Prof. Meister has drawn attention to this and another allied problem. "The transfer of light industry to zones of cheap, competent and docile labour — as is the case today in South-East Asia — means a comparable reduction in the number of immigrant workers at home, and hence helps to diminish racial ill-feeling with its unfortunate consequences of industrial and social unrest. Similarly, on the model of tax havens the absence of anti-pollution legislation (or the floating therefore) in the poor countries creates real 'havens for polluters' — so a new style of international division of labour is gradually coming into being, the rich countries keeping the highly capitalized industries with the clean factors to themselves, while the poor countries manufacture labour intensive products involving dirty factories."[4]

In this milieu, it is becoming increasingly difficult for any single country to find a national and indigenous solution for its socio-economic problem. (This inability leads to serious political complications). It is not surprising that for decades both Washington and Moscow denounced the so-called narrow nationalism of the poor and newly independent countries which were slowly sucked in every new economic order without their consent, an order which condemned them to live first in dependency and then in global slums. Even the poor country is forced to put all its eggs in the export basket. This is the practice today. It was not so ten or fifteen years ago, even when the economic plight of these countries was unevenable.

Modern technological regimes are formed not by nations but by economic organisations and interests, on the one hand and by scientists and technological experts, on the other. Every nation tries to keep control on both because in the final analysis their competitiveness and productivity increases depend upon their control of technologies. Economic nationalism of the ADCs is most fiercely reflected in their national as well as MNC alliance technological regimes. Even within the alliance system secretiveness, jealousies and desire for appropriation in respect of technologies remain a critical barrier to further integration. Unlike the international trading regimes such as GATT and other organisations etc. there is no trading international technological regime. The day such a regime comes into being the monopoly of the control of a few powerful nations over the rest would be complete. At present only EEC is moving in that direction. Before such a calamity comes down on the world from all sides, it is important that a more equitable, ecologically justifiable and aesthically satisfying technological progress must be created right now.

Notwithstanding all the promises that the emerging technological regimes are making, they are neither able nor find it in their interest to reach out to vast starving millions whose survival is so much jeopardised by the technological regimes themselves.

The prevailing technological and scientific regimes are dominated by the production of weapon system, on the one hand, and those other technologies which are either focussing on consumer durables or on the information on the other. Of course, there are new frontiers of space bio-technology, genetics etc. about which the world is still as much trembling as it is hopeful. It seems that the global economic system, knowledge, order and the security system are now dominated by technological regimes in which economic, security and knowledge themselves become the components.

The choice before every nation is how to (a) formulate its own policies, and (b) how to negotiate with multi-nationals. Ideas are free but their economic application is a costly affair, which people only as a nation can undertake. The case for economic nationalism as well as of genuine globalization refers to laying down of investment and technological priorities and having by deliberate conscious choice a spectrum of techniques from the best downward.

But more important, as the Korean and the Japanese experiences teach us, will be the capacity to play one multi-national against another; one developed country against another; and one international regime against another. It is a ruthless world, and we have to resort to every conceiveable method used by others to get designs and integrate them with our own with the help of scientists and technologists, of which there is no dearth. We will also have to sell most of our research institutions to those Indian industrialists who along with the Government would be ready to engage in this extremely complicated defensive-offensive strategy.

References

1. Barnet R.J. and Muller. R.E. Global Reach : The power of the Multinational Corporations, Simon and Schuster.
2. Colman D. and Nixson F., Economics of Change in Less Developed Countries, Philip Allan, U.K., p. 219.
3. *Ibid.*
4. *Ibid.*, quoted.

DISCUSSIONS

I

A. Rahman

Dr. A. Rahman explained that in his theme paper he had given a synoptic view of the historical development of technology as he saw it. He had also traced the development of our approach to science and technology, both before and after independence.

Dr. Rahman was of the view that technology should be classified from the point of view of the use to which it was put, and also from that of the degree of sophistication required. He pointed out that science and technology were elitist activities. They were the cutting edge of the development of knowledge. The major problem was how they should be utilised. It was for the political leaders, he thought, to decide what use should be made of them.

Referring to labour-intensive technology, Dr. Rahman, observed that while labour-intensiveness was a must in certain areas, it was counter-productive in others. Proceeding, he pointed out that science and technology as part of the culture of society came into existence after the Rennaissance, and were concretised by the Industrial Revolution. They came as a result of a revolt against the power complexes which existed before, that is, the nobility and the church. The present power complex has arisen out of the growth of industries for centuries. Most of the innovations made were for military power. Indeed, it was only after World War II, when Japan was prohibited from re-arming, that technology was developed for Civilian use. Even so, the innovations could be used for military purposes.

India was concerned with import or transfer of technology, Dr. Rahman continued, but he had not discussed this problem because those who had the technology naturally wanted to use this advantage for their own benefit. In the absence of political clout there was nothing that a country seeking transfer of technology could do. This was very evident now from the attitude of the United States. There was not much point therefore discussing terms and conditions of transfer.

Why cannot we have a consensus about science and technology, Dr. Rahman asked, but pointed out that the decision was for the political leadership to take. The scientific community could only interact with the politicians. For this purpose the scientists should have a lobby, as there are lobbies in other areas, but in this instance this was difficult because 90 per cent of the scientists worked in government establishments. Apart from that, Dr. Rahman thought that even the scientific community did not have any clear idea of the development required. He referred in this connection to a report by some very eminent persons. It was a good report, he thought, but it lacked direction.

India was spending far too much on internal security. This was partly because, he felt, of the internal crises arising out of growing inequality and of rising expectations. If at least a portion of the resources spent on the security of the VIPs could be diverted, more funds would be available for education and for the uplift of the people.

Indian scientists, Dr. Rahman observed, had not been able to interact with artisans and craftsmen because of their prejudices, the nature of development, and of the language in which science was taught. Unless, however, arts and crafts were developed, unless artisans and craftsmen were made aware of technology, development could not take place. In India skills existed, Dr. Rahman emphasised, but they had been ignored. This is shown by the fact that while sophisticated technology had been imported, "traditional" crafts not only continued but supplied a good proportion of the needs of the people. Also, when sophisticated technologies were imported, our illiterate workers were able not only to work them, but repair the machinery and maintain them.

In consumer industries, such as food, as also in entertainment, repair and in such items as in cosmetics, which have been neglected, whole areas existed, according to Dr. Rahman, which could be made into cottage industries employing large numbers of workers.

Environmental degradation was certainly a problem, Dr. Rahman agreed, but a total change in outlook was needed to meet this danger. People living below the poverty line, struggling for day to day existence could not be aware of this danger unless they were made to see that it was to their interest to prevent such degradation.

In conclusion, Dr. Rahman pointed out that when technology developed in Europe the whole class of aristocracy was wiped out. In India too, if science and technology is to develop, they must ally themselves with people deprived under the present system. This is, however, what scientists and technologists in India are not prepared to do because of their linkages with those who have benefited from development. What is therefore needed is a national consensus to bring in the deprived people.

II

Ashok Parthasarathi

Dr. Ashok Parthasarathi initiated the discussions by presenting his theme paper. What is the strategy of development that India has followed, he asked. There are many dimensions of such a strategy, he pointed out, of which technology was only one. He also pointed out that the use of the expression, "science and technology" as if a single entity was being described was incorrect. "Science and technology" are not the same. They are two different things.

Science and technology was no magic wand to wave over a poor country to make it rich. The concept that the highly industrialised countries constituted a storehouse of science based knowledge waiting to be utilised, was very misleading. To extend this mistaken notion to believe that those countries also constituted a storehouse of technology, available to the developing countries for the asking, was even more deleterious to the interests of the developing countries. What is more, the countries which became politically independent from 1947 onwards do not really have "the advantage of late comers", as has often been argued. Our experience, as well as that of other newly industrialised countries like Brazil and Indonesia, shows that there is no super market of technology in the North from which we can draw on easy terms. There is only a technology market involving harsh terms of purchase including arbitrary prices.

Dr. Parthasarathi stated that the dominant elements in the development process were political and social. Technology was not an independent variable, it was not the causal factor but, rather, a dependent variable. Cultural values, social mores, economic institutions, the political process and the character of the State and the private sector, were much more important in determining the nature, directions and pace of social and economic changes than the work done in the technology generation system, viz. the R & D system.

In India, we have an explicit policy on science and technology, lumped together, in the Scientific Policy Resolution of 1958, supplemented by the Technology Policy Statement of 1983. These are politically validated documents representing the prevailing national consensus at the time they were adopted. But do they continue to remain valid over time ?

The Scientific Policy Resolution (SPR), prepared by Bhabha, Mahalanobis and Nehru himself states that "the key to national prosperity, apart from the spirit of the people, lies in a combination of three factors, technology, raw material and capital, of which the first is the most important because the creation and adoption of new scientific techniques could make up for the deficiencies of natural resources and reduce the demand for labour". However, except for this brief reference, it made no mention of technology. Hence, it was that the Technology Policy Statement was announced by the Government in 1983.

Continuing, he pointed out that, in countries which were labour-surplus and capital-short like India, the concern was very different from that in the highly industrialised countries which were capital-rich and labour-short. We have, however, followed that "Northern" pattern of development. The Green Revolution, which is highly capital intensive, is an instance in point. What is more, the net energy generation per hectare in terms of the calorific content of the crops produced, he pointed out, minus the energy input that goes to produce that crop is rapidly approaching zero, raising serious questions about its sustainability.

Such capital-intensive development happens because Government have priced capital low, that is, low with respect to the social rate at which it should be priced. As a result, the Rs. 30,000 crores which have been invested in our industrial system since Independence, has given us substantial industrial "muscle", but has made little impression on the problem of unemployment.

Dr. Parthasarathi then turned to the problem of population. Most recent analysis of the problem lead to the conclusion that, on an optimistic estimate, India's population will stabilise between 1500 and 1700 million by around 2025 depending on the progress made in our efforts at population control. China, on the other hand, is likely to stabilise at around 1300 million. In the next generation i.e. during the life - time of our children, this is going to present problems which have no parallel in history. How can technology help in this respect ? In Dr. Parthasarathi's opinion, technology, which was a variable dependent on economic and social policies, could only lead to the development of new contraceptives; it could not ensure their adoption. Such adoption calls for social technologies designed around new values and the meeting of basic needs of the whole of our population.

Dr. Parthasarathi then went on to say that we have built up a scientific community, but, in the absence of a clear indication to the contrary, the nature of the scientific R & D and technology development undertaken has followed the Western pattern of development. Of the many new areas on science and technology which have emerged since 1945, the area of biotechnology is one which holds enormous potential for tropical countries like ours. For example, so far we have been building plants to produce chemcial fertilisers at costs of Rs. 1500 crores for 1300 tonnes/day capacities. However, now bio-fertiliser plants could be set up to achieve the same result at one-tenth of that cost, occupying one - twentieth of the same space and with one-hundreth the energy input.

India has the competence, Dr. Parthasarathi asserted, to produce the technology required to meet its social and economic needs. The scientific and technological communities have excelled themselves and attained the highest world standards in areas like Space, Atomic Energy, professional Electronics and some areas of defence technology. This has happened because the objectives were clearly framed and the targets set. It could happen in areas of decentralised rural development too. He cited, in this connection, the impressive achievements of our Solar Photo - Voltaic industry, in designing, manufacturing and deploying 25 per cent of the world's solar energy systems predominantly in our rural areas.

III

P.D. Hajela

Prof. Hajela stated that Technology was not merely a normative concept, of wanting something and having it. There are macro-economic paramenters, and it is only within the framework of such parameters that one could hope that one's dreams would be fulfilled. It is the macro-economic framework, the parameters they set, their definitions and of the economic processes involved that have been engaging his attention. He felt that efficiency was not merely a question of what benefit the individual producers get as a result of the application of new technology. The crucial issue was whether the added efficiency of the individual producer or firm, or the surplus he derived therefrom was compatible with the efficiency of the economic system.

The issue was highlighted, Prof. Hajela continued, by John Maynard Keynes who faced a situation of abundance of capital, but poor opportunity or will to use it. His remedy was public sector which would use the capital in public works and thus boost the will to utilise it. In the Keynesian scheme the focus was not on the efficiency of the public sector, Prof. Hajela pointed out, but on the efficiency of the economy as a whole. The concept of State intervention was thus linked to the efficiency of the economic system rather than on the efficiency of individual public undertakings.

In India the situation is just the reverse. There is no capital abundance. The problem in this country is how to combine equity with growth in such a manner that the efficiency of individual enterprise is kept in view as also the efficiency of the whole system.

It was a big mistake to apply Keynes's mixed economy system to Indian conditions. Dr. Parthasarathi is right that low interest rates discourage the use of labour. Naturally, by using capital intensive techniques, we are misapplying Keynes.

As pointed out by Dr. Parthasarathi, the efforts of the CSIR have been successful in the Defence Sector. This is because defence is a captive sector. In the non-defence sector, on the other hand, the CSIR has not been so successful. This is so because, according to Prof. Hajela, in the non-defence sector the composition of the output was sought to be changed in favour of capital goods. It was hoped that the output of the capital sector would boost the wage-goods sector. In fact, it has been used for the manufacture of durable consumer goods, because we have failed to tackle the structure of demand. There has been a mismatch between the capital goods and the growth of the consumer goods sector.

The point to be emphasised thus is that technological advance must be correlated with macro-economic policies. Unless this is done, growth cannot be reconciled with equity.

With regard to Dr. Rahman's paper, Prof. Hajela wished to mention three factors which have come in the way of technological advance. They are :

(i) Excess demand

(ii) Entrepreneurial inertia, and

(iii) Low real wages.

Dealing with the last factor, that is low real wages, Prof.

Hajela stated that it was a misconception that multinational Corporations wished to invest in countries with low real wages. The Japanese have invested substantially in the United States where the wage-rates are high. Apart from incremental changes in technology, there are technological revolutions as in Electronics and also changes in techno-economic system which provide a favourable ethos to high-fly investment. It is because such ethos exists in the United States that the Japanese are attracted to that country.

Prof. Hajela regarded high real wages as an important factor that influenced technological advance. It was only after full or near full employment in agriculture, and in many types of industries, that Japan and South Korea advanced technologically. High real wages created the right motivation, he thought, for technological innovation.

Another factor that has militated against technological advance in India is excess demand, Prof. Hajela concluded. Public investment has created excess demand, and this has given rise to conditions of oligopoly rather than of perfect competition. He referred to a recent survey which showed that the more growth intensive sectors have higher concentration ratios. Such oligopolitic conditions combined with low real wages induce entrepreneurial inertia, and are not conducive to technological advances.

IV

Siddharta

Dr. Siddharta referred to the Government statement in between the Scientific Policy Resolution, 1958 and the Technology Policy Statement 1983. This was the statement of Approach to Science and Technology, January 1973. This statement acted as a sort of bridge between what was happening in the fifties and the types of problems referred to by Dr. Parthasarathi which had been thrown up during this decade and later.

The articulation of demand for technology, whether such technologies were generated domestically or abroad, occurred, Dr. Siddharta pointed out, through the exertion of an array of instrumentalities which had nothing to do with technology *per se*. These instrumentalities related to social, political and other areas. Except in vertically integrated structures as in Defence, Space, Atomic Energy and now in the vertically integrated multinationals, where there was internal articulation of demands, it was the economic demand that determined whether a particular technology would find a place in the market, free or otherwise.

The scientific policy resolution did not deal with science, Dr. Siddharta continued, except as an instrumentality. Its concern was to inject science into other policies which have nothing to do with Science *per se*. The Drugs Policy, for instance, has to incorporate the findings of bio-medical science to ensure their efficacy and prevent adulteration. Similarly, the primary education systems to be effective have to incorporate findings on children's ability to learn. This was indeed the theme of the Approach paper of 1973.

Science policy, according to Dr. Siddharta, occupied a comparatively small area. Much larger areas were occupied by economic policies, environmental policies and foreign policies. The concern was how to implement the strategy to incorporate scientific findings to the national purpose, if there was one. In the absence of a grand ideology valid all the world over, India cannot borrow the designs of institutions from outside. Such institutions can be based only on national consensus.

Dr. Siddharta deplored the fact that the economic community in India was unaware not only of the Science and Technology system but also of the history of this system, that is, how the system evolved different types of organisations in the country. Science institutions do not mean only CSIR, the Tele-Communication Centre or Defence Science. It should include the Survey of India, the GSI and the meteorological establishments which are science institutions and have a long history.

Referring to the population problem in India, Dr. Siddharta emphasised the need for a moral order which would determine the conditions for human interaction among 1.5 billion human beings which India is likely to have before the population stabilises. Without such a moral order, he thought, we are likely to have a society where every transaction would be violent. In this context he referred to the need to articulate carefully our international position on biotechnology and intellectual property rights without which we shall not be able to use biotechnology in the country in a non-violent manner.

In conclusion, Dr. Siddharta warned against the white—white collaboration policy hitherto followed in the west being extended to white-brown and white-yellow collaboration to include the middle classes of India and other countries of Asia. If the Indian middle class got into this kind of a moral order a situation will arise, he warned, when in the absence of a grand ideology to deal with the major instruments of social change, namely technology, violence will be inevitable.

V

P.G. Menon

Shri P.G. Menon stated that his Critical Note contained his reaction to Dr. Rahman's paper. Some of the concerns he had in mind had also featured in Dr. Parthasarathi's paper.

Shri Menon referred to the slogan used by some of the participants, namely, "To catch up with the West" by a process of leap-frogging. We wanted to play the game of development which they had invented, and to play it better than they. Is that possible, he asked, considering how far behind those dynamic societies we are in terms of our industrial R & D, and our industrial Infrastructure.

Referring to the ordinary people for whom "appropriate technology" is supposed to be meant, Shri Menon stated that since time immemorial, scientists and technologists never normally thought in terms of making easier. As a result the artifacts and equipment designed and manufactured by them were not user—friendly. As a typical example of this approach he cited the foot-operated mini-spinning machine of the Schumacher group. To use it was to be tortured, he said.

Shri Menon continued that we should concentrate on profitable industries from which the West was pulling out, such as those which were skill-intensive, and required long years of apprenticeship. Optical lenses was one such 'industry', with an annual global demand of about $ 10 billion. However, India needed to improve its marketing skills considerably, in order to be able to export profitably.

Shri Menon concluded by stating that in order to be sustainable, models of development should be "people-led", and in which scientists, technologists and the Government participated. He invited the participants to visit one such model with which he was involved, namely, that for the Eco-Regeneration of the Pushkar Lake Valley System in Rajasthan.

VI

V.P. Gupta

Shri V.P. Gupta stated that he intended to convey the mundane, down to earth reactions of a common man. He did not agree with the impression he got from Dr. Rahman's paper that technology had something made to order. According to him, technology meant knowledge based on science which was used for the welfare of man.

Shri Gupta also differed from Dr. Rahman's categorisation of technology into groups, such as entertainment, food and communication. These according to him were applications of technology. Technology could be utilised, he pointed out, for various purposes, such as pollution control or prevention of waste, but technology itself was something distinct, which knew no boundaries.

Shri Gupta was of the view that India never took to technology in earnest. Our effort at industrialisation was also halting, he thought, for we talked of small scale industries and put in restrictions as in the MRTP Act. But where do we go from here, Shri Gupta asked. In Shri Gupta's opinion, India should develop her own technology. Technology could be borrowed from abroad but not at the cost of our macro-economic requirements. He concluded by suggesting that the industry collectively, or the private sector as a whole, and not individual undertakings should take decisions about import of technology.

VII

Kamal A. Mitra Chenoy

Dr. Kamal A. Mitra Chenoy wondered how application of technology for development could be discussed without discussing the Dunkel proposals which had not been referred to so far. These proposals hinder development in developing countries in a variety of ways. It permits, for instance, product patents instead of process patents which the Indian law allows, and extends patentable products well beyond those allowed by the world International Patents Organisation (WIPO), and even by the U.S. Patents Act. In fact, it extends patentiability to natural processes including areas of bio-technology, thereby privatising the most promising priority areas. It is indeed ironical that the same Northern Countries which are talking about common global resources, about bio-sphere being common property, want to privatise what is taken from bio-diversity, that is bio-technology.

The Dunkel Draft, Dr. Chenoy, continued was essentially marking out new growth area in technology, and seeking not only to privatise them to the advantage of the developed countries, but also to ensure that such privatisation became unchallengeable. It seeks to make patents valid for 20 years as against the Indian low which provides for 5 to 14 years. It also shifts the burden of proof to the defendant so that any one accused of infringing a patent has, in order to prove that he has not done so, reveal his patented method.

The Dunkel text has no provision for compulsory licensing. Import of a patent product is treated as actual operation of license, so that there is no incentive at all to allow indigenous production.

The ambit of General Agreement or Trade and Tariff (GATT) which was restricted to commodities traded is now being extended to Services and to Patents.

The quantum of research needed for the developing countries, Dr. Chenoy observed, required South-South Co-operation, and to a policy which seeks, not to dovetail our technological requirements with the foreign policy needs of a unipolar world, but to multilateral co-operation in the South. The South Commission did go into this problem, but the possibilities and priorities of such multilateral co-operation need to be examined further.

On the question of import of technology, Dr. Chenoy pointed out, that in spite of the warning against concentration of the means of production contained in Article 39 (c) of the Constitution, and in spite of the Preamble to the Constitution declaring India to be a "Socialist" Republic the reality had to be faced that there has been a secular increase in the concentration of asset holding, and that in spite of the incentives given the large private companies have gone in, not for R & D, but for repetitive import of technology. Indeed, such repetitive import, and import of obsolescent technology to cater to the affluent market will be inevitable if development is left to the motive of profit maximisation. That is why in countries like South Korea and Taiwan, which are regarded as having performed economic miracles, and even in Japan, the State has actively intervened in the matter of technology import.

Choice of technology, Dr. Chenoy asserted, should be a sub-set of the entire role of development and of development policy. It is not only the potential of increased violence that can occur if the hierarchial stratification further worsens, but also the ecological damage arising out of particular technological choices that need to be taken into account. If, for instance, we now allow destruction of our indigenous genetic resources through our development model these resources will not be available in future.

There has been a slashing of funds in the recent Budget for the Social sector, including education. There is also an argument that there should be more emphasis on Science and Technology than on soft items like humanities. Dr. Chenoy, however, pointed out that apart from the brain-drain from the IITs, the entire notion of development and the understanding of the social, economic and cultural dimensions of the situation can come only through education.

Technology was labour displacing, Dr. Chenoy said, and unless technology could be based on equity there could be no consensus. Consensus was often used to support elite-friendly development, but the poor were not a party to this consensus.

Technology and development, Dr. Chenoy concluded, were predicated on international politics and international development. Technology policy can be viable only if it is a part of the overall effort to internationalise its important issues. There was a need in this context to link up our efforts with such movements in the West as the Green movement or the Peace movement.

VIII

Indiresan

Dr. Indiresan, as a former Director IIT, and one who still kept in touch with the institution, stated that though brain-drain was a matter of concern he did not think it could be linked up with elitism. Nor was the migration of IIT graduates as heavy as had been stated. According to a study conducted in IIT Madras and IIT Bombay, the figure was between 25-30 per cent.

Referring to the problem of population and the consequent increase in the demand for employment, Dr. Indiresan said he was all in favour of labour-intensive production, but that even on this type of production employment had to be limited to the need to produce economically—with no more than the minimum labour required. Employment in productive units should not be regarded as a welfare measure—as a dole. By treating it as such we have created a high wage cost economy, though our real wages are low.

Dr. Indiresan deplored the prevailing corruption and stated that the TELCO car referred to by Dr. Parthasarathi was a matter of technological pride, but the profit derived from the production of this car would be miniscule compared to the profit made by some companies by successfully manipulating custom and excise duties. So long as investment on technology was less profitable than on "politicking", technology will be at a discount.

On labour-intensive activities, Dr. Indiresan referred to housing. He pointed out that if 200 sq. mts. of land was made available to every household it would generate tremendous labour-intensive demands for house construction, furniture-making et.al.

He thought this was quite feasible, for distribution of 200 sq. meters per household would mean not more than one per cent of the total land area. This was, however, not being done because vested interests had an interest in land shortage, and consequent rise in land prices.

Dr. Indiresan also referred to the services sector where, in his opinion, unlike in the production sector, quality improved with increase in the number of persons employed. There was a scope for large employment in this sector, and for better quality of service to make our economy internationally competitive.

Finally, Dr. Indiresan emphasised the need for greater investment in human capital, as had indeed been suggested by the World Bank report. There was also a need to nurture indigenous technology, he said.

IX

B. Joshi

Shri B. Joshi wished to confine himself to the two theme papers and to raise some questions thereon.

First, we have indeed a galaxy of Science policy experts, but they seem to be good only at hindsight. Why have we not been able to see things at the right time? The present policy of structural adjustments in the form of liberalisations and marketisations was, Shri Joshi observed, silent on science policy. He wanted to know from the present speakers what their views were on the structural adjustment, policy and how it would affect Science and Technology.

Secondly, about intellectual property rights. We seem to be gradually yielding to pressure, but have we done a thorough analysis? Have we weighed the arguments and counter- arguments and come to conclusions?

Thirdly, the whole problem of technology and development seemed to Shri Joshi to be out of context. In the current debate, he thought, issues have changed, but have we adjusted ourselves to the change, and if so, how thoroughly? In India we had comparative advantage in some spheres, e.g. information technology, bio-technology, with our large scientific infrastructure. But how do we take advantage of this infrastructure?

Finally, Shri Joshi said that about 80 laboratories have been taken out of the CSIR and attached to the Ministries. Nothing has however been thought of the future. How are we going to adjust ourselves to the current globalisation?

X

Paulose Mar Gregorios

Dr. Paulose Mar Gregorios wished to make several observations on the subject and sought confirmation of his perceptions. First, he felt that our own cultural elites, when they reflected on the problems of development, seemed to accept one of Hegel's theses that development was a force in which, not man but history was the principal actor. Men could co-operate, oppose or ignore the force, but there was a spontaneity about the process. Consequently, when, because of our mistakes or otherwise, we are forced to integrate with the World Bank/IMF, it was regarded as futile to resist. Opposition had infact been made obsolete, according to this view, by the collapse of the Socialist countries. Was this perception correct? Dr. Gregorios was doubtful about it.

Secondly, in addition to the three sectors of the economy, viz. agriculture, industry and services which we have hitherto recognised a new sector, information, had become important, Dr. Gregorios thought. It was the most profitable sector, more so than the Services, and there was an attempt to capture information market so that the capitalist system could go forward.

Thirdly, technological renovation had become a monopoly, should this be subverted or controlled ?

Dr. Siddharta, Dr. Gregorios pointed out, had drawn a distinction between science and scientific policy, and Dr. Rahman had added to it technology policy. In the speakers opinion, scientific policy did not mean that science was the subject or object of the policy, but only that the method used should be empirical. On the other hand, science policy meant how to develop science and scientific temper, and also how to foresee and deal with the possible consequences of these policies. He however, did not agree with Dr. Rajni Kothari that science and technology were two different, parallel streams. It was the understanding of Dr. Gregorios that though technology came after science, it revealed the true nature of science. All research and development in science, he observed, was based on technology.

Dr. Gregorios stated that he had participated in the 1979 UN conference at Vienna to which reference had been made. It was found there that of the total resources spent on research and development, the developing countries spent only 5.4 per cent, while the remaining 94.6 per cent was spent by the developed countries. The Conference debated fruitlessly how much more funds should be made available to the developing countries for R & D. But were R & D mere functions of funds, Dr. Gregorios asked. In his opinion the necessary climate for R & D had not been developed in developing countries. The lack of team spirit, where individuals claimed credit for achievements, nepotism in recruitment of personnel and lack of community feeling between researchers and industries were, according to him, some of the impediments to R & D, more important than availability of funds.

In conclusion, Dr. Gregorios stated he was happy that Dr. Siddharta had spoken of a moral order. But who orders this morality, and what is the technology that generates the moral order, he asked. In the opinion of Dr. Gregorios moral order could develop only in the process of developing a social and economic order. It was relevant in this connection, he thought, to go back to European history and trace the development of their moral order, and identify the factors operating in Europe for this purpose. It was also relevant, he concluded, to go back to our own history and ask the same questions.

XI

N.K. Seth

Shri N.K. Seth was of the view that having opted for a policy of liberalisation the country had also decided its technological policy.

Massive foreign investment, as the Government of India desires, is hardly possible, he thought, unless foreign technology was also accepted.

Technology was a key factor of development, Shri Seth continued, but there was a big gap in technology between developed and developing countries. India's technological backwardness was due, in his opinion, to the concepts of self-reliance, import substitution, labour-intensiveness and appropriate technology being over-stretched.

Shri Seth disagreed with Prof. Brahmananda that technology should be imported only for the manufacture of wage goods. Such a limitation, he thought, was not possible. Scientists should, in his opinion, discuss and decide the extent to which technology should be imported and to what extent such import should be ruled out.

XII

V.G. Bhatia

Dr. V.G. Bhatia was of opinion that India's technological backwardness was due to the fact that there was no demand for technology. This in turn followed, in his view, from the economic policies we had adopted during the last four decades. These policies have been inward-oriented with no competition, either domestic or foreign. There was therefore no incentive to reduce cost by adopting new technologies. He cited the automobile industry in India as an example.

India had spent billions of dollars on scientific research, but, according to Dr. Bhatia all this had been wasted; indeed had been counter-productive. Government's ability to mobilise resources was, Dr. Bhatia concluded, limited. The available resources should be spent on compulsory education and on health measures; areas which had been grossly neglected so far.

XIII

J.S. Bali

Shri J.S. Bali, while complementing the organisers for a very interesting and informative Seminar, made the following points:

(i) Although the seminar had been very good and covered all aspects of development, there was lack of specific suggestions as to what we should do ?

(ii) Politics had ceased to be a vehicle of social change, politicians could no longer bring about such changes.

(iii) All changes, technological, economic or any other have to concentrate on improving the quality of life, but in this respect population-growth was the biggest impediment. He doubted if population would stabilise itself in India at 1500 or 1600 million. He thought the present population will at least double itself to 1800 million, by 2025 AD. There can be no change in quality of life of millions without population stabilisation.

(iv) Shri Bali did not understand how higher interest rates, as suggested, would make the entrepreneurs invest more. On the contrary, he thought, it would add to the volume of unemployment because of lesser industrial expansion.

(v) There has been some discussions of a "grand ideology", but the mood of the people had changed. A consumer-oriented middle class had grown up, so much so that even a Gandhi or a Nehru would now find it difficult to have an ideology accepted. There is no grand design now, for the programmes, if any, do not reach down to the people. On the other hand there is excessive emphasis on consumerism.

(vi) What does globalisation mean, Shri Bali asked. Survival of the fittest? A chain of supermarkets and constellation of shopping arcades? We must have selectivity in our development. We must decide what is basic. Wage goods are basic. There may be others. It is only in the spheres where we have comparative advantage that technology should be imported. We cannot afford to import technology *ad lib*.

(vii) Excess demand had been referred to as a problem. But what do we do? There was an ideology in the fifties and the sixties of austerity of demand in living. There is none now. This is, however, not a task for the scientists or the bureaucrats. The answer is improving the supply side which must be found by economists and scientists.

(viii) Technology displaces labour, Shri Bali warned, and the benefits arising there from hardly trickle down to the masses. We must, therefore, be very discriminating about technology. In particular, it should be decided carefully when technology should be imported and when it should be developed indigenously.

(ix) To me it seems that having lost the spirit of 1950s and early 1960s i.e. living within our means, we have entered into cultural imperialism of TV. etc., and consumerism.

(x) Technology changes have to fit in larger framework of economic reforms and changes of policy. The aim of technology as well as economic reforms is to get the optimum results out of the working of our natural resources. Therefore, we should have our own technology policy considering our own resources and environment.

(xi) I stressed the need for standardisation for a large range of products in order to reduce costs and achieve economy of scale particularly as the future cycles are going to be shorter in life.

(xii) R & D linkage with industry must expand, and the industry itself must spend much more on the R & D. There are areas of high technology, intermediate technology, appropriate technology and incremental technology. Several million patents are registered. We have to work out our demand and choose whatever is necessary according to our environment and surplus labour. It is not necessary to go in for high technology all the time. On the other hand, recourse must be to have adaptation and innovation. There are no fixed formulae, every country must device its own paradigms of development and must do so according to our needs. Suppy side must increase and the demand must come down, voluntarily or be controlled by economic factors.

XIV

Susheela Mehta

Ms. Susheela Mehta observed that in spite of high population growth the developing countries were doing much less damage to the environment than the developed countries. About population itself, she pointed out, that, as the example of Kerala had shown, its growth cannot be controlled unless there was some social development, and unless some egalitarian measures were taken.

All family planning measures, Ms. Mehta continued, had been imported. They were unsuitable to the Indian conditions where people were so poor and so under-nourished. There must be widespread literacy and some social awareness for these measures to succeed.

The so-called liberalisation measures and the consequent indiscriminate import of technology, she concluded, would do a lot of harm to women and to the poorest strata of society, the landless labour.

XV

O.P. Gupta

Shri O.P. Gupta, speaking from the point of view of small scale industries, stated that machinery and equipment were imported by small scale units without giving any thought to the choice of technology. The Industrial Policy Resolutions of 1948 and 1956 did provide an ideology for industrial development, but provided no guidelines in the matter of choice of technology. We are now concerned with technology upgradation, but again there are no specific guidelines to evaluate and select the technologies to achieve a particular form of development. Various types of technology—appropriate, intermediate, labour intensive *et al.* are talked about, but no choice has been made and all kinds of technology are being imported.

Several countries have been organising TECHMARTS where technologies are displayed, demonstrated and traded, but we have no such system in our country. Shri Gupta's organisation proposed to organise the first TECHMART of its type during India International Trade Fair 1992, and was also in the process of setting up a technology information centre.

Some units have developed, Shri Gupta concluded, technologies for themselves, through their own R & D, but these are generally not documented, or shared with others. There is a need to provide adequate venture capital to this sector for development, adaptation and absorption of technologies.

XVI

P.S. Gupta

Shri Prem Sagar Gupta wished to make certain observations on some of the points raised in the discussions.

Brain-drain from the Indian Institute of Technology had been referred to, but apart from such brain-drain another unfortunate phenomenon was noticeable which involved considerable waste of training, as when trained chemical engineers took up jobs and careers, totally unconnected with the education they had, as sales executive trainees in subsidiaries of multinational firms. Whose fault is this, he asked. But no one seems to be worried about this Brain-Waste.

On the question of population, Shri Gupta observed that it

was an universal experience that birth rates declined with improved standards of living. This did not mean, he emphasised, that there should be no population control measures and efforts to meet the present situation of population explosion. It only meant that the basic approach to control population and handle the problem was to improve the quality of life.

With regard to industries, Shri Gupta deplored the lack of quality control, and cited, the instance of the Premier Automobiles manufacturing the same model of FIAT II00 that Italy had produced in 1948. Even so the quality is going down everyday simultaneously with increased prices, he added.

Finally, Shri Gupta was of the view that the devaluation in June 1991 had resulted in a change in the character of our foreign trade. With the sole exception of engineering goods (and as was pointed out during the discussions, Pharmaceuticals also) our exports now comprised increasingly and mainly of agricultural and primary commodities, instead of value added products, taking us back to the days of colonial economy and reversing the pre - devaluation situation.

XVII

Baren Ray

Shri Baren Ray in his intervention referred to scientific temper, a phrase which had been coined about four decades ago. There was indeed a great need for scientific temper to meet the forces of traditionalism and conservatism, so deeply entrenched in our society, but while this phrase was widely propagated there was hardly a week when the contrary view was not also articulated that all modern developments in science and technology had been anticipated by our ancient scientists about fifteen hundred or two thousand years ago.

Shri Ray also referred to the dichotomy between intellectual and manual labour, and deplored the fact that nothing had been done to bridge the gap. There was no schools, he pointed out, for carpenters and blacksmiths. One reason for this was perhaps that such schools attracted trainees from all castes. This was resented by the castes of carpenters and blacksmiths, as the case may be, who regarded the professions as reserved for them. The caste system was as strongly entrenched at the lower levels in the hierarchy as it was in the higher.

Even among scientists at the higher levels, Shri Ray thought, the freedom necessary for research did not exist. This had, in his opinion, led to a high rate of suicide among the scientists. (Voices from the participants saying that the suicide rate was not so high).

Finally, at the risk of great unpopularity, as he put it, he expressed the view that it was impractical that the multinational corporations, who alone had the necessary environment for the purpose and who had made concerted effort to advance technology, should be denied the incentive to do so. The Dunkel proposals could not be rejected out of hand, he said. There should be give and take in a process of negotiations, he concluded.

XVIII

Balraj Mehta

Shri Balraj Mehta, while complementing the writers of the theme paper and the Critical Notes on their presentations, observed that what was missing in the discussions was the contact, economic, political and social, in which the scientists had to function. The parameters which dominated the fifties, the sixties, the seventies and even the eighties were, albeit with many omissions and commissions, the concept of transfer of technology from developed countries and from multi-national Corporations. There were bargains, and there was give and take. All this had now changed. The concept of transfer of technology was itself being belittled. Indeed, there could be no transfer of technology when 100 per cent equity was held by foreigners, or even when 51 per cent was held by them, with the remaining 49 per cent held, not by Indian collaborators, but by unidentified share-holders. In this context the very talk of adaptation of technology, of development and of Indianisation have become redundant.

Secondly, Shri Mehta continued, while we talked of reform of economic policies what was happening was retrogression.

There was also a tendency to regard politics as a crime. Indeed, a good proportion of our armed forces were being used against our own people. But this was not politics, Shri Mehta asserted. Politics was still in command, he said. It could still be an agent for social change.

Finally, Shri Mehta concluded, instead of taking sides on issues at stake we tend to become merely carping critics.

XIX

Ramaswamy Iyer

Shri Ramaswamy Iyer agreed with Dr. Ashok Parthasarathi that low interest rates encouraged capital-intensity. The prevailing tax system (with certain incentives related to investment) also did the same, and even administered prices (with an element of return on capital necessarily included) had the same effect. There was also a tendency among managers to opt for the latest technologies, he pointed out, and these were capital intensive; besides, managers always found it easier to deal with machines than with men, and so they tended to have a preference for capital intensive technologies.

The new economic policy, Shri Iyer thought, might bring in not merely capital-intensive but also sophisticated and ready made technologies backed by the power and resources of giant multi-nationals. The indigenous technological development that had taken place in the past may become very difficult in the future.

Shri Iyer was of the opinion that the ever accelerating pace of technological change was not necessarily good. A pathology of technology, as he described it, had developed. There was a tendency to believe that technology had the answers to all problems, including those created by technology. For instance, one response (heard at a recent meeting) to suggestions for the development of alternative sources of energy, such as solar power, was to propose the installation of large satellite to capture solar power and transmit it to earth. Again, at a recent symposium on environmental problems it had been suggested that the generation and emission of methane gas by cattle could be reduced by injecting all cattle with certain anti-biotics which would inhibit the production of methane; and that methane generation in paddy fields could also be countered by developing strains of bacteria that would absorb the gas. These were examples of technology gone crazy, he thought.

Finally, he pointed out that other groups such as the Economic Affairs group, could be concerned with the industrial and economic aspects of technology. If the social affairs group was also to deal with technology, its approach should be distinctive; it should be concerned with problems of poverty, the rural urban divide, the emergence of a dualistic society, the growth of social tensions, and so on, and with the question whether technology could help to solve such problems or could aggravate them.

XX

Siddharta

Dr. Siddharta in his concluding remarks observed that availability of funds was not main problem of R & D. He pointed out that with the exception of the CSIR laboratories, the others, that is those under the Ministries, never spent the funds allocated to them for research. In his opinion the absorptive capacity of the laboratories funded by Government was no more than one percent of the GNP. What was therefore necessary was industry - scale technologies to be developed by the industries for themselves. Such development should be funded by Government as had been done in Japan and South Korea. The locus of R & D should shift, he thought, from the laboratories to the industries.

One of the instrumentalities which helped a great deal in Germany and Japan, Dr. Siddharta continued, was legislation on utility models and petty inventions. There is no such legislation in India. There were two types of sources of technology for the small scale sectors. One was what he called "embodied", which related to Capital goods. The other was non-embodied, and dealt with process technology. In regard to the latter, they were at present mainly "stolen", that is used unacknowledged from other sources. This cannot continue long. What is needed, Dr. Siddharta concluded, was legislation and a policy regime for transfer of technology, vertically from large scale industries to the small scale sector.

XXI

Ashok Parthasarathi

Dr. Ashok Parthasarathi referred to the comments made by the speakers in course of the discussions. He agreed with Prof. Hajela's view that in the context of excess demand in all sectors the new Economic Policy of liberalisation was likely to result in a high cost economy.

Dr. Parthasarathi pointed out that many inventions and initial commercialisation took place in small firms, but in the United States these smalls firms, which did not have adequate resources for marketing, were soon bought up by larger companies. However, in Europe and in Japan such ownership transfers are rare.

On the basis of his experience in the Department of Scientific and Industrial Research which deals with R & D in Industry, Dr. Parthasarathi told the seminar that 1150 companies were registered with the department and they spent on R & D an aggregate of Rs. 820 crores a year, or about 0.74 per cent of the annual sales/turnover of these companies. There were, however, large variations of R & D expenditure in these companies. As categories, the public sector ranked highest in R & D expenditure, the national private sector next, and the foreign sector last. In fact, the foreign sector figured at a very low level in R & D spending in this country.

On concentration, Dr. Parthasarathi, conceded that it could lead to higher spending on R & D . In fact, however, this did not happen. He regretted that Indian companies looked more for foreign brand names in collaboration agreements than for technology transfer.

Dr. Parthasarathi agreed with Dr. Indiresan about the

tremendous potential for employment in the services sector and in civil construction work. As for the latter, apart from house-building, and road making, activities such as construction of silos for storage of grains could employ large numbers productively. But he wished to emphasise that all this was not enough to absorb the numbers seeking employment. On the question of population, he said in reply to the point raised by Shri Bali that the projection that the population would stabilise at 1500/1600 million had been made by Dr. Ashis Bose in a lecture. This projection was, however, based on certain assumptions. If these assumptions proved wrong, the projected figures could even be exceeded. In this context, Dr. Parthasarathi said that the Prime Minister had rendered a service by putting family planning back on the agenda at a meeting of the National Development Council. This was a very necessary step.

Reverting to the problem of employment, Dr. Parthasarathi regretted that India had no concerted plan to find employment for the vast numbers that would seek employment in the coming years. China had a plan to generate 80 million additional jobs in the rural areas over the period 1990-2000. Even if this did not fully materialise, they would be able to generate at least 40/50 million jobs. The Finance Minister had suggested as part of his speech on the Union-Budget for 1992-93, the setting up of a Small Farmers' Agro-Business Consortium. It was a good idea, but not adequate to meet our requirements for employment. Bio-Technology based rural industry had tremendous potential for productive employment in rural areas, but no plan had yet been drawn up in that regard. Meanwhile agricultural operations in the green revolution areas, Dr. Parthasarathi pointed out were using less man days per hectare than before. This had compounded the problem.

In regard to employment generation in industries, Dr. Parthasarathi warned that the basic fact should be noted that managers preferred machines to men because the latter were often aggressive and militant. Trade Unionists should pay adequate heed to this factor as otherwise owners in both the public and private sectors would place ever greater emphasis on automation, thereby destroying even the available employment potential in industry. Dr. Parthasarathi also pleaded for a more discriminating use of "investment allowance" by Government. While such an allowance was justified, for instance, in high technology and intrinsically capital intensive areas, such as the manufacture of Semiconductors or Computers or the production of Chemical Fertilisers, there was no justification for such allowances to be given for low technology areas of high employment potential, such as assembling TV or radio receivers.

Developing this point further in relation to the associated question of choice of technology, Dr. Parthasarathi regretted that the Government economists were more concerned about "modern technology " than the technologists themselves. The key concern, should be how to increase the wage bill per unit of production, rather than the capital employed per unit of production. Fiscal and financial incentives and wages, incomes and price policy should be oriented to such an objective.

Referring to the Dunkel Draft Text (DDT), Dr. Parthasarathi complemented Dr. Kamal A. Chenoy on the Very relevant points raised by him. The Reason why India was concerned about DDT, Dr. Parthasarathi explained, was that the product patent, as distinguished from the process patent, envisaged by DDT, would force our industry to seek patents for a large number of products, even when we had the technology to make those products through one process route or the other. Apart from the unnecessary cost in foreign exchange this would entail, our experience and that of other newly industrialised countries was that the patent holders in the OECD countries use the opportunity to attach conditions for the grant of licences to use their patents, of which restricting exports was a major conditionality. This is a danger which the Commerce Ministry should take serious note of.

With all the dangers that DDT posed to this country, there was one feature which our industrialists should take advantage of. According to the DDT, Dr. Parthasarathi pointed out, if the provisions of the Text were accepted and came into force, on January 1, 1993, the new patent law provided that product patents would come into force ten years later, i.e. January 1, 2003. During this ten-year period, applications for product patents could be made and would be received by the Controller General of Patents but kept in a sealed cover. The applications would be taken out and processed for acceptance only in 2003. What is more, they would take effect only in the order of priority of their receipt. In the meantime, i.e. between 1993 and 2003, process patents under our existing law of 1971 would continue to be granted, and though the product patents granted after 2003, will have retrospective effect from the dates of the application, the process patents granted meanwhile will have precedence. It was, therefore, to the advantage of our industrialists to apply for and obtain as many patents as possible, until the new patent law mandated under DDT came into force.

Dr. Parthasarathi agreed with Father Gregorios that information should be added to labour, capital and technology as a key factor in the development of industry, agriculture and services.

Major areas of domestic technological development, Dr. Parthasarathi pointed out, had already been successfully done and commercialised. Thousands of crores of rupees of domestic production were already based on locally developed technology. He agreed there was some concern, as pointed out by Shri Prem Sagar Gupta, that the new economic policy might result in the export of primary products, but stated that there were sizeable exports already in chemical and pharmaceutical products, textiles and engineering goods, and these were not expected to decline.

There must, however, be what Dr. Parthasarathi called technological pluralism. High technology needed for export must co-exist with simpler products for the domestic market. As regards the complaint that the model for our FIAT cars had not changed since 1948, Dr. Parthasarathi pointed out that a change in the model required very expensive re-tooling which would not be remunerative unless there was a large enough market for these cars. Such a market was only beginning to come about today.

Another feature worth noting, according to Dr. Parthasarathi, was that the hiring and firing of employees and workers which was characteristic of the U.S. Industrial system did not exist in Japan or even in Europe. The trade unions in India should, however, accept a new social contract which, while protecting employment, dealt adequately with the problem of technological change.

In conclusion, Dr. Pathasarathi stated that while he was concerned about several aspects of the New Economic Policy, he also felt that it had introduced some measure of competition which should force managers to improve quality and reduce costs of production, and hence sale-prices. India could not afford to continue a cost plus economy. The changes had to come some time, though it was debatable whether the changes had been brought about at too fast a pace. We need to pressurise our industries, but we cannot afford to let them die. A delicate balance had, therefore, to be maintained, and the success or otherwise of the new policy would depend on how the balance is struck.

XXII

A. Rahman

Dr. A. Rahman in concluding the debate on his presentation wished to make two points.

His first observation was that we must deal with the problem of mass education, and with the connected problem of diffusion of technology. In India, he pointed out, we identify problems and have long debates, but we fail to look at the realities and solve them. In regard to technology we must look at different sectors, see what must be done. We must also look at linkages of one sector with another. All this requires ground work.

Secondly, Dr. Rahman continued, we must decide on the role of the scientific community. One of their roles is undoubtedly to generate knowledge and scientific technology, but another important role was to act as critics, with a number of single-issue groups, such as the Environment group or the women's group, in action today. It was important, Dr. Rahman observed, to bring about the required integration in order to work out a significant perspective of development, and interact for this purpose with the political decision- makers. This was a role for which the scientific community was well suited.

In conclusion, Dr. Rahman quoted from poet Iqbal that laws are made by the powerful in the interests of their own states. One can criticise these laws, but that has little effect to be effective one has to be powerful, but no State can be powerful if the power is confined to 10 per cent of its citizens to the exclusion of the remaining 90 per cent.

Part III

SECULARISM AND SOCIAL TRANSFORMATION

SECULARISM AND SOCIAL TRANSFORMATION IN INDIA

Rasheeduddin Khan*

I : The Context of Socio-Economic Transformation

Four-and-a-half decades of national independence is an appropriate occasion to reflect on the nature of the contemporary Indian polity that has emerged. We must examine the contradictions and conflicting interests that beset it, in the process of the gigantic socio-economic transformation of our continental federal polity.

In the time scale of history of such an ancient land like India, spanning five millenia of continuous civilisation, 45 years would appear a small, even a negligible and an inconsequential period of time, not worthy of any reckoning. But in the dynamic phase of our contemporary times marked by incremental revolution, exponential curve and telescopic changes these very 45 years appear as a recognisable epoch, a watershed, a nodal point of transformation in the annals of our five thousand years of continuing existence.

---

* Director, Indian Institute of Federal Studies, New Delhi, Former Professor of Political Science, Jawaharlal Nehru University, New Delhi-110067; Former Member -Rajya Sabha.

A new civilisation is emerging in India, around a new polity, by the interaction of different, sometime opposing and sometime converging set of forces and factors domestic and global, in a highly interdependent world setting. An ancient society is getting transformed into a modern polity, at a time when national isolation is an impossibility, and global interdependence a major reality specially for a geopolitically strategic country that stands on the cross roads of international transactions.

India is one of the world's most complex plural society. Complexity of India is basically a function of its 'size' and 'scale'. The sub-continental polity, in the past as in the present, acquires its defined personality essentially as an agglomeration of regions and sub-regions. This has been recognised throughout the centuries as evidenced for instance in the *Vayu Purana*, the *Ain-i-Akbari*, the *Imperial Gazetteers of India*, the reports of the pre-independence National Planning Committee (Presided over by Jawahar Lal Nehru) and in the several relevant documents of the planning of India after independence. It is around these well defined socio-economic sub-regions (about 60 to 70) that distinctive sub-national communities (but not nationalities) exist, whose indices of inclusive identity can be measured in terms of specific jatiformation, tribal patterns, religious communities and sects, dialects and literary heritage, variations in common beliefs and rituals and in the manner in which classics of myths and wisdom like the *Ramayana*, *Mahabharata* and the *Gita* and the wide-range of *Puranas* and folk-lore interpreted, together with peculiarities of culture-pattern, folk music, dance and drama, familiarities, and local history etc. The roots of socio-cultural federalism in India are very deep, even as the framework of political federalism is still in a process of evolution of change, seeking to acquire a stable shape and form under democratic dispensation.

India's continental territorial dimension and its teeming millions constituting one-fifth of humanity, introduces the factor of 'scale' in any discussion of the Indian reality. Length of history underlines the depth of the roots. In a country of more or less unbroken succession of social history, continuity of traditions, customs, conventions, and rituals, result in over-laying the contemporary framework of society with certain continuing forms of primordial ties. These bonds continue to project their cohesion even within the parameters of democratic system, that is, post-primordial and post-colonial political system. But the point to note is that these ties and bonds still evoke strong primordial loyalties around a wide range of identities, sometimes even at the expense of loyalties around modernized focil of allegiences like class, strata, union, professional association, ideology, party, etc.

The social composition of the Indian polity today may be visualised as representing a gigantic mosaic in which primordial cleavages both intersect and inter-mix with contemporary socio-economic segments. The social situation in India therefore reveals in co-existence of multi-level and multi-structured groups. New class formation that have come into being as a consequence of the process of industrialisation and urbanisation, compete for cohesion and loyalty with the persisting feudal-cum-tribal pattern in rural hinterland and jati-cum-religious community loyalties in urban situation.

There is a peculiar pattern of interaction and inter twining, between the pre-industrial and industrial class formations, particularly because of the tenacious hold of feudal agro craft bonds in large tracts of the country. But Since the political system is democratic based on the constitutional recognition of rights and equality of all the citizens, irrespective of caste, creed, gender and domicile, and since the system functions on the principle of adult franchise, periodic elections and divisions of power, as between the Centre and the States and within the organs of government we find the manifestation of primordial loyalties taking diverse forms.

The contradiction between the modernized political system and social situation marked by a patch work of tradition and modernity, is all too apparent in several sectors of national life. As long as the democratic social revolution remains incomplete, political democracy would continue to bear the brunt of the infighting of the dominant caste -cum-class force for power, and for increasing acquisition of goods and services. They seek to keep the lower classes outside the pale of the beneficial effect of national development and the range of national prosperity. In the situation of unequal advantage, every increase in the GNP and in national standards of living would continue to give unequal benefits to the entrenched 'haves' at the expense of the disinherited and dislocated 'have notes', notwithstanding the slogans about democratization, distributive justice and socialism.

With the dawn of political independence, the process of industrialization gained momentum and acquired a certain direction. Planned development within the matrix of a mixed economy has its own points of contradictions. Public sector, in the framework of the capitalist mode of production has not promoted the prospects of socialism (even if that was intended, as it is sometimes naively believed) but provided, at public and State cost, the infrastructure of power, energy, coal, iron and steel, transportation, communication etc. that facilitated the growth and expansion of a sprawling capitalist system in India. At best public sector represents the segment of State capitalism, more as a cooperative rather than as a competitive element of the given economic system, creating a contradictory tableau of growth and poverty. The process of industrialization is still far behind the requisite level of development that could stabilise the basis of self reliant and self generating economy. This is clear from justaposing the facts that while we are 15th in rank in terms of our GNP, we have the dubious distinction of being 106th in terms of *per capita* income. It is instructive to remember that during the decades of planned development, while the net national product at constant prices has increased by 165% the per capita share has increased only by 45% (that is almost one-fourth less), hence, the contradictory phenomenon of growth *and* poverty, and not growth eleminating poverty.

By unofficial reckoning about 38 to 40% of our people are below the poverty-line. To comprehend this phenomenon of contradiction that has precluded the percolation of benefits to the disinherited populace, one has to examine carefully, the pattern of interaction and dialectics between the 'given' market forces (controlled and manipulated by expanded business-commercial-industrial linkage among the propertied classes) and the role and expectation of the emerging classes (constituting segments of the formerly alienated and oppressed groups and middle castes) in a situation of expanding and protected capitalist system in India.

In this process, while part of the poor have certainly not remained poor despite the fact that part of the rich have become richer, yet the more crucial truth remains that a bulk of the poor have continued to remain poor, if not in absolute, certainly in relative terms, because of the gulf between the rich and the poor segments have grown in terms of income-distribution, civic amenities, availability of goods and services, and the potential of using the opportunities provided by growth itself.

There are two sides of this picture. The positive side is that in 45 years, there has been a phenomenal rise and expansion of the middle and working class. Probably nowhere in world history, this size and diversity of professionals and occupational groups of the middle class and working class has emerged in such large proportions jointly accounting for more than 300 million people. The negative side is that in terms of the total human situation in the country, this growth of the middle and working class, is offset by the existence of millions constituting the lower classes and poor peasantry, comprising the massive impoverished segment in the continental rural hinterland and in myriad pockets of urban agglomeration.

In India one might identify 5 propertied and 5 non-propertied classes, that play economic, social and political roles, as aggregate groups in the working of the Indian polity. These classes in broad strokes are :

5 propertied classes

i. Major capitalists, with an all-India spread and controlling major industries; top businessmen and traders ; big contractors;

ii. Middle bourgeoisie, with regional relevance;

iii. Traditional commercial classes;

iv. Rural rich ;

v. Upper segment of professional groups, top managers and senior bureaucrats.

5 non-propertied classes

i. Middle and lower middle classes - i.e., middle

professional groups; small traders; middle and lower bureaucracy;

ii. Working classes;

iii. Marginal and small cultivators;

iv. Land-less labourers, poor peasants;

v. Lower service sector and menial workers unemployed and destitutes.

India's political system with its liberal democratic overtones, leans towards a coalescence of power comprising the upper classes and middle castes (led by the captains of industry and commerce and the land-based rural rich), whose joint interest-orientation runs counter to the programme of an all inclusive egalitarian transformation. The four sub-systems, of the politial system, namely the party system, the electoral system, the parliamentary system and the administrative system, functions each within itself and all together, in a manner that contributes to the maintenance of a power-equation, in which the dominance of the propertied classes and their interests is assured.

II : Characteristics of the Indian Party System

The spectrum of the party system in India is such that with the exception of the communist parties, all parties, when the chips are down, cater to the multiple interests of the propertied classes, in varying degrees and in many forms. Electoral system is manipulated by vote-banks, and powerful caste-cum-interest factions, greased by the effective use of black money (which today has become almost a parallel economy, vitiating many assumptions of investment, taxation, resource mobilization etc.) in financing the ever increasing costs of elections. Parliamentary elections have become an exercise in severely limited options. At the federal apex of power at least, even now, the Congress looms large on the political horizon as the only all India party with branches in every State and Union Territory, and in practically every district and several tehsil towns.

Indian party-system is asymmetrical. The Centre piece is the Congress, dominating the all-India scene by its numerical preponderance, and habitual support that it receives from the administration, the vested interests, local toughs and dadas, as the more-or-less permanent ruling party in majority of the States. Next to this gigantasaurus, there are two types of parties, the trans-regional parties covering few States like the BJP, Janata and Lok Dal on the Right, and CPM and CPI on the Left; and the uni-regional parties like the DMK and AIADMK in Tamil Nadu; Kranti Ranga in Karnataka; Telugu Desham Party in Andhra Pradesh, National Conference in Jammu and Kashmir; Akali Dal in Punjab; Jarkhand Mukti Morcha in Bihar; Forward Bloc and RSP in Bengal etc. and few parties, groups, and factions of local relevance. Since 1989 election, the BJP has emerged as the main opposition party in the Parliament, and a ruling party in large States of the Hindi Belt—UP, Madhya Pradesh, Rajasthan and Himachal Pradesh. Because of this situation naturally the effective range of choice for the election to the Vidhan Sabhas of the States is little wider. Hence the DMK or AIADMK government in Tamil Nadu; CPM in West Bengal and Tripura; occasional coalitions of opposition parties in Kerala, Gujarat and Rajasthan. Non-Communist left the erstwhile PSP, SSP, Socialist Party have dissolved in cauldron of anti-Congressism . What remains in Janata and Lok Dal are frustrated ramnants, whose socialist identity pales into irrelevance in the alchemy of heterogeneous coalition.

The Congress has been in power both at the federal level and in a majority of States of the Union for most of the past four-and-a-half decades, essentially because of three reasons—as a main successor to the national movement, as the only All-India party that unites or multi-ethnic, multi-lingual and multi-religious people, and as the party that represents what may be called the 'GCM' of Indian politics by trying to unite the many ideological segments into an operational unity. Being a multi-class party, it has points of contradiction but its dominant leadership ever since the time of Jawaharlal Nehru has maintained a centrist position that despite its alternate tilting towards the 'left' and the 'right' had nevertheless kept a balance between the many forces and ideological strands and worked out a pragmatic alternative which did transform India in the course of just four decades into a stable political community, integrating the many streams of linguistic, cultural and religious diversities and laid the foundations of a self reliant economic base and generated the long-drawn process of cumbersome social change.

III : Aberrations in the Political System

Reflection on the functioning of the political system, four obvious aberrations stand-out as severe impediments in the process of socio-economic transformation, namely, *populism, economism, parochialism,* and *the breakdown of the national consensus.*

In countries like India that have suffered for centuries, first under feudal autocracies and oppression, and then under colonial exploitation and foreign domination, the accumulated problem of social inequality, economic imbalances, blatant discrimination based on caste, creed, language and region are so many that it creates a situation propitious for populism particularly in a polity that depends on periodic elections and competing party system for the continuance and legitimacy of its power structure. This has generated widespread *political permissiveness,* signifying palpable erosion of values to a shameless degree. Nothing is beyond a typical politician—lying, cheating, duplicity, blackmail, indecency, exhortation of money, land-grab, you name it and it is there. Since success is the only goal, leaders and parties indulge in blatant propaganda, and in the game of toppling and defection. The populism of the ruling party is matched by the populism of the opposition. Removal of the Congress becomes the single major point of opposition unity.

To maintain themselves in power, the manipulative instinct of the Indian political elite often make them cultivate, what may be called the dualistic style of functioning marked by public promises and private betrayals. Without promises mass-support in the shape of popular votes is not possible, and without betrayal the interests of the dominant classes cannot be served. Without the help of the dominant classes, the political elites cannot remain in power, even as without mass acquiescence they cannot pretend to retain the facade of the 'consent of the governed'. This is probably endemic in the system.

To repeat, in the situation obtaining within the parameters of the Indian political system, a party cannot come into power without people's vote, and cannot remain in power without upper class support. The political system as functioning in India, is predicated on maintaining its power and legitimacy by manipulating the mutually contradictory, but jointly reinforcing pulls and pressures, from opposite class formations. This in-built contradiction lends itself to populism on the one side and the strengthening of economic oligarchy on the other. The politicians in a liberal democracy are like brokers who strive to sell *political democracy* to the masses and enjoy the pay-off from the *economic hegemony* of the upper classes, in a bid to retain their own power by mediating between the two within a *tolerable level of tension*, and reconcilable conflict, whose management then becomes their main pre-occupation.

Economism and trade unionism flourish in the situation of 'Libertarianism' that is an off-shoot of the prevalent political atmosphere marked by over-emphasis on worker's rights at the expense of concomitant obligations of the workers towards national development. The liberties taken by the propertied classes coupled with the mis-management, inefficiency and corruption that is rampant in industrial complexes, vitiate the atmosphere for the maintenance of an equilibrium, between rights and duties, privileges and obligations. In an unequal society while the 'haves' still command disproportionate share in the national wealth, whatever be the level of production and GNP, it is the working class and the discriminated sections, that have to face the adverse effect of maldevelopment, low production, topsy-turvy scale of priorities and low rate of growth of GNP. Therefore, at this stage of economic development in India, marked by imbalances and low production level, unequal to the national requirement, inordinate pre-occupation with the rights, wages, bonus, concessions, is counter-productive. Without the fulfilment of production targets and improvement of efficiency, the very prospects of generating more wealth and greater opportunities for the completion of the socio-economic transformation would remain bleak, thereby adversely effecting the working class, the poor peasantry and backward sections.

In this situation, obviously the working-class segments are caught-up as it were in a vicious circle. Pre-occupation with their own rights, however, important, cuts them away from the sympathy of the larger citizenry, apart from attracting the might of law and the oppressive apparatus of the State. Economism has robbed the working-class of its radical edge and revolutionary role.

Parochialism in India, takes two main forms : communalism and casteism. Each of the two forms tries to fragment the national identity and fracture the national body-politic. They Counter-pose allegiance to a sub-national segment at the expense of the larger whole, the nation, and weakens the slow and precarious process of the growth of an equipoised federal polity. A responsible and responsive federal authority alone can reconcile the legitimate and well-coordinated autonomies of regions and sub-regions, within which most of the genuine demands of the linguistic, cultural and religious communities can be met. A viable pattern of 'unity in diversity', that is, unity of political integration tempered by the diversities of language and cultural, religious communities, caste and tribes, is a pre-requisite for the flowering of India's peculiar national genius. Parochialism destroys this very possibility by promoting group-rivalry, animosity, tension and violence. Quite often their idiom, slogans, methods of organisation and agitation (particularly of caste and communal parochialism) are reminiscent of fascistic politics. "Communalism" said Jawaharlal Nehru "is the fascism of India".

All the parties, at one or the other time, and in one or the other form are guilty of formenting parochial loyalties for the ulterior motive of winning an election or mounting and agitation, or settling a partisan score. But what is alarming is the fact that in the specturm of the Indian party-system, there are parties, groups and fora which thrive on the exclusive basis of promoting communalism and casteism. And this in the name of democracy, and even quite invoking perversely the concept of genuine secularism. The BJP supported by the RSS, the Shiv Sena, the Vishwa Hindu Parishad, etc. and the Dal Khalsa work in the full glare of the people, the midia and the Government of India. There are other parties, some even with socialist pretensions, whose main support-base is round certain middle-jatis, and which inevitably cater to the protection and promotion of the interests of these jatis variously under the cover of rural development, egalitarianism, greater benefit for the agricultural classes, inter-regional and inter-sectoral balance, etc.

It is in this context that there is a constant tussle between the two alternative processes of 'secularism' and secularation of the polity on the one hand and 'communalism' and communal polarisation between religious communities on the other.

IV : Communalism and National Fragmentation

Let us first comprehend the meaning and implication of Communalism' in the context of India's politics and polity.

What is Communalism ? Adherence to religion and religious system is not communalism. Exploitation of religion is communalism. Attachment to a religious community or religiosity is not communalism. Using a religious community against other communities and against the nation is communalism. 'Affliction' to ritualism, superstition, obscurantism, magic, charm and occult practices like astrology is not communalism. These are merely irrational, unscientific and primordial orientations, due to conformism to traditions, or to fear of the unknown and unbounded ambition. Even commitment to conservative values in social life and conservative orientation in politics is not communalism. It can be called social backwardness and political reaction. However, it should be recognised that all these aspects can be inputs into the development of communal consciousness, and indeed the communalists, in various permutation and combination have utilised most of these aspects in order to build their communal, political base. But 'communalism' as a specific phenomenon in Indian polity is something different and more specific.

Let us pause at this point to realize that a real man of god, i.e., a true believer in religion, is also expected to be a good human-being and indeed most of the time he is. It is not uncommon to see deeply religious people, not only as good humanists and excellent neighbours but also as committed nationalists and patriots in their own way and their own terms. It is wrong to assume that communalists are religious people, in the real sense of the word. Even those few who are both 'religious' and 'communal' act as communalists in politics largely by emphasizing the dubious and contentious belief that their religion is a 'complete code of life and hereafter' for all time, hence politics and civic affairs cannot be segregated from religion. Historical experience in all parts of the world, and most clearly in India has shown that this world of fancy and illusion soon degenerates into religious, bigotry and political intolerance in the context of the politics of modern States, which are mostly multi-ethnic national sovereignties, integrating diverse religious communities. Indeed communalists become communalists precisely because they are ignorant of the moral teachings and universalists underpinning of their own religion, which makes them, in essence, not only irreligious but also anti-national and anti-human. A communalist may not even respect and adhere to a religion except as a public posture, for a communalist is basically interested in 'using' religion, and that too not for any religious, spiritual or moral ends, but on the contrary for 'secular' ends (in the sense of statecraft and politics), therefore for meta-religious or non-religious mundane political ends attuned for aggrandisement of power, position and wealth.

Communalism is perversion of religion from a moral order to a temporal arrangement of contemporary convenience from a faith into a constituency, from a strategy of living into tactics of politics, from an end to a means. Communalism exploits parts of religious dogma for expedient political purposes. Communalism seeks to conform arbitrarily religious tenets, tradition and values to suit the exigencies of current political life and subtle, of religion, and of genuine attachment to a religious community. Communalism is promoted by a real or an imaginary fear of the other communities, communalism is conversion of religiosity into political bellicosity. Communalism is the enemy of progress, revolution, democracy and of federal nation-state building on national scientific lines. In this sense communalism is not a phenomenon of conservative reaction but of modernised reaction.

Then how do we define communalism ? Communalism is basically an ideology of *political allegiance to a religious community* as a primary and decisive group in the polity, and for political action. Communalism is a modern phenomenon, and not a phenomenon of the medieval past . It is a sectarian, restrictive and negative response to the process of modernisation and modern nation-building. Communalism envisages a religious community alone as a base and universe of its political ambition and action. Communalism is perception of other religious communities as inimical entities within a polity and within a nation, arranged in an unfriendly antagonistic and belligerant equation one to another.

Communalism is a political orientation that recognises religious community and not the nation and the nation-state as the terminal community—the final point of political allegience. Therefore, communalism is a political strategy opposed to nationalism as an aggregation of multi-ethnic, multi-religious and multi-lingual communities.

Communalism is opposed to secularism as a pattern of socio-cultural co-existence and political integration. Communalism is opposed to a rational civic basis of party formation and political system. Communalism perceive majorities and minorities segments and divisions within a polity and a nation, based essentially on religious communities and not even on any other ascriptive basis, (like that of family, clan, tribe, jati, language, region or domicile) and certainly not on the basis of political, ideological, party, class, interests or strata considerations, which is the hall-mark of a modern political system. Politicisation of religious community opposed to other communities and the nation then, is the main plank of communalism.

V : Colonialism and Communalism

It is interesting to remember that communalism as a term used in the special connotation of religious and racial antagonism especially in India entered the English lexicon at about the same time i.e., mid 19th century, when the British Crown became the imperial sovereign. This simultaneity is not a mere coincidence. It establishes on the one hand casuality link between 'occurrence in history' and on the other, an organic link between the role of imperialism and the rise of communalism in India. Not that communities in the same religious sense did not exist earlier nor that antagonism between them was completely absent. The pertinent point is that in the activisation of this very antagonism, and its transformation from a latent and inward looking religious cleavage into the most articulate socio-political divisive conflict, the presence and policy of British imperialism played a decisive and negative role.

Separatism in politics and politicisation of religious communities have been the two most detrimental contribution of British colonial administration in the emerging body-politic of undivided India. It should be realized that it was this structure, style and process of politics which eventually resulted in the vivisection of the nation and the partition of the country due to the manipulaton of the withdrawing British imperial power in collaboration with the reactionary political exertion of the Muslim League, aided and abetted by other separatist forces of Hindu communalism.

The recognition of the fallacious and pernicious 'two nation theory' implying that Hindus and Muslims *per se* and by definition were two separate monolith communities was historically and sociologically a fallacious assumption. It completely overlooked not only the regional and linguistic variation in the Hindu and the Muslim communities in India, it also overlooked the centuries old heritage of intercommunal co-existence marked by mutual understanding between them as neighbours in villages, localities, cities, regions etc., The false slogan that Hindus and Muslims constituted 'separate nations', and therefore were entitled to 'separate territorial sovereignty' once British paramountly lapses, was the most monumental blunder of contemporary Indian history. It destroyed not only the civilizational unity built over the centuries and the dominant pattern of composite culture evolved by a long drawn historic process of interaction, assimilation and synthesis of diverse ethnic groups and trends, but also violated the time tested and universally accepted basic assumption of modern federal nation-building. It gave a disastrous shock to some of the cherished traditions of Indian polity and social life-traditions of accommodation and reconciliation, of respect and recognition of diversities of toleration and goodwill, of creative and innovative harmonisation of trends, tendencies, beliefs, customs, etc. It annihilated a gracious part of India's historical personality, and projected instead an irrational, invidious and untenable proposition that 'religion' alone is the criterion of identifying a nation and therefore of state building.

The recognition of the principle of religion alone as the basis of modern state-formation and state-craft, had far-reaching repercussions on the polity and politics of the sub-continent of South Asia, or what is historically referred to as the Hindustan sub-continent. In Pakistan it has given a handle to the religious groups to assert their political ambition in the name of Islam. This has led to an endless crisis of political identity in Pakistan, and has weakened the process of secular modern politics there. In India, as a repercussion it has legitimised communal politics. These two structural developments have vitiated secular politics in the sub-continent. They have distorted contemporary political traditions, political culture and political functioning, whose negative impact on the evolution of new national identities both in India and Pakistan, are all too apparent.

The first consequence of this development was the birth of an avowedly Muslim communal State of Pakistan, whose politics domestically has been marked by the persistence of the 'mullan-in-mufti' syndrome, signifying an alliance of theologians, the military-Junta and a combination of bureaucratic and commercial elite, which has repudiated not only the pretention of secular-democracy, envisaged in Jinnah's speeches and statements after independence, but also frustrated all attempts of civilian rule and restoration of genuine representative political system in Pakistan.

The spill-over of Pakistan's persistant Muslim communalism (despite its formal masquerading as Muslim nationalism and national identity) across the borders has created problems for India, especially in the wake of Sikh militancy-marked by the Bhrindanwala phenomenon, the Khalistan demand, Indira Gandhi's assassination, November riots in Delhi, the see-saw in Akali politics, all contributing to inter-communal tensions and conflicts and to unabated terrorists with Pakistan, has given a new edge to inter-state communal politics within India, itself.

Another consequence of the recognition of religion as the *raison d' etre* of politics, as exemplified by the creation of Pakistan, has been the strengthening of the communalist ideology in India. It has contributed in no small measure in providing a tradition, a base and a legitimacy to communal politics in sovereign democratic India. Partition has not only divided the country, but it had also divided the language and idiom of politics in the sub-continent, by promoting and legitimising the communal diction, as a recognized and acceptable idiom, together with the other idiom, namely the national idiom of politics. The repercussion of partition on domestic Indian politics has been to divide Indian politics itself into one based on multi-religious, multi-lingual and multi-regional aggregation, orientation and articulation.

Further, by so doing it has not only fragmented national politics on erroneous and irrational lines, but it has also distorted the process of democratic federal nation building in India, and impaired the foundations of the emerging edifice of secular-civic culture. Communalisation of politics has also postponed the shift from a scriptive based feudal, atavistic, emotionally charged passion-politics, which in essence is anti-democratic, to interest-cum-class based democratic politics, resting on the recognition of individual citizens, as equal and free member of the polity, without discrimnation made on the basis of tribe, *jati*, domicile, language, gender etc.

VI : Repercussion of Communalism on the Indian Polity

Given this context and the prevalent political traditions of communalisation of politics, the working of the Indian political system could not steer clear of the communal idiom and aggregation. The logic and processes of adult franchise, periodic elections, competing party-system, etc., has provided legitimacy and protection of law to all political parties, socio-cultural organisations, formations, groups, etc., both communal and nationalistic. Therefore, this otherwise positive framework of political system and processes, has ironically also provided a 'blanked protection' to all manifestly and proclaimed communal formations. Democratic protection is provided to non-democratic even anti-democratic elements, on the assumption that discrimination between parties or groups on any count might be arbitrary and authoritarian, and anyhow it is against the principles of democratic open society, and that these elements should be fought 'politically' and 'socially' and not by resorting to legal means, much less to executive and administrative action.

Undoubtedly there is considerable weight in this argument. And in an ideal or near ideal situation its efficacy can be proved and admired. But the situation which India is facing in terms of the historical background of communalism, the stage of socio-economic development, the level of political consciousness, the political experience of the last four decades, the increases in communal tensions, riots, conflicts, violence, and group and individual terrorism, calls for a sobering re-appraisal of our political values, processes and the working of our political system.

India, today appears a society prone to continuing communal violence and, political destablisation. Much of this had been tolerated over the years under the mistaken belief that this is an unavoidable stage in the building of an open democratic polity. This was supposed to be a part of evolution. However, this might be one aspect of the situation, but frankly it also indicates a pathetic incapacity of the system. This is reflected in the indecision of the executive, alternated by vacillation between 'firmness', and 'accommodation', in the divided counsel of parliamentarians and legislators based on their party tactics and power game, in the limited juristic view taken by the courts that occasionally give protection of law to criminals, anti-social elements, violent fanatics and habitual offenders. And all this is resulting in demoralisation of the administration and the police. This has contributed to a persistently bizzarre situation in national life for years that can be described as an unmanageable tragic drift.

What are the current manifestations of communalism in India? To use the issues of the bygone past for settling scores in the present against another community is communalism. To punish the present generation for the real or imaginary misdeeds of the past generation is communalism. Communalism is also an attempt to generate inter-communal psychosis by raking up events and episodes of the mediaeval past. The communalists seek to use the past as a continuum of the present, for promoting inter-communal discord. They overlook themselves and confuse the other people about the basic characteristic of the ancient and the mediaeval ages marked as they were by feudal autocracy, religious bigotry, dynastic ambitions, migratory movements for empire-building, invasions, annexations, conquests, vandalism and tyranny. Dynasts, empire-builders and potentates, often indulged in vain-glorious acts to acquire false recognition and prestige in one's own community and to exploit the impulse of the army and the bureaucracy to perpetuate their worldly ambitions by projecting the false garb of religious mandate. To punish innocent members of a community due to acts of commission or omission of few rulers or leaders of the same community in the past or in the present time, is rank communalism. To attack and murder a human being in a frenzy or riot, only because he belongs to another community, is the worst form of communalism. To incite communal animosity and hate by word of mouth or publication, particularly by using one's privileged position in profession and society, especially the media, is wicked and manifests communalism.

Today communalism, in its varied shapes has acquired a most dangerous form and an alarming proportion. It is a multi-pronged challenge that seeks to disrupt India's multi-religious fraternity. It is an affront to India's nationalist identity and tragic set-back to our evolving secular culture. It is subversive of our political stability and economic development, and therefore manifests itself as enemy number one of our democratic polity.

VII : The implications of the terms secularism and secular polity in European experience in the Indian context

The term secularism has been subjected in India, by the academic experts specially, and the intelligentsia generally, to needless scrutiny in terms of its meaning and implication. The fact is that every term indeed has three different meanings—literal, historical and contemporary. These three meanings, namely in terms of etymology (i.e., linguistic roots), historical connotation (i.e., based on different uses put to it over the centuries and in different countries), and contemporary meaning (i.e., current common usage) may not be, and indeed are rarely identical to each other. A classic example is of the term democracy. Aristotle, if resurrected would be terrified to realize that democracy is being advocated as one of the ideals for a good and just society.

There are, however, two valid objections to the term secularism, by the detractors, the nit-picking critics, and even the well-meaning objective analysts. One is that the term is heavily overlaid by its European/Western connotation, of 'separation of Church from the State', and the 'separation of the School from the Church'. Hence it is ethno-centric in its historical context and relevance, and therefore cannot be universalised, obviously due to diversity of social and religious traditions, in the world. Second objection is that the suffix 'ism', gives it a dogmatic veneer and an orientation of unquestioned certitude, and thus transforms is from a worthy ideal into a rigid doctrine. Both the objections are indeed valid, if one is taking too literal a view of the terms secular and secularism and perceive them only within the strait-jacket of West European experience.

Secularism as a term, used freely in public discourse in India, implies a concept and process, that seeks to change a traditional society into a modern polity, by emphasizing certain values and norms of civic life and political culture. It has both a negative and a positive connotation.

In its negative connotation, secularism implies for instance, a process which is *opposed* to: (i) domination of religion in politics; (ii) building a mono-religious state structure (like for instance Islamic Republic, Buddhist-State, Hindutva etc.); (iii) the idea of a theocratic or quasi-theocratic State controlled and directed by a religious - community; (iv) discrimination between religious segments in society, State and government for purposes of civic life, and in the political system and in the making of constitution, laws, rules and procedures, etc.; (v) counterposing religious identities to the unified national identity; (vi) fragmentation of the citizens into exclusive electoral constituency, based on ascriptive grounds of sects, tribes, caste, religious community etc.

Positively, secularism means the following: (i) recognition of religion and beliefs as personal and devotional aspects of life, (ii) affirmation of equal respect to all religions and belief systems, (iii) promotion of understanding, harmony and cooperation between different religious segment for national unity and integration, (iv) assertion of the supremacy of state and its laws equally for all citizens, (v) liberation of the civic polity from religion-dominated groups and parties, (vi) enforcement of the common civil laws, made and modified by elected representative of the citizens, (vii) recognition of equality of status and opportunity for all citizens irrespective of caste, colour, creed, gender or any other basis primordial discrimination, and (viii) enforcement of the principle of fraternity of the citizens as *citizens* and not members of primordial groups—religious, linguistic, ethnic or regional.

Since there is no organised Church in India of the two major religious segments, constituting the Hindu and Muslim population, acounting for about 94% of the people, the basic question of the separation of the Church from the State, as the guiding principle of secularism, as was the case in Western civilization, does not arise. In Western Europe it was the question of horizontal segregation of the State from the Church, because the emergent secular State was to be emancipated from an organised church which had for centuries usurped the powers and prerogatives of a State. In India due to our own peculiar religious background, belief system and historical demands, consequent on the emergence of an independent State in the wake of the success of the national liberation movement, the question is of vertical segregation between newly constituted republican democratic States, and the many segments of primordial loyalties based on caste, religion, language, region, etc. In brief, in India it is the basic question of the supremacy of State power, in civic, social and political affairs of the newly liberated people, who, were earlier fragmented in their basic loyalties to their respective ascriptive groups and to their concerned feudal principalities. In a word, secularism in India means and ought to mean, the supremacy of State, as the terminal point of political loyalty, over and above all other focii of loyalties, no less and no more. In the West, secularism emerged in the process of struggle between feudal political authority and the traditional Catholic Church which exercised political hegemony. In India, and in most of the Third World countries, Secularism as a phenomenon represents a struggle for building an integrated political community, in a multi-religious situation. Our struggle for secularism is against religious separatism, religious bigotry and religious belligerency, that seeks to divide our national unity and political solidarity. It is a struggle against the processes of fragmentation of our integrity and community as a sovereign people. It is an assertion of a new legitimacy of a multi-religious plural society, seeking to respect all religions, yet refusing to be dominated in its political culture by any one or all of them. Thus here is a wide difference in the historical context and social situation and therefore in the nature of challenges to a secular polity, between Western Europe of the 16th to 19th century and in India and the Third World countries in the 20th century.

VIII : Two Traditions in All Religions

There are two competing traditions in each religious system namely, the *orthodox* tradition and the *humanist* tradition. The orthodox tradition enjoins attachment to dogma and rituals. It is conformist in its orientation, and lends itself to rigidity, of belief, bigotry in propagation of the faith, intolerence of deviation and dissent, promotion of militancy among the faithful and belligerency towards other belief-systems. The humanist tradition on the other hand is heterodox, pluralistic, fairly open and broadly accommodative of varied orientations and divergent interpretations.

The orthodox tradition emphasizes the exclusive, even superior, nature of each religion. It has a history of recurrent efforts at 'purification' and 'fundamentalisation' of religious beliefs and practices, of 'revivalism' of myths, legends and heroic images of the past. It has a tradition of the total rejection of other beliefs and faiths. It is not surprising therefore, to perceive a 'totalitarian' approach to religion and society in the orthodox tradition. As an extension of this 'holistic' approach, the orthodox tradition has continuously exhibited its prediliction to play a political role, a power-game, a hegemonistic impulse to dominate the devout, their groups, and society at large, cultural institutions, and exclude 'the others', the 'infidels' the 'melechs' the 'outsiders', call them what you will.

The humanist tradition in all religions underline commonality of approach in several aspects of social life. It lays stress on individual moral code. It propagates universal ethical norms for common welfare. It promotes the values of love and compassion in human life. It seeks to build bridges of understanding between diverse religious traditions, by identifying similarities of images and values, despite divergences in nomenclature. It projects the basic values of life and happiness for all, adherence to truth, goodness, justice, fairplay, toleration, mutual respect and accommodation of dissent. It seeks to transcend dogma, by asserting the basic fraternity of the human species. It uses moral exhortation to influence human consciousness. It speaks of God as a universal God, of religion as a humanistic endeavour, of society as a common responsibility. It points out to the futility of doctrinnaire disputation and dogmatic fights, and extols the lasting benefit of the values of 'live and let live', of plurality of perception but unification of human goodness and concern for all. The sufi tradition in Islam, and the Bhakti tradition in different parts of India, are examples of this heritage.

The humanist tradition promotes religiosity but not formal religion. One must make a distinction between formal, habitual and bigoted attachment to organised religion, and the mystic and ethical individual sense of religiosity. A widespread adherence to religiosity is apparent in the common people, most of whom due to lack of systematic scientific education and enlightenment are not entirely committed to rationalism and scientific temper. The impact of religion in its many varied manifestations, has percolated in different shapes and forms, in various parts of the world, even in this age and time of massive scientific and technological revolution. The deep social, moral and cultural roots of religion in almost all civilizations make it an integral, even unconscious, habitual and primordial part of human existence. It is an invariable influence, and a 'given' factor of collective life. Such a deep-rooted factor is susceptible of use and misuse by the power elite, especially in an age of mass mobilization for politics and universal electoral participation in a democracy for legitimisation of power and authority. And this is happening in different shapes and forms in various parts of world, especially in the developing countries marked by rampant poverty, illiteracy, low political consciousness, competing party system, and high profile of religious identity as a significant sub-stratum of new nation-building process.

IX : Secularism and Composite Nationalism

Now let us focus attention on the process of secularisation

of the polity for socio-economic transformation.

The process of modernized federal nation-building in India depends particularly on three major engineers of change : democracy, secularism, and social justice. In a simplistic formalation one might add that they respectively are conceived as the main instruments of gigantic change in the political, social and economic transformation of our continental polity.

Democracy is expected to transform the political ethos of new India by inducting into the processes and the structures of the polity the many segments and groups most of whom had hitherto remained outside the purview of *political activity*. By universal politicization of the Indian citizens, democracy is expected to promote mass mobilisation and participation for stabilising the foundations of a new political culture in this ancient land. Naturally against the background of India's social composition and sociological foundations of its politics, democracy acquires the characteristic of being both a response and a challenge. It is a response to the exploitation, decades of colonial rampage and maladjustments, and the overall heritage of 'sanctified' social inequality implicit in the caste system, economic stagnation, political hierarchy and autocracy. It is a challenge and an intervention for building a new edifice for the future, based on equality, liberty, justice, and fraternity, coalescing the world's most complex and diverse plural society into political integration and national solidarity. It is for this reason that democracy with social justice has been the main slogan of national political will, the operative principle of our new political system, the universally recognised major premise of all our socio-economic development.

Secularism in India theoretically meant three things: (i) the rejection of the quasi-theocratic State form like that of Pakistan, and the affirmation of a non-religion-based democracy; (ii) the proclamation that religion is of private or group concern ; and (iii) the assertion of the unity of the people of India and the inalienable equality of all citizens of the republic irrespective of their caste and creed.

In the peculiar situation of India, secularism as an instrument of social change and political transformation has at least three operational dimensions (i) as a process of *non-communal* political integration (as between religion-based segments such as Hindus, Muslims, Christians, Sikhs, etc.);(ii) as a process of inter-community social integration (as between the varna-cum-jati segments of the Hindus and the social strata among the Muslims, Christians, etc.); and (iii) as the dominant political idiom, method, and objective of general socio-political change in order to transform a religion-dominated ethos into an ethos of enlightened humanism.

Secularism in India therefore, appears both as an ideal as a reality. It is evident that in many ways we are far from the realization of the ideal. But it is equally apparent that there is a national consensus for the steady realization of secularism as an operative principle of national politics. Secularism in India is an evolving reality through an agonising process, but then that is probably also true of the other major ideals before the country.

Secularism in the imagination of religiously devout politicians and many other well-meaning nationalists meant no more than political reconciliation of religious communities and harmonization of communalism. The argument was that individual communalism was bad but multiple communalism held in balance by State would lead to compulsory toleration and unavoidable appreciation of each other, by mutual acceptance of each other's separate identity. This is the implication of the much publicised vedantic ideal of equal respect to all faiths (serva dharma samabhava), which is proclaimed as the genuine Indian interpretation of secularism. As an extension of this assumption it follows, for example, that to chant Vedas alone or to recite only Quran at a State or national function might be communal and non-secular. But to simultaneously chant the Vedas, recite the Quran, sing the Psalms of David, read passages from Dhammapada, and listen to the devotional songs from the Granth Sahib and to the verses of a Zindavasta would be the pure assertion of secularism and indeed an affirmation of national integration. Secularism meant, so to say compound communalism, resulting in the cheerful fusion of religious symbols, idioms and social rituals through the theosophical Ram-Rahim approach to politics.

In the name of defining Indian form of secularism, we overlook its basic universal ingredients of adherence to rationalism and scientific temper, and on the contrary we almost always defined secularism in India to mean some sort of multi-communalism. In the name of toleration of all communities, and their eventual harmonisation, what we finally achieved is reconciliation of multiple communalism, promotion of multiple obscurantism, universal superstition and mixing of all mythologies. Only uni-communalism is assumed to be against secularism, and that too, not always-while multi-communalism is facilely recognised as the very hall-mark of authentic Indian nationalism and an affirmation of our patriotism. If at a State function, if all the scriptures are recited, simultaneously or one after another it is recognised as the very ethos of Indian identity—a celebration of genuine Indian fraternity. There can be no more spurious interpretation of secularism than this. Because of our peculiar facility in living a life of hypocracy, we declare that we are secular while we indulge in practices and rituals, openly and formally, with pomp and fanfare, which are the very negation of a secular culture, secular values and secular orientation.

But even this pretence today is being by and large avoided by more powerful communal lobbies. So far we have heard *ad-nauseum* that the religious minorities and their culture and so-called identities are in 'danger . For generations Islam in India, in the imagination of certain votaries, has some how always been in 'danger' One thought this to be a peculiar form of 'Muslim melancholy', and learned to live with it, sometime in bewilderment, sometime in anger, sometime in despair, and all the time in disbelief. Now since 1980, or near about, we are told that Sikhism (Which was once even claimed to be the sheild of Hinduism) is also in abject and moral 'danger' and that too only and exclusively due to the Hindus! Small mercy that the Buddhists and the Jains have so far not expressed themselves in this dismal idiom; on the contrary some of the leading Jain intellectuals and journalist have become crusading defenders of Hindutva. But the most bizzare development on the communal horizon today is that we hear, with recurrent emphasises and woe, and in strident tones, that Hinduism and the mighty Hindu community comprising a little more than 80% of our people, are in 'danger' and that its traditions, religious practices, values, culture and identity is threatened as never before, by the minorities in India, with the connivance of the powers that be !

It is maintained by otherwise well-meaning persons with scholarly predilection that secularism is a slogan and an orientation that is essentially meant to weaken the so-called 'Hindu solidarity'. Some even hold that secularism has only a relevance in politics dominated by an organised Church—like the Catholics, the Protestants, the Church of England, the Muslim, the Mahayana Buddhists, etc.—and not in India, where the majority Hindu community is not only without an organised Church but is also an amorphous, heterogeneous religious community, attuned by its very teachings to all religions. Few others assert that since Hinduism is pluralistic, therefore, it has a primordial secular approach itself. They say : What is then the need to go on speaking about secularism in a predominantly Hindu polity? Because to be Hindu is to be secular.

It is in this situation confused by pseudo-theorist of Hindu religious revivalism that it is necessary to remember that while all communalism is bad, but the majority communalism is worst. Majority community ordinarily determines the basic social ethos of a country. Communalism of the minority exhibits itself in forms like 'separatism', 'exclusivism', 'withdrawal', 'anarchism' and it focuses itself on limited symbols, specific and divisive traditions, and on a wide range of difference and dichotomies away from the mainstream commonalities. On the other hand communalism of the majority can pass-off as nationalism itself, because it is pervasive, dominant and with deeper historical roots and greater range of commonalities. It is capable of focusing on the many symbols of the past and of drawing sustenance from the basic structure of traditions, customs, conventions, festivities, etc. of the nation. But what is more frightening is that if the majority community exhibits the besieged psychology of the minorities and feel threatened, either in fact or in imagination, then it also exhibits minority traits of 'separatism', 'exclusivism', 'withdrawal' and 'anarchism' and thereby in its approach and transaction, transforms itself into the mould of the gigantic minority, arrayed in combat formation and in belligerent equation with other minorities. It seems in India, we are passing through this alarming and dismal phase in our national life.

Thanks to the enlightened and democratic heritage of composite federal-nationalism, India, did not become formally a Hindu State. But neither did it become an authentic Secular State. Due to the pulls and pressures of communal politics, and confusion in the ranks of the secularists, the shape that the Indian State has acquired is a Hindu version of psuedo-secular State.

It is this crisis that has to be overcome by the concerted efforts of the democratic and secular forces in India today in order to restore to the Indian State the authentic secular image, and help it play the catalytic role as an instrument of socio-economic transformation, in order to change a classic traditional society into a vibrant modern polity.

SECULARISM AND SOCIAL TRANSFORMATION IN INDIA

COMMENTS

Prof. Yoginder K. Alagh

Prof. Rasheeduddin Khan's paper is comprehensive and discusses all the relevant approaches and issues. The comments that are being made in this letter are therefore, of an incremental nature.

Prof. Khan's description of the Indian economy as one which has grown fairly rapidly, particularly in the last decade or so, but one in which on account of historical reasons substantial dualities still remain is basically a correct insight. I find that in my own somewhat tortured style of an economic statistician I have made some of the poinτs in a rather longish article in the July Issue of the Journal, "Developing Economics" published from Japan.

There are, however, three additional points which need to be emphasised in Prof. Khan's analysis. First there is no discussion in his paper of the role the Indian abroad is playing in the rising ethnic tension, terrorists violence and communal tension in India. This is an important aspect and it would be a serious shortcoming to ignore it completely, although I would accept the position that our basic problems are Indian and have to be handled within the country.

Prof. Khan's analysis does not come to grips with the fact that some of the most communalised States in India are those that have developed very fast. This is true both of Gujarat and Punjab. Punjab has shown some of the highest agricultural growth rate in the world and Gujarat similar performance in the manufacturing sector. In Gujarat there has also been a decisive change in the structure of employment, the share of the agricultural sector falling from around 70% in 1960's to around 54% at present. The percentage decline of the agriculture share in the labour force in Gujarat compares with that in South Korea from 1960 to 1990. Gujarat also has a fast rate of in-migration as some studies show. Such problems need not necessarily lead to communal tension. In our case we do not seem to be managing the problem of fast change well.

Another major aspect to be looked into some detail is the criminalisation of Indian politics. The trends discussed by Prof. Khan are a part of this overall back-drop.

SECULARISM AND SOCIAL TRANSFORMATION IN INDIA

COMMENTS

J.S. Bali

I am in agreement with the broad analysis of Prof. Khan and his conclusion. In particular, in agreeing with him, I do maintain that the roots of our social cultural federalism are deep and historic. But I feel that political or economic federalism deserves a lot more attention in order that it becomes substantial.

I also agree that in the gigantic mosaic of India, you have a mosaic of particular model, trades, interests and habits vis-a-vis modern elements of aggressive selfishness, consumerism and the like. There is tradition on the one hand, which demands loyalties of the conservative kind and there is the new social situation in which there is no regard or respect for the old or the ancient tradition. It is also true that added to this diversity of mosaic is the new emergence in aggressive form of the class forces and caste forces in a bid for power.

It is also true that in the existing economic set up any increase in the GNP goes to the benefit of the "haves" largely, and not proportionately to the "have nots". Recent study shows that consumer expenditure of the poor which on average used to rise by 3-4% during the last 5 years rose only by 1.5% in 1991-92, the year of economic reforms and that poverty has increased.

According to CSO estimates 0.34% per annum meaning 6.1 million, have been added to the poor in 1990-91. The total impact in 1991-92 amounts to 22 million, according to CSO estimates. Further, growth in consumption declined per capita, from 3.7% to 1.5% and this has maximum effect on the welfare of people in the lower belt who are on the poverty line or just above.

I also agree that public sector represents a segment of State capitalism which has contributed neither to growth nor to economic betterment of poor nor production of surplus revenue.

I agree that in the last 15 years there has been a phenomenal rise of the so-called middle class. The estimates were 200 million so far but it might as well be 300 million as assessed by the Professor. It is also true that the existing political system depends upon coalition of power between upper class and middle class, a union of the businessmen, politicians and the bureaucrats, in which there is dominance of middle class, upper class and the property class, each making sure of their own interest.

I also agree that the Indian political system has made full use of the above nexus. A party cannot come into power without people votes which is exercised once in 5 years and it cannot remain in power without the support from the upper class. I have therefore, been advocating instead of 5 years general elections, 4 yearly, so that the voter will suffer for one year less before expressing his mind. It is only during the general election that the voter really gets the chance to express his preference. No wonder the political functioning is marketed by public promises and private betrayals, promises having been made for mass support. Undoubtedly, therefore, the political practices of cheating, lying and duplicity are, all in the name of populism.

But all this or some of it can be set right in the shortest period by introducing electoral reforms in addition to economic and social reorientation. Exploitation of religion is communalism but to be religious is not "communal". In other words religion is the private affair of individual in a secular society. Unfortunately, parties have cropped up under the existing system which excel in creating communalism and casteism, based upon superstition, ritualism and the like . In other words religion is being perverted and when it is perverted, it becomes communalism, the enemy of progress. All this in the name of the nation-state.

Europe turned away from religion to secularism because of the fight between the Church and the Monarch, and the State thus became secular. Those conditions do not apply to India at all; If I may say so India has been secular throughout history, whether ruled by Hindus, Guptas, Lodis, Mughals, Sikhs or the British.

In a secular State the following are necessary :

a. Supremacy of national over local interest.

b. Equality of laws to all its citizens, common civil laws for all citizens.

c. Equality of States.

d. Opportunity for all citizens irrespective of caste, colour, creed.

On the question of secularism playing a role in social transformation, I am afraid, I have different views. I do not subscribe to the theory that secularism can be an instrument of change towards social transformation. Social transformation in my country has to be brought about by a series of institutional measures and several political, economic and social changes.

It is true that 80% of the population in India is Hindus (it declined from 82%). It is a great tribute to the 'national players' that they did not make it a Hindu State nor declared the State religion to be the Hindu religion as is the case in England where the Church of England is the State religion. That does not however, mean that a Hindu should support the feeling that there is something wrong with him, that he should be on the defensive all the time and that even for his basic fundamental rights he should seek dependency on some political group or the like. I maintain that the majority Hindu culture or civilisation is (Sarva Dharma i.e. the way of life) 'Dharma' meaning philosophy of life and not the narrow definition of faith in a particular deity. Therefore, Hinduism retains its identity and adds to it the basic element of rationalsim.

Hindu secularism thus contains scientific temper and tempo combined with rationalism. This is what the Vedas, Upanishads and other documents will show. Hindu secularism therefore, cannot be defined as the cumulative communalism of the largest community. On the other hand, Hindu secularism preaches tolerance and respect of all religions and faiths and also enjoins that religion is a private affair of the individual not to be meddled with politics.

Secularism or the secular State cannot expect to become the engine for social transformation because in my view social transformation or social change which is required in the society accross the board can be achieved by some of the following institutional measures :

- Universal education particularly primary education.
- Less University Education and more of Vocational Education.
- Less of unionised activity and more of hard work and efficiency.
- 4 yearly general election with minimum qualification for the candidate.
- Regeneration of value system and code of morality.
- Complete negation of communalism or casteism for the sake of winning votes and derecognition of any party which indulges in such approach.
- Freeze University Grants.

All religions and all parties should support a national consensus on the subject of social transformation through democratic means, some of which are suggested above.

We wanted social change to be brought about by the political parties but they have deviated and gone into their own selfish needs, so the people will have to do it. What can help is 'Institutional reforms.' One of the main objects of social change should be empowerment of the poor, i.e. large segment of the society like two thirds being outside the capital market.

Social change cannot be divorced from economic change and the economic change would be effective only if the so-called 20 crores middle class become 50 crores of middle class at least.

SECULARISM AND SOCIAL TRANSFORMATION IN INDIA

Kamal A. Mitra Chenoy

Prof. Rasheeduddin Khan in his learned and stimulating paper has sharply pointed out that "Today communalism, in its varied shapes has acquired a most dangerous form and an alarming proportion....It is subversive of our political stability and economic development, and, therefore, manifests itself as enemy number one of our democratic polity." (p.16). This growth of communalism is not fortitious, and is arguably a product of specific features of social transformation in this country. In the course of this necessarily short comment, I would like to sketch some of these features, based on the increasingly influential work of some Indian, and foreign, social scientists.

The Indian political elite, or ruling elite, also called the 'dominant coalition' (Bardhan, 1984; Kaviraj, 1988), includes the Indian bourgeoisie or Indian capitalist class as a whole, including also the agrarian bourgeoisie, in which big business or the big bourgeoisie plays an increasingly leading role; and also the upper strata of bureaucracy in both state and industry. But, in recent years the balance in the ruling coalition has shifted, in favour of the big capitalists, thus the withdrawal of the fertiliser subsidy, and the dismantling of controls and talk of debureaucratisation. This coalition is, of course, both upper class as well as upper caste, though intermediate castes influential in rural areas, are through the pro-Mandal agitation etc. challenging this dominance.

This dominant coalition was never ideologically hegemonic, as the ideology of a liberal or welfarist capitalism did not have unchallenged popular support. Thus the powerful appeal from the 1930s, of 'socialism' espoused by the young Nehru, JP, Netaji, et. al. Paradoxically, even today while India 'structurally adjusts', parties ranging from the BJP to the CPI (ML) factions, are all committed to some variant of socialism, which after the 42nd Amendment is also enshrined in the Preamble of the Constitution. This hypocrisy, however indicates the severity of the crisis we now find ourselves in. But this crisis has been long in the making.

India went in for a capitalist modernisation which was doubly belated. In the first place, India was a late starter, and secondly, it was attempting capital accumulation not only without colonies, but while placed in an unfavourable position in the international capitalist division of labour. But what made this task insuperable were the political obstacles. The liberal metropolitan elite led by Nehru tried to bring in a 'revolution from above', what following Gramsci has been termed a `passive revolution', in which the activity of the State is substituted for the more active mobilisation by a hegemonic capitalist class. (Kaviraj, 1988; Chatterjee, 1986). Nehru, as is now generally accepted, had a rather optimistic view about the beneficial political consequences of economic development. The young Nehru, who theorised the conversion of nationalism into a state ideology, also vastly underestimated the resilience of communalism.

For instance, in his *The Discovery of India*, Nehru argued that once the independent State "assured the protection of religion and culture, etc., the major problems that were bound to come up were economic ones which has nothing to do with a person's religion. Class conflicts there might well be, but not religious conflicts, except in so far as religion itself represented some vested interest". (Nehru, 1946, p. 387). A couple of years later, speaking about communalism, he said, "I do not think it is a very difficult problem to soive. If social and economic issues come to the front the communal problem falls into the background". (Press interview, London, 27 January 1936 quoted in Chatterjee, 1986, Chap. 5). Life proved him tragically wrong, as he himself realised. The communal problem, as his most able biographer has noted, "darkened his last days". (Gopal, 1984, p. 265).

Independent India was indeed born out of a communal partition, and its greatest fighter against communalism, the Mahatma, fell at the hands of a Hindu fanatic within months of freedom. The Nehruvian elite endeavoured to build the 'modern temples of India' and thereby displace communal prejudice by a scientific temper. But the 'Passive revolution' strategy despite all their efforts was aborted, and its failure and degeneration enabled the renewed assault by Hindu communalism. When the Congress came to power, it had to build liberal political institutions against the logic of traditional social structures. (Kaviraj, 1984). From the outset this type of political modernisation was resisted by important elements in the Congress, who were dominant at regional and lower levels of the party; major sections of the bureaucracy, especially at the lower levels which even the British had not sought to substantially reform the bulk of the landed elites; large segments of the urban bourgeoisie, particularly its trading and rentier elements; and significant sections of the intelligentsia, especially in non-metropolitan areas.

Some scholars have argued that the drive for political institutionalisation slackened in the second phase of Nehru's leadership (Kaviraj, 1984,1988), or later after the initial phase of Mrs. Gandhi's regime. (Kothari, 1980, 1983). At any rate, the internal emergency is seen as a watershed. (also Blair, 1980; Manor, 1983; Sheth, 1982). By this stage the process of the decline of democratic institutions definitely set in. The centrepiece of the party system, which political scientists often dubbed the 'Congress party system' or 'dominant one party system', itself degenerated with its democratic internal mechanisms suppressed and power centralised around Mrs. Gandhi and her coterie. This process continued under Rajiv Gandhi, and despite the recent AICC elections, continues to this day.

The independence and efficacy of the judiciary has been undermined, both by the partisan nature of the selection of the higher levels of the judiciary, as well as the mounting overload on the system wherein justice is delayed if not denied. The vaunted 'steelframe' of the bureaucracy has buckled, and recent events including the stock scam, highlight how ineffective and self-serving it has become. Even the legislature, particularly at State and municipal levels, is a pale shadow of its past. And as the joke goes, whereas in Russia they send criminals to the firing squad, in Italy to jail, in India we send them to the legislature.

The reasons behind this are structural, not merely because of a decline in national character. Major social/class factors retarding political institutionalisation have already been mentioned. But, a major, and arguably decisive, role in the degeneration of the political process has been played by the lumpenised nature of economic development. The black economy, never parallel, (since parallel lines by definition never meet), but always interpenetrated with the 'white' economy has grown exponentially. (Kabra, 1982). Black money is the major source of electoral funding and later political corruption. As Kabra has noted, "the symbiotic relation between politics and black economy makes many laws concerning economic regulation, controls and taxation nearly a dead letter, (and) it also enfeebles the machinery for their enforcement and implementation. As a result, the actual outcomes of the economic processes is sharply at a variance from those intended by the stated policy framework". (Ibid., p. 163) Lumpen elements which were earlier utilised to bring in the votes or to capture booths, are now themselves seeking legitimacy and increased political clout as legislators. This has significantly contributed to the decline in the functioning and legitimacy of legislatures.

In the backdrop of this secular decline in political institutions, the concomitant decline in secular politics could only be expected. The same Congress whose pre-eminent leader Nehru repeatedly re-affirmed a commitment to separate religion and politics, went in, particularly after 1980, for opportunist policies of communal votebank appeasement. (Singh, 1992). Part of the justification of this shift was provided by the shift in the definition of secularism to *'sarva dharma sambhava'* i.e. religions should be treated equally by the State. In other words, politicians were no longer supposed to confine religion to their private lives, but to arbitrate between religions to ensure that they were treated, or perceived they were treated, equally. Given the imperatives and exigencies of electoral politics, such a distorted notion of secularism, would be bound to favour majorities, or perceived majorities e.g. 'Hindus'; balanced by compromises with representatives of influential minorities as in the Shah Bano case.

Of course, this is not to say that major communal compromises or ploys were not indulged in by major Congress leaders, even in the Nehruvian period. Conservative Congress men led by Rajendra Prasad successfully diluted the provisions of the Hindu Code Bill, virtually forcing Ambedkar out of the Congress. It should be remembered that Shyama Prasad Mukherjee, the founder of the Jana Sangh, was given a major portfolio in Nehru's cabinet. Even the Ramjanambhoomi problem is largely a creation of Congress manoeuvres.

The Ramjanambhoomi Card was first played by the Congress when the Pant -C.B. Gupta faction sought to counter the potential threat from the socialist Acharya Narendra Dev in the forthcoming elections to Faizabad East in the U.P. assembly. Faizabad was Narendra Dev's home town, and he had represented it in 1937 and 1946 as a Congressman, but had lost in 1948 after leaving the Congress. The destruction of a small mosque near the Babri Masjid, and the digging up of a Muslim graveyard in the vicinity in November 1949, followed by the forcible insertion of the Ram Lila idols the next month, in the backdrop of sustained religious mobilisation including the chanting of religious prayers in the area for more than a month, was only possible because of direct support from the State Congress leadership including the then CM. (Gould, 1990). In the 1952 elections in which both the Congress and the Ram Rajya Parishad put up candidates against Narendra Dev, the 'Hindu' wave was enough to ensure the latter's defeat by less than 450 votes. The rest is fairly well known history.

What I have tried to indicate, very briefly, in the preceding pages, is how the political space, as it were, for the rise and spread of communalism, is the direct consequence of the nature of social transformation that took place, and did not take place, in India. The secular decline in secular political institutions, and their legitimacy, as well as the deepening of socio-political crises, facilitated the rise of an authoritarian 'communal nationalism', or an upper-caste Hindu chauvinist nationalism, which is what the RSS-BJP-VHP actually represent.

The decline of democratic institutions is also strongly correlated with the increasing crisis of the particular form of capitalist development followed in India, particularly in the post-Nehruvian period. (Singh, 1992). As the crisis deepens, particularly after the negative impact of the IMF-World Bank prescribed new economic policies is felt more acutely by the poor and large sections of the middle strata, the regime is likely to resort to increasing doses of authoritarianism. A large part of the middle strata is sympathetic to State repression, and even State terrorism, as a reaction to the threat of terrorism and secessionism in Punjab and Kashmir, in particular. Laws such as the Armed Forces Special Powers Acts, NSA, TADA and ESMA already exist, and have already been widely used against peaceful and constitutional dissenters. There is every possibility that this trend will grow significantly in the foreseeable future. The vicious cycle will then get accentuated: increased doses of State repression will further alienate sections of the affected people, in turn leading to more violence and alienation, resulting in even more State terror, and so on. This, after all, is what has happened quite starkly in Kashmir.

Events in the Kashmir valley and Punjab, however, provide grist to the RSS-VHP-BJP mill. Increased terrorism there is used to justify the communal belief that religious minorities are fundamentally anti-national, as well as to legitimise authoritarian measures against them, by making full use of the siege mentality of the middle strata.

Viewed in this light, the current scenario is more dangerous than many of us realise. A mere reiteration of the dangers posed by this communal resurgence will, unfortunately not suffice. An effective struggle against communalism therefore, will have to simultaneously mobilise both for social and political justice, for the expansion of real democracy. This is obviously an enormous task. But the future of this country hinges on it.

References

1. Bardhan (1984), Pranab, *The Political Economy of Development in India.* Delhi : Oxford University Press.

2. Blair (1980), Harry W., "Mrs. Gandhi's Emergency : Indian Elections of 1977, Pluralism and Marxism : Problems with Paradigms", *Modern Asian Studies,* Vol. 14, No. 2, 1980

3. Chatterjee (1986), Partha, *Nationalist Thought and the Colonial World* : a *Derivative Discourse.* Delhi :

4. Gopal (1984), Sarvepalli, Jawaharlal Nehru : *A Biography,* Delhi : Oxford University Press, Vol. III.

5. Gould (1990), Harold, "Modern Politics in an Indian District", in Richard Sisson & Ramashray Roy, (eds.), *Diversity and Dominance in Indian Politics,* New Delhi : Sage, Vol. 1.

6. Kabra (1982), Kamal N., *Black Economy in India : Problems and Policies,* Delhi : Chanakya.

7. Kaviraj (1984), Sudipta, "On the Crisis of Political Institutions in India", *Contributions to Indian Sociology,* (New Series), 18/2.

8. Kaviraj (1988), Sudipta, "A Critique of the Passive Revoltion", *Economic & Political Weekly,* Special No., November.

9. Kothari (1980), Rajni, "The Call of the Eighties", *Seminar,* January.

10. Kothari (1983), Rajni, "The Crisis of the Moderate State and the Decline of Democracy", in Peter Lyon & James manor. (eds.), *Transfer & Transformation : Political Institutions in the New Commonwealth,* Leicester University Press.

11. Manor (1983), James, "Anomie in Indian Politics", *Economic & Political Weekly,* Annual No.

12. Sheth (1982), D.L. , Social Basis of the Political Crisis", *Seminar,* January.

13. Singh (1992), Randhir, "Communalism in Contemporary India : Some Theoretical Considerations", *Mainstream,* Annual No., November.

SECULARISM AND SOCIAL TRANSFORMATION IN INDIA

A CRITICAL NOTE

R.C. Dutt

It is a pleasure to read through Prof. Khan's paper on "Secularism and Social Transformation in India" with its perceptive, insightful observations on various aspects of India's socio-political, economic life, and perhaps a greater pleasure still to analyse these observations, discern their consistencies and their inconsistencies, if any, their adequacies and inadequacies, in order to draw out concrete conclusions for action. The following comments are therefore offered, not in a spirit of carping criticism, but in order to derive a plan of action from the highly relevant observations scattered throughout the paper.

Prof. Khan is right that "continuity of traditions, customs, conventions, and rituals" in a country like India "with more or less unbroken succession of social history" has resulted in "over laying the contemporary framework of society with certain continuing forms of primordialties" (p.2). I presume he agrees, though it has not been stated categorically, that this has created problems, which needs to be overcome, in building a modern society. I find it difficult, however, to agree with his observation about the public sector (p.3) for I have the "naivete" to believe that the public sector was intended and would in fact have promoted "the prospects of socialism" if it had been pursued in the spirit in which it was launched. My reason for this belief is that the public sector was not being built up *ad hoc* in the infrastructural sector to facilitate "the growth and expansion of a sprawling capitalist system in India". It had a plan and that plan was that it should "play the dominant role in shaping the entire pattern of investments in the economy whether it makes the investments directly or whether these are made by the private sector" (Second Five Year Plan, Chapter II, para 2). That it did not succeed, as socialism did not succeed even in the erst-while Soviet Union, is a different matter. Nor can the failure be assessed by the contradiction between the growth of GNP on the one hand, and the comparative stagnation, on the other, of per capita income, for the latter being merely an average, is influenced by the increase in numbers. The real failure was a failure of distribution reflected, as Prof. Khan has rightly pointed out, in the increasing gulf between the rich and the poor. This happened because investments in the economy instead of being determined by the planned growth of the public sector, as the Second Five Year Plan had ordained, was increasingly determined by market forces which had an inherent bias to cater to the rich.

Prof. Khan's analysis of the political system calls for no criticism. He has very appropriately characterised its "dualistic style of functioning" as "marked by public promises and private betrayals, and has rightly pointed out that a party cannot come into power without people's vote, and cannot remain in power without upper class support". One could wish, however, that this line of thought was pushed a little farther to consider some allied questions : is this inevitable in a liberal democracy? If not, how can this characteristic be overcome without abandoning democracy itself ?

In India, we have, indeed, two exceptions to this phenomenon, namely, West Bengal and Kerala, which deserve consideration. Left parties in these States have acquired a measure of influence, and in the former state at any rate, have retained power for about a decade and a half without upper class support. It is not on the basis of competitive populism that this influence has been acquired and retained. This has been done, on the other hand, by political cadres of these parties working with the deprived masses and identifying themselves with them in their day to day struggle for existence. Have these two instances any lesson for the rest of the country?

I am glad Prof. Khan has referred to the role of "a responsible and responsive federal authority" (Botton 7 to 7) in reconciling "the legitimate and well coordinated autonomies of regions and sub-regions within which most of the genuine demands of the linguistic, cultural and religious communities can be met". To my mind, this role is vital and should not be overlooked in the well meaning but over-enthusiastic desire to promote pluralism, or by drawing on the theory and practice of federalism in other countries functioning in entirely different contexts.

In regard to Prof. Khan's analysis of the phenomenon of communalism, with most of which I agree, I find it difficult to accept his view on religiosity. Religiosity in the true sense of the word may not be communal, and those among them who are communal are so because, as Prof. Khan has pointed out, "they are ignorant of the moral teachings and universalist underpinning of their own religion". The fact, however, remains that in the real world religiosity means for the overwhelming majority of people "affliction to ritualism, superstition, obscurantism, magic, charn and ocult practices .....", as Prof. Khan puts it (p. 10). And these " can be inputs into the development of communal consciousness", as Prof. Khan has pointed out in the same paragraph. It is the people so "afflicted" who respond almost spontaneously to the cry of the communalists that the religion he belongs to is in danger. In a devotee of this type the lofty Vedantic dictum, "*Sarva Dharma Samabhav*" has no meaning, for he cannot have the same feeling towards another religion which does not uphold what he believes is the "truth" which his religion preaches. A Hindu, for instance, who believes that his religion tells him that Ram is an *avatar* of God cannot have the same feeling towards another religion which does not recognise Ram as such. He can still be *tolerant* of other religions, but he cannot have "*Samabhav*".

It follows that secularism, while it may not conflict with religiosity in the highest and truest sense of the word, is certainly incosistant with religiosity which pre-dominates in the real world.

A secular State must, therefore, avoid doing anything that promotes religiosity, for by doing so it will only promote religiosity of the wrong type. It is for this reason, and not because it is "Compound Communalism" (P. 21) that the practice of inaugurating state functions with brief prayers from all faiths is open to objection. If chanting Vedic hymns, reciting the Holy Quran, or singing Christian Psalms by individuals is not communal, as indeed it is not, doing so collectively does not amount to "compound communalism". On the other hand, the practice does promote religiosity, and there is no assurance that the religiosity so promoted would be of the non-communal type. Even more open to objection is high dignitaries of the State indulging publicly in obscurantist practices, such as paying obeisance by prostrating themselves before "Holy" men, or rolling on the ground in accordance with "religious" injunctions.

Prof. Khan is entirely right in holding that "Secularism in India means, and ought to mean, the loyalty...", for in India the State professes to be secular. It is, however, necessary to watch and ensure that practice does not vitiate the profession. It is also necessary to be clear as to what constitutes the sphere in which the state is, or ought to be, supreme, and what could be left to religion, organised or unorganised. There is no unanimity on this. Indeed, there is a constant struggle to push "religious liberty" in the name of conscience to justify practices which conflict with national policies as defined by the State. In India, for instance, are the activities of *Anand Marg* who are reported to have indulged in violence and terrorism and are said to have promoted narrow chauvinism to be regarded as religious? And yet, the special Rappoteur of the United Nations has questioned the government of India about alleged harassment of members of the *Anand Marg* community. To take a more familiar example, is a religious community justified in creating disaffection against, and in trying to subvert a Socialist government, because the latter believes in atheism, or at least agnosticism? There are indeed limits to religious, or for that matter to any type of freedom, and these need to be defined.

A further point, since the paper is on Secularism and Social Transformation, that needs to be pointed out is that there can be no social transformation except in a secular environment. Religion undoubtedly serves a basic human need. Man has a fear of the unknown, and is not satisfied with the answer that the unknown is unknowable. Religion by providing a set of answers, whether based on reason or on faith, gives solace to human beings, specially in times of stress and strain. Science has no answer to these questions, and as long as it has not, it is undesirable, and futile too, to deny human beings the solace that religion brings to them. By the same token, however, religion which deals with man's relation to the unknown has little contribution to make in determining human relations in concrete situations, which can be scientifically studied. The codes of conduct prescribed, which vary from one religion to another, relate to a different sphere altogether. A theocratic State, which is the reverse of a secular State, by drawing on the precepts on one religion, not only misapplies them to areas for which they have no special competence, but in the process accords superiority to one denomination, even though others may be tolerated. This negates the principle of equality which is the prime objective of social transformation to promote. Social transformation is possible only when there is a clear-cut and well-defined dichotomy between the sphere of religion and that of the State. Any transgression by the state on the religious spheres causes widespread disaffection, which weakens, if it does not subvert the State. Conversely any transgression by religion on the State sphere breeds not only inequality but revivalism and retrogression.

Finally, a point which needs to be noted in this context is that the conflict arising out of the primordial instructs, be it religious exclusiveness, casteism, ethnicity or language, cannot be resolved, nor can the primacy of secularism asserted, except in societies which are developing reasonably fast economically to the benefit of all sections of the people. In the absence of such development, the deprived sections place the blame on rival groups, religions, caste or ethnic, and competition takes the form of assertion of primordial differences. This is borne out by recent history. Secularism has asserted itself in developed countries not because of intellectual acceptance of its superiority, but because religious conflicts have become irrelevant in these countries. On the other hand, there has been a re-emergence of religions and ethnic differences in East Europe and in the erstwhile Soviet Union following the economic hardships that have appeared in these countries, and there has been a re-emergence of racism in Germany following its unification which has disrupted economic life. The lesson for India is that secularism will not be safe, nor will the primordial differences of caste, ethnicity and language be obliterated as long as millions of its citizens are left out of the process of development and made to fend for themselves in an unequal struggle for existence.

SECULARISM AND SOCIAL TRANSFORMATION IN INDIA

COMMENTS

Paulose Mar Gregorios

Prof. Rasheeduddin Khan's paper is comprehensive and deals with some of the problems of the concept of 'Secularism' as used in India. These comments are meant to advance the discussion further.

I personally suggest two things: one, that we abandon the concept of secularism as we have recently developed it in India, for reasons I shall seek to give; two, that we get used to a more meaningful concept like Democratic pluralism, as a better name for the objectives we seek in India. I shall specify some of the implications of the latter concept.

On pp 16 ff, Prof. Rasheeduddin Khan has sought to give a fair summary of the difficulties involved in the concept of secularism as currently used in India. He mentions mainly two: that the associations of the concept with particular developments in western history make it unsuitable for India, and that the suffix "ism" gives the term the flavour of a dogmatic system.

The difficulty for me is with Prof. Khan's initial premise : namely that the contemporary use of a word can be arbitrarily fixed without reference to its etymology, or to the historical development of the concept. He points to our current positive use of the word 'democracy' which in classical Greek thought had a somewhat pejorative sense. I submit that even conceding that point, we are using the word "secularism" in India in a sense quite different from its contemporary use in the rest of the world. This is not the case with the word "democracy". But I also contend that the concept of secularism as now used in the rest of the world cannot be acceptable at all as a conscious option for all Indians in the present situation.

I submit that current international dictionary meanings as well as usage have to be seriously considered. After having typed that sentence I picked up The Concise English Dictionary, without knowing what I was going to find. That dictionary gives only one meaning to the term secularism : *The elimination of the religious element from life*. The prestigious, exhaustive and finally (!) authoritative multi-volume *Oxford English Dictionary* gives the meaning of secularism as "*the doctrine that morality should be based solely on regard to the well-being of mankind in the present life, to the exclusion of all considerations drawn from belief in God or in a future state*". My submission is that if that is the general international usage of the word, it seems quite illegitimate for Indians to use it in a sense so contrary to it, for all Indians who commend "secularism" insist that they do not mean elimination of the religious element from life. If they do not mean what the word means they should use some other word.

I have another reason for strongly objecting to the use of the word secularism in the way some Indians are using it. It is the name of an existing ideology, a pseudo-religion which pervades our culture; this religion is anti-human in the sense of being arrogantly and self-destructively anthropo-centric, while claiming to be pro-progress. It ought to be opposed by all people who desire humanity's welfare. It is a crypto-religious ideology created by the European enlightenment of the 18th and 19th centuries. It came to be articulated and organised as a religion around the middle of the 19th century ; though Immanuel Kant had much earlier advocated a "Religion within the limits of reason alone", meaning a religion based on the Critical Rationality of the European Enlightenment, which acknowledges no authority above human reason, whether of scripture or of tradition. But Kant did not call his new religion "secularism"; his followers may have called it The Religion of Duty (Felix Adler, 1905), Ethical Religion (W.M. Salter, 1889, H.J. Bridges, 1926), or Ethical Society.

Secularism as an explicit religious ideology carrying the specific name 'secularism' begins with G.J. Holyoake (1817-1906). The first English use of the word 'secularism' seems to have been by Holyoake, around 1850. His contention was that all the ancient religions had become obsolete in the age of science because they retained unscientific world views. He intentionally created a new religion called precisely 'Secularism', designed for consumption by 'modern scientific man', equipped with all the paraphernalia of traditional religions: Sunday meetings, catechisms, Sunday schools, hymns, and even a new set of 'scriptures' drawn from the then budding modern science. This new religion was espoused by a number of distinguished practitioners of science in America and the UK in the early part of this century. It flourished into the 1930s, then broke up into various splintergroups. I certainly do not want to espouse that religion-shades of scientology!

Quite apart form G.J. Holyoake's religion called secularism, a kind of pervasive religion of secularism has developed and spread within the elite Western system of education and culture. Our children are exposed to this religion all the time that they go to a modern school. The school teaches modern science as the main source of all knowledge; often it gives the child the impression that what is known to science is the only truth. Even grown up academicians, including most University Professors, seem to be scared to utter something which cannot be scientifically demonstrated. Science forbids the introduction of the transcendent as a principle of explanation. Modern science, without ostensible claiming to be so, in effect becomes a new religious system, which teaches that the world open to our senses and our measuring instruments is the only world that exists, and that it is knowable by the human reason without any external assistance. That world is also believed to be self-existent and self-sustaining, an assumption which is obviously dogmatic and totally unscientific. This is the new religion of secularism. Many thoughtful scientists repudiate these assumptions, as having no scientific basis. But the general run of educated people are pervasively influenced by this un-scientific religion. I am committed to exposing this pseudo-crypto-religion as anti-human, and will not espouse it or propose it as the remedy for our communal conflicts.

This religion of secularism which pervades the culture of the educated Indian elite constitutes part of the problem. It alienates the common people of India from this pseudo educated elite class. It erodes confidence in the leadership of the elite. It imposes an identity on the Indian people which they are unwilling to accept. They would much rather follow the Mullahs or accept 5 '5 fundamentalist' movements, or espouse a distorted Hindutva rather than this pseudo secularist religion as the badge of their identity. I therefore , submit that this secularism is one of the causes of the present communal malaise, and, therefore, part of the problem rather than the solution for communal conflicts.

As regards Democratic pluralism only a few brief comments are needed in this commentary paper. Pluralism is a word used with differing meanings in different contexts. In philosophy, it is opposed to Monism, or to the idea that everything can be traced back to a single principle, e.g. Vedantic idealism or Marxist materialism, both of which are monist (though Sankara himself may not have been a strict Monist, and Marx fiercely attacked the idealist Monism of Hegel). In advocating democratic pluralism we are not advocating any particular philosophical position. In sociology, pluralism is opposed to a single or monistic principle of interpretation for social reality (historical materialism or dialectical materialism). Pluralism is the ideology of liberalism in its anti-Marxist, pragmatic stand. We do not espouse this position either.

In proposing democratic pluralism as an alternative to secularism, we do not espouse any particular ideology in philosophy or sociology. We do not, however mean just a variety of ideologically or religiously differing communities simply co-existing either. We are definitely opposed to the melting pot ideology of pluralism, symbolized in the inscription on American currency : "epluribus unum" or "out of the many, one", this ideology implies that all particularities have to be melted to form one composite identity. We mean a social system in which communities with varying religious, cultural and linguistic backgrounds commit themselves to live together as a single (federal or integral) polity, in which all citizens are equal and each is committed to seek the welfare of the whole and the whole is committed to the welfare of each. Pluralism is not mere co-existence of variety; it is the living together of variety bound together by a common commitment. Pluralism is not possible without a core of so common commitment. The range of that common commitment can be expanded from time to time.

In the Indian situation a democratic pluralist polity would imply at least the following :

a. Commitment by all to the welfare of the whole and to the welfare of each.

b. Equality of status before the law for all; there are no minorities or majorities.

c. No special privilege based on religion or caste; no job reservations, no special electoral constituencies based on merit or economic need; Constitution to be amended if necessary; for backward communities there should be a system of registration for admissions, fee concessions, scholarships, jobs etc., based on proved economic need rather than on caste.

A national comprehensive scheme and campaign for rural work creation and literacy , to be run by an independent body, with government as well as peoples' contribution funding, participation of teachers and senior students and armed forces, to create a national ferment. This should not be under the aegis of political parties, but should make use of the voluntary agencies and public bodies to be set up where necessary. Democratic pluralism demands the direct participation of the people in national reconstruction.

Many more details can be worked out. The important first step is to abandon the concept of secularism as solution to our communal problems, and to create a vision and movement in which the people can themselves be the arbitrators of their own destiny, creating a new and dynamic unity based on peoples, own actions and attitudes. Call it *Democratic pluralism* or by some other name, but never Secularism.

If I may venture an additional thought, I would suggest that we have to make a distinction between society and community. The basic difference is in the type of relationship which each concept implies. Society (Gesell Schaft) implies more impersonal and faceless structures of relationship, whereas in Community (Gemeinschaft) there is a common commitment which is binding on all, and the relationships have to be on a more personal basis. What we need is an emphasis on the global community, rather than on a just society bound by rules and laws. A global community, however, has to be a community of local communities. The local community does not exist in isolation, but in the framework of regional, national and international communities. There will have to be rules and regulations to govern the conduct of people within these communities, but more important than the rules are the basic commitment of each individual and each member community in a larger community. This idea is also given in shorthand here, and needs to be further developed.

One important consequence of shifting from society to community as the primary emphasis is that the role of the State is considerably reduced in the framework of the community. In a society the State is the arbiter of justice and the people sometimes become helpless when the State is unable to produce justice. In communities the people are the primary agents, and they will have to be the primary actors, through appropriate persons and institutions, to see that the best interests of both the community and of each individual member of it are always fostered.

The other point that I would like to touch upon is my frequent affirmation in the past that the root cause is to be sought in a political economy which does not assure the people of democratic justice. In a polity where the way to get justice is through clout and bribe and pressure tactics, people tend to organise themselves around identities smaller and more manageable than the national identity, for the majority community as well as for the minorities, for power broking, bargaining and for jockeying for position. If the issue of Communalism is to be solved, strive for a polity in which majority and minorities alike can be assured of a semblance of justice.

SECULARISM AND SOCIAL TRANSFORMATION IN INDIA

COMMENTS

V.P. GUPTA

Let me, at the outset, place on record my deep appreciation of the excellent presentation by Prof. Rasheeduddin Khan. His paper is a testimony to his scholarship and deep insight into the subject. He has done a lot of original thinking and tried to diagnose the ills we are presently afflicted with. Everyone may not necessarily agree with him. After all, it is a question of perception. Again the very object of presenting a paper is not to deal with a subject on comprehensive and conclusive basis but to make the readers sit up, think and re-act. I am sure Prof. Khan has acquitted, himself admirably.

One may not agree with the Prof. Khan's assertion that a new civilisation is emerging in India and an ancient society is getting transformed into a modern polity, at a time when national isolation is an impossibility, and global interdependence a major reality especially for a geo-politically strategic country that stands on the cross-roads of international transactions. Read with his own statement that we are 15th in rank in terms of our GNP and have the dubious distinction of being 106th in terms of per-capita income, the foregoing assertion of his may sound a

'Manmohanism'. Similarly one may at best wink when he talks of socio-cultural federalism of India of yester-years. By now, it is widely held that before the advent of East India Company's rule, the modes of travel, for ordinary people at least, were few and far between and before embarking on a journey they would wish farewell to all their dear and near ones who would entrust them to God by tying a coin as 'Imamzamin'. We never had one -India as of now. His statement that Congress being a muti-class party by keeping a balance between the many forces and ideological strands worked out a pragmatic alternative which transformed India into a stable political community integrating the many streams of linguistic, cultural and religious diversities and laid down the foundations of a self reliant economic base and generated the long-drawn process of cumbersome social change is belied by facts. How we wish, he were right and we had an integrated society. The fact is that we still have a society divided on linguistic lines and culturally differentiated. Prof. Khan's statement to the effect that at the present stage of economic development, inordinate preoccupation with the rights, wages, bonus, concessions of the workers is counter-productive is a debatable issue. Is the low level of our production cause or the effect of lack of reasonable wages, conditions of work and social security enjoined by the Directive Principles of State Policy ?

One cannot, however, fail to agree with Prof. Khan when he says "while part of the poor have certainly not remained poor despite the fact that part of the rich have become richer, yet the more crucial truth remains that a bulk of the poor have continued to remain poor, if not in absolute, certainly in relative terms because the gulf between the rich and poor segments has grown in terms of income-distribution, civic amenities, availability of goods and services and the potential of using the opportunities provided by growth itself. " His forthright statement that secularism in India is both an ideal and a reality and in many ways we are far from the realisation of the ideal would evoke wide response. It is the cause of this failure on our part, which we have to fathom. One could not agree with him more when he says that secularism represents a struggle for building an integrated political community in a multi-religious situation. It is the isolationism and exclusivity bordering on revolt on the part of some sections of society that we have to ponder over and find causes leading to this attitude.

The fact of the matter is that while during the last 45 years we have been able to successfully solve a few of our problems or potential problems, like influx of refugees, role of fundamentalism and obscurantism, military versus civilian rule, there are a few issues on which we have not been able to make any progress at all. I am referring to problem of sex, inferiority of women at least in social life, conditions of the working class, unemployment and providing people with at least the basic necessities of life. Not only we have failed in solving our problems, we seem to have lost all faith in the sincerity of our leadership to solve our problems. This seems to be one of our greatest tragedies. We seem to have lost faith in the rule of law. Barring a few (who may be termed 'naive') everybody feels that anything can be 'managed' including the legislature, the executive and the judiciary. It is not the supermacy of the right but supermacy of the 'might'. One can get away with anything. It is this lack of faith in the 'high and mighty' that has inter alien stood in the way of cohesiveness of society.

Prof. Khan, in his efforts, to identify the causes of our present state of affairs arising from power equation, has tried to delve into the four sub-systems of the political system—the Party System, the Electoral System, the Parliamentary System and the Administrative System. He has dealt at some length with the Party System but then he got bogged down by the pseudo secularism and the communalism of the majority.

In the matter of economy New Delhi is not the right window on India. Eighty per cent of India still lives in the villages and is connected with agriculture, solely or partly, in one way or the other. The majority of them still use the wooden plough, pair of bullocks as a means of locomotion, human labour for harvesting and for separating grain from the chaff and a bullock-cart to carry the produce to the storage-bins. They still live in the pre-industrial age if we over-look their use of artificial manure. As for industry we never took to industrialism 'without reservations'. Even now a substantial portion of our production comes from handicraft or village sector. We never had a working class movement in the sense it is understood the world over. The reason was that barring the metropolitan towns, wherever the industry grew up, it attracted workers from the nearby villages who went in droves impelled by primordial ties referred to by Prof. Rasheeduddin Khan. They seldom severed their ties with the villages. Moreover, their problems as members of the working class were also debated with their employers in a language unknown to them which on the one hand gave rise to an intermediate class who called themselves labour leaders and on the other hand never let them have faith in their own might as working class. After independence too, the same situation continued with the difference that the white-collar workers tried to arrogate to themselves all that really belonged to the manual workers. Even now the same situation continues. Barring fraction of one per cent who may be engaged in foreign or international undertakings or the highly sophisticated Indian units which have taken to computer and other technological devices, the working class in India is still in the pre-industrial stage. There is little transformation. The highly educated persons and professionals are of course, looking up to big industrial houses, if not to migration abroad.

On the social plane, there has come about an upheaval, more or less. The placid sea, after Independence, is now turbulent. The Muslims, not withstanding the 'sins' of their parents, refuse to remain the second-class citizens; the Akalis insist on their 'Khalistan', the adivasis want their own State, backward classes press for their rights based on population percentage and the low and the lowly want a change in their condition over-night not to mention extremists all over and foreign agents. This is not to suggest that in J & K they are wrong. They are absolutely right, from their point of view. But why has such a state of affairs come about?

My guess is that the chief villain of the piece is our 'over-protection of the interests of the minorities'. The minorities have come to look upon their minoritism as a vested interest. They refuse to play their secular role and try to evade their responsibility in the garb of 'preservation of their rights'. Whether it is a case of wages and working conditions of teachers in Frank Anthony School or the question of maintenance of a destitute woman divorced by her husband, the minorities have taken the things to ill-logical ends with the result that even the majority finds it profitable to be labelled as a 'minority'. Even the Arya Samaj, an out and out Hindu body, has tried to prove itself a 'minority' and thereby enjoy the privileges of minority in the matter of administration of its schools. Not only that, whenever anybody has tried to put its foot down, the issue has been given a political colour and the whole community has cried 'wolf' forcing the weak and impotent authority to cave in. Shah Bano is a case in point. This state of things has led to a reaction among the majority during the last few years and they are flexing their muscles to cry a halt to this state of affairs.

Let us be honest to ourselves. Our ideal to make a multilayered cake has collapsed. Let us take to the 'melting pot' theory, prevalent the world over. The earlier we do, the better.

SECULARISM AND SOCIAL TRANSFORMATION IN INDIA

COMMENTS

P.G. Menon

I am on the side of the Professor Khan. My comments are intended to strengthen his case.

He avers that "national isolation is an impossibility" (p.3, para 3) at this time. 'National isolation' is not like a go-no go gauge. The real issue is: from what foreign forces or things should who all in India be isolated to what extent? Should the Muria be partly or wholly isolated, now, from the global demand for the hardwoods in his area? Should we attempt to isolate our children from the foreign tobacco lobby?

There is much merit in the logical positivism school of philosophy's contention that "the meaning of a proposition is the method of its verification". Meaningful discussion requires that important general concepts such as 'national isolation', and others mentioned below be 'dis-aggregated' into the numerous specifics to which our national boundaries should be partly or completely permeable (e.g. refugees). The absence of such 'dis-aggregation' leads to confusion, to platitudes, to unnecessary ideological confrontation, as between the supporters of the global village economy and those who believe that Trans-National Corporations empower the forces of 'anomie'.

"Primordial ties" and "primordial loyalties". These, too, need to be spelt out. Only then can we meaningfully discuss the pros and cons of each, and whether and how, differing value-systems and goals can either be synergised, harmonised or enabled to co-exist.

"A contradictory tableaux of growth and poverty." (P. 3, para 2, line14, and passim). It is vital, if socio-economic transformation is to be a sustainable process, to realise that India's current system of laws and of government ensures that National economic development directly promotes in increase in both relative and absolute poverty. Because :-

(a) A large percentage of what could 'trickle down' either evaporates in transit or is corruptly siphoned off.

(b) Before a factory has reached the stage of hiring production workers, land must be acquired for it to come one on, and land must be acquired for the powerhouse to generate electricity for such factories. We have created between 12 million and 20 million project-affected persons since Independence in the name of creating employment. The PAPs are marginalised by the current model of national development. For they are neither given adequate compensation, nor are they trained for the alternative livelihood that industrialisation promises in principle.

(c) If the 'economic development', such as mining or the 'harvesting of trees' takes place in one place (e.g. Jharkhand), and the 'value-added' is retained (say in the form of share-dividends) elsewhere, then the 'in-group versus out-group' syndrome gets powerfully energised. Too many people in the Jharkhand area are not impressed by the arguments of the nation-state apologists that it is India that gets the fruits of such development. Peoples (and their paradigms) that the Emperor Ashoka is alleged to have extinguished are beginning to re-assert certain primordial loyalties.

(d) I fear that the IIC has added some fuel through its publication "The Indigenous Vision". It would be nit-picking to argue that 'indigenous peoples' were not used as a synonym for 'tribal' or 'adivasi' (original inhabitant).

This concept of 'indigenous people' is potently divisive in our over-populated land with its diminishing "ecological commons'. The concept implies that they who are not 'adivasi' (original inhabitant) are not, really, first-class Indians; it implies that some are nothing more than long-terms squatters who should be repatriated to Turkey or Mongolia or wherever their ancestors came from.

(e) Frustration and other forms of excess stress result in anger, anxiety, flight (from reality) or regression, as well as displacement and projection—these, then are contributory causes of communalism.

(f) Max Weber has familiarised us with 'the autonomous life of an institution". The Union and State Governments of India manifest this 'autonomous life' For they operate according to the rules framed by the British to rule a conquered people. And these rules, in turn, are based on repressive laws enacted after the Mutiny, to take away the traditional rights of people in India to own manage common property resources through their own local institutions. The GOI, therefore, in the name of development, is able to allow a paper factory to harvest bamboo at two rupees a tonne from what was tribal forest before the post-Mutiny Forest Act, and the same Government charges the local tribal fourteen rupees a kilo for the same bamboo.

The above is one reason for Prof. Khan to reconsider in what way the "nation and the nation state" can be "the terminal community—the final point of political allegiance". (P.II). For one thing, any self-defined in-group which believes that it is being exploited by the nation-state in order to benefit some other group or groups is going to protest. Its protest may be violent, e.g. 'naxalitism'. Its protest may extend to wanting autonomy, or even full political independence, especially if its numbers are large enough, and if enough of them believe that they are 'indigenous people'. The long-term solution has to be based on this *axiom* : that the members of any political or economic union *must feel that they gain enough* from that relationship. Otherwise, they are not likely to manifest that spirit of give-and-take necessary for the peace of our plural society.

SECULARISM AND SOCIAL TRANSFORMATION IN INDIA

COMMENTS

E.M.S. Namboodiripad

Dr. Rasheeduddin Khan's paper on "Secularism and social transformation in India" is an instructive document which throws light on many important aspects of the problem. I, however, have my reservations on two parts of the paper.

Firstly, he says "The sub-continental polity, in the past as in the present, acquires its defined personality essentially as an agglomeration of regions and sub-regions" and adds "these well-defined socio-economic sub-regions (about 60 to 70) are distinctive sub-national communities (but not nationalities).

Secondly, he considers as valid two objections to the term "secularism". The term, he says, is "overlaid by its European/Western connotation, of 'separation of Church from the State' and the 'separation of the School from the Church'", Again, "the suffix 'ism', gives it a dogmatic veneer and an orientation of unquestioned certitude, and thus transforms it from a worthy ideal into a rigid doctrine."

I agree that there is a point in each of these formulations. I, however, feel that the essence of the question is distorted by Professor Khan. For a correct understanding of the reality conveyed by the two terms "sub-national communities and not nationalities" and the term "secularism being heavily overlaid by its European/ Western context" will be seen to be untenable if India's historical context is taken into account.

I remember in this context the controversy between the first generation of Indian nationalists and the ideologues of British imperialism. The former asserted that, like England, India is a nation : the latter on the other hand pointed out that India is a mere "geographical expression" and not a nation.

Pointing out to the existence of innumerable castes and sub-castes, religious communities, linguistic-cultural groups and tribes, the British rulers tried to substantiate their thesis that "India is not a nation". Early nationalists on the other hand asserted that, in spite of these diversities, there is a unity among the Indian people who constitute a nation.

Which of these two stand-points was correct? I am of the view that there is an element of truth in both. India was at that time a developing nation. The innumerable castes, sub-castes, religious communities, linguistic-cultural groups, tribes etc. were slowly merging into one nation with its aspiration for freedom from the British rulers. As the freedom movement grew, the unity of the various sections of the Indian people grew stronger.

This however, did not negate the fact that the emerging unity was an agglomeration of diversities which were cleverly utilised by the British rulers to deny the Indian people freedom and independence. The two aspects of 'unity in diversity' were not contradictory to but complimented each other. However, after the nation attained freedom (in 1947), the diversity in the broad framework of unity started asserting itself more and more. Hence, the growth of casteism, communalism, tribalism, linguism, regionalism, etc. in free India.

It was through this process that what Professor Rasheeduddin Khan calls "the agglomeration of regions and sub-regions which are sub-national communities but not nationalities" emerged. It is significant that, in the course of the development of the freedom movement, the concept of linguistic States in a united but federal India arose.

It was when the freedom movement embraced the mass of marking people whom Mahatma Gandhi called "*Darindra Narayanan*" that the concepts of federal unity in diversity, State autonomy within the context of Indian unity, the formation of linguistic States etc. arose. This may, therefore, be considered the development of a united Indian nation and simultaneously the existence of several politically and administratively autonomous sub-regions which the Professor calls "sub-national communities but not nationalities".

For one would not quarrel over the word "nationality". I am more concerned with the essence of the concept. The various "sub-national communities" which according to some are nationalities should be and are integral but fully autonomous parts of United India. Professor Khan probably thinks that, if the word 'nationality' is used, it would mean a unit which is not an integral part of united India. That I differ from him in this interpretation of the connotations of the term is a different matter.

I am in full agreement with him that the nation-State in India is the federal (central) State. But I would insist that what the Professor calls "sub-national communities" should have the right to enjoy the essence of State as it relates to subjects which are left to the federating units in federal India. Correct balance between a Centre which enjoys the right of keeping the country united and the maximum possible autonomy for the federating units—this according to me is the essence of the matter.

Coming to the second question, I agree that, unlike in Europe where the established Christian Church enjoyed wide powers and was almost indistinguishable from the State, India has had no established Church: neither the Hindu nor the Muslim religious community had the authority which the Christian Church possessed in Europe. Secularism in the sense of separation of Church and State therefore, does not have the same relevance in India that it had in Europe. But the caste and the religious community in India had the same control over the minds of the Indian people as the Christian Church had in Europe.

The princes of Indian States before the formal integration of their States into United India after freedom were the heads of the two major institutions of society—the caste and the religious community. In British Indian provinces too, the leaders of Hindu castes and Non-Hindu religious communities were simultaneously feudal landlords and, therefore, possessed enormous powers. The democratic freedom movement, therefore, inscribed on its banner (a) fundamental land reforms all over India, and (b) the ending of princely rule in what was once called "Indian India". Anti-feudal struggle in the sense of struggle for the abolition of feudal landlordism and the disintegration of princely states became part and parcel of India's struggle for freedom.

It was in this context that the demand arose for the integration of all parts of British Indian provinces and princely states which were inhabited by people speaking a single language into a new linguistic State. After protracted struggle, this demand was, by and large, conceded in the 1956 Act of Parliament, abolishing all princely States and constituting by and large linguistically re-organised States.

What was left unfinished in the 1956 Act was finished subsequently by the formation of the Maharashtra, Gujarat, Punjab and Haryana States. With this, each of the "sub-regional communities" referred to by Professor Khan, constituted a nation-State within the broad framework of a united and indivisible Indian State.

It is in this context that the problem of 'secularism' and national integration has to be analysed. It is not only a question of separating religion from the State but also of building a caste-less democratic India in which, cutting across all castes, religious, linguistic-cultural, tribal and other diversities, the Indian people are united in a single nation inhabited by a large number of sub-regional communities each of which has its own autonomous states. This is the real unity in diversity.

I have no major difference with the Professor Khan's analysis of the negative and positive connotations of the term "secularism" (as spelt out in paras 2 and 3 on Page 17). I, however, want to make it clear that "recognition of religion and beliefs as personal and devotional aspects of life" should include recognition of atheism. This, in fact, is recognised in the Indian Constitution which provides two forms in which the religious and the irreligious can take their oaths on assuming public office : while the religious (the followers of all religions) "swear by God", the irreligious "solemnly affirm". Freedom to people to believe in and practice any religion or no religion is thus the essence of secularism. From this naturally arises the obligation of religion not to interfere in State affairs, while the State and non-official organisations are obliged not to interfere in religious affairs. In this sense 'secularism' in India as in Europe means the separation of religion and politics from each other.

SECULARISM AND SOCIAL TRANSFORMATION IN INDIA

COMMENTS

Y.S. Rajan

Some quick points

On page 5, Prof. Khan describes about some segmentation of the propertied and non-propertied classes. Probably as a sixth entity under non-propertied classes, it will be good to add a group totally untouched by our economic system (they might have been "pushed away by the system"). Some tribal groups, people in remote areas etc. will qualify for this. The description is "beyond destitutes"

In the same page second paragraph starting "India's political system with its liberal democratic overtones, leans towards a coalescence of power comprising the upper classes and middle castes .." does Prof. Khan mean middle classes or castes? I think it was a typo considering the development of his thesis.

While pointing out these nitty-gritty details, I personally think that looking at India as a multi-segmented society on the lines suggested by Prof. Khan would give much better clues to handle the issues realistically. Simple divides such as rural urban, etc. cannot even provide rudimentary approximations of the complex reality.

The reality of requiring people's support (essentially through votes) and upper segments' support for remaining in power—is well brought out in pages 7, 8, and 9. Intra-system pulls and pressures of a very complex nature results from this stark and perhaps unresolvable reality. Tendencies for experimenting (even dangerously with) newer fragmentations or newer (albeit temporally transient) group identities emerge from this situation. Such experiments and (sometimes irreversible) results thereof become a part of social transformation in India.

Another complicating feature is the time-compression of events in the present day world. Complex readjustments towards modern secular systems, elsewhere in the globe, could take place at a slower pace spread over centuries. In India we are attempting to bridge the gaps of centuries in several fronts in a matter of few decades. In any case slowing down is *not* possible. One could even say, that some tendencies towards smaller group identities take place because of pace of changes in many fronts (whether it is economic growth or social equity etc.) has *not* kept pace with the subjective expectations.

On pages 22-23 Prof. Khan has brought out an issue "What is more frightening is that if the majority community exhibits the besieged psychology of the minorities and feel threatened, either in fact or in imagination, then it also exhibits minority traits of 'separatism', 'exclusivism', 'withdrawal' and 'anarchism' and thereby in its approach and transaction, transforms itself into the mould of the gigantic minority, arrayed in combat formation and in belligerent equation with other minorities." On the one hand, it is necessary to analyse as to the root causes of such besieged psychology. On the other hand, it is also perhaps necessary to question whether a *majority* feels besieged. It may well be, that in the complex milieu of segmentation and (transient) group identities, a group is able to project a scenario for a smaller period. Even then, why it is so, is worth examining.

It is in this context, I would specially like to draw attention to the article by Prof. P.N. Haksar on "Fundamentalism and Secularism" which appeared in *Man and Development*, December 1991 and was reproduced in *Current Science* with a brief introduction by Prof. Satish Dhawan. I reproduce here the brief introduction by Prof. Dhawan in *Current Science* as it provides a basic view on the creation of modern India.

In the turmoil—social, political and economic—that India is passing through, nothing stands out as the strife spawned by friction between communities, castes and religion often fomented and manipulated by politicians and their henchmen. There seems to be a growing distrust of reason, a forgetting of the roots of Indian tolerance and adherence to morality. While some members of the Indian intelligentsia have on a few occasions taken courage to speak out against the whipped up frenzy and its disastrous consequences, the Indian Science community has generally not discussed or taken a public stand in its usual gathering places such as conferences, Symposia, Congresses, etc.

Although many see this phenomenon as a menace not only to the strengthening of the roots of science in India but to virtually all civilised development, few do much about it. Haksar's editorial note (reproduced below) in *Man and Development* is worth reading by all our colleagues. It is a sober and reasoned analysis in the light of history by a respected intellectual who has been active for many decades in the endeavour to help create a modern India, which is rational and humane, where the power bestowed by knowledge and status is tempered by wisdom and sensitiveness—he has been in the thick of the fight and yet above it. It is good, sobering message for all Indian intellectuals.

Lastly I would like to bring out a concept.

Modernisation process in (political) economy has been looked as *Land-Labour-Capital-Technology*. Whether it was pastoral Aryans or Genghis Khan, it is totally unimportant now. But other elements tend to dominate. Present day dominion is by capital and technology. Even while such elements operate in the economic plane, modernisation process in social plane has perhaps followed: Tribe-*Religion-Caste-Language-Class-Nation Humanity*. In the present day world strength of adherence of large segments or people to *nation* is the litmus test of the modernisation though other elements may "pop up" in sometime. Some of these are considered secular e.g. language or class groupings.

Conflicts in the economic plane between the possessors of Land-Labour-Capital-Technolgy, can fall back upon divisions of Tribe-Religion-Caste-Language-Class of social plane, and in practice these interact in a complex manner. Economic conflict being reflected as social conflict and vice versa. Still, I feel, to use these concepts for the two planes can help to understand several situations.

As in the economic plane one *cannot* "get rid of" some strengths of those possessing Land and Labour, in the social plane other group adherences cannot be totally "gotten rid of" even in a fully conscious rational and humanistic Nation. The layers will remain similar to geological formations causing occasional tremors, landslides etc.

Our present dilemma is to strike an operating balance. Other elements from Tribe-Religion-Caste-Language-Class may "pop up" continually: but when imaginative social movement, can keep the hopes and aspirations of people around issues of nation, relative importance of other elements will go down. Classic example is the early stages of our Independence movement.

The question before us, is perhaps how to generate such a movement even while being engaged in the mundane activity of economic growth and implementation of nitty gritty social welfare activities like health, education etc. Answer perhaps is partly linked with the method of accelerating these mundane activities and making them more equitable (contradictory requirements?) I don't claim to know the answers. But providing material comforts rapidly to the several segments of people listed by Prof. Khan (aspirations and expectations of whom vary considerably and are often opposing each other in a situation of limited public resources) is one crucial element. In addition, we have to search for other elements that could act as secular common-factors : science is one. Can mass media like television be made one? Let us *not* overlook the role of cinema in early years of Tamil Nadu and the role of Hindi cinema. Can we think of more elements? If we can find a few and *energise the binding forces* resulting from these elements (of common factors) we can transition the process of social transformation to a modern Nation which is secularisation in true sense.

COMMENTS ON PROF. RASHEEDUDDIN KHAN'S 'SECULARISM AND SOCIAL TRANSFORMATION IN INDIA'

Nirmal Singh

Professor Khan in this synoptic paper on the complex relationship that developed in India, mainly in the post independence period, between secularism and social transformation has advanced many seminal ideas. A number of contradictory readings exist among social scientists and political commentators about the course social transformation has taken since 1947 and there is no universally acceptable social science terminology either to comprehend and describe/analyse the related developments. This makes it all the more necessary to take up the challenge of clarifying issues as Prof. Khan has done.

In section 1 the author has succinctly referred to the development of capitalism, as the process of industrialisation was taken up through the planned process by the Indian State, resulting in 'the contradictory phenomenon of growth *and* poverty.............In this process, while part of the poor have certainly not remained poor despite the fact that the rich have become richer, yet the more crucial truth remains that a bulk of the poor have continued to remain poor, if not absolutely certainly in relative terms'. From this formulation, a correct logical inference has been drawn that the ruling party/parties have to bid for legitimacy by mouthing populist slogans, while structurally continuing to rely on a symbiotic dependence on the propertied classes 'led by the captains of industry and commerce and the land based rural rich'. Unfortunately, the logic of this contradictory character of the ruling party (Classes) has not been fully worked out.

I suggest that we could consider the proposition that by the mid-sixties, the early success in building of the public sector as segment of State capitalism more as a cooperative rather as a competitive element of the given economic system, creating a contradictory tableau of growth *and* poverty had entered a critical phase. The balance between growth and poverty began to be titled, more and more, though not in a straight line, towards more poverty and less growth. The wars with Pakistan and China also played contributory roles. This resulted in partial withdrawal of the legitimacy by the poor in the 1967 General Elections and in a section of the leaders of the ruling classes openly challenging the continuity of public sector and planning, symptomised by the formation of Swatantra Party. Similarly the success of building productive capitalism in some advanced regions of agriculture, aided by State action abolishing absentee landlordism and other forms of feudal excesses, of helping rich peasants to own the land they controlled and providing modern technology—machinery, irrigation facilities, fertilisers and HYV seeds etc.—resulted in the new rural rich demanding greater economic autonomy and share of power from the industrial capitalists. The rise of the Charan Singh phenomenon was visible in all Green Revolution areas. In short the very success of growth as an aspect of social transformation resulted in the ongoing transformation being questioned both by the poor who were systemically denied access to the growth benefits and the beneficiaries of the development.

Prof. Khan has referred to 60 to 70 well defined socio-economic sub-regions. These sub-regions cut across the mappings of 'specific jati-formation, tribal patterns, religious communities and sects, dialects and literary heritage, variations in common beliefs and rituals', etc. that he writes about. The term 'federal' when applied to more or less territorially demarcated regions has a very different meaning for constructing a political/constitutional arrangement, from the one that answers the difference of primordial loyalties of caste, religion, interspersed language affinities etc. No arrangement can be worked out, in a modern democratic set-up, on any relatively stable basis, wherein these identities define political actors/actions for social transformation. Some of these identities do legitimately define social action as community action but should be constitutionally confined to aspects directly bearing upon these commonalities and barred from interfering with similar community actions by other such groupings and also from political, economic, secular, educational and cultural structures open to all irrespective of these primordial loyalties. This is the ideal towards which we have to move, if social transformation processes are to be freed from divisions and dissensions extraneous to these processes. Not decrees but consent through education have to move, if social transformation processes are to be freed from divisions and dissension extraneous to these processes. Not decrees but consent and education could be the basis of moving in this direction. If the societal organisations we inherited at independence were built on a long tradition along ascriptive and hierarchical, and partially exclusivist lines, no transformational task can be completed if the sense of direction is lost or the forced pace of moving on modern lines results in generating massive alienation.

The critical situation for social transformation that we referred to created a situation, which has been aggrevated of late, wherein the denial of benefits of growth to the weaker sections of society has prompted them to take to oppositional role, and also to open their flanks for manipulation by such political forces that mobilise them on primordial lines in wider economic political or cultural arena. The shrinking constituency of the incumbent political leadership of the State carrying out social transformation even among the propertied classes resulted in populist competitions to control State leadership, breakdown of the earlier consensus among the propertied classes and opportunistic appeals to primordial loyalties, even pitching one set of these against such other identities for retaining or capturing political power. This has only compounded the problems for social transformation. Hence the need for a relook at the question of relationship with secularism.

It is true as Prof. Khan states in Section II that Congress

looms large on the political horizon as the only all-India party with branches in practically every district and several tehsils, has been in power at the Union level and in majority of States for most of the part for the last 45 years and unites within it multi-ethnic, multi-lingual and multi-religious people to a great extent. But it is also true that the contradictions of 'growth and poverty' model of social transformation that it has pursued have adversely affected this 'Greatest Common Measure' of Indian politics. Unfortunately, it is not true, as Prof. Khan erroneously asserts, that Congress 'worked out a programmatic alternative which did transform India in the course of just four decades into a stable political community, integrating the many streams of linguistic, cultural and religious diversities, laid the foundations of a self-reliant economic base and generated the long drawn process of cumbersome social change'. The New Economic Policy, the acceptance of the conditionalities imposed by international monetary agencies, and the massive borrowing resulting in the burden of unbearable foreign debt, etc. are too glaring a contradiction of the claim of having built a self-reliant economic base.

The aberrations in the political system, the spread of communalism and national fragmentation, and the repercussions of communalism on the Indian polity that Prof. Rasheeduddin Khan discusses in his paper bring out enough empirical evidence to question his formulation that the ruling party has transformed India into a stable political community, integrating the many streams of linguistic, cultural and religious diversities'. Khan's counter propositions are spread all over his paper and they depict the prevailing empirical reality, and not his loose formulation cited above. Populism, economism, parochialism and the breakdown of the national consensus, public promises and private betrayals, strengthening of economic oligarchy, selling political democracy to the masses, and enjoying pay off from the hegemonic upper classes, that the author has written about do apply to the political parties also but the Congress party as the ruling party and the party that launched and stayed with 'growth and poverty' model of transformation has contributed more than any other to these developments.

colonial masters, in the rise of communalism in India, eventually resulting in the partition in 1947. The false two nation theory, based on the principle of religious community forming a nation, was fostered by the British. The fact of partition was not only a success story of the imperialist design, as Prof. Khan exposes, but it aslo represented a failure on the part of secular national movement to stem the lid of communalism, a fact that he glosses over. It has vitiated secular politics in the sub-continent as a whole. The weakness of the leadership of Indian national movement to thwart the imperialist design of fomenting communal strife and identifying a religious community as a nation has not been analysed, and no clear lessons have been drawn from history. Prof. Khan has also brought out the importance of the ever present process of all religions being the carriers of two competing traditions—the *orthodox* and the *humanist*. Conformism, rigidity of belief, bigotry in propagation of faith, intolerance of dissent, promotion of militancy among the faithful and beligerency towards other belief systems constituted the orthodox tradition. Heterodoxy, pluralism, fairly open and broadly accommodative and divergent interpretations characterised the humanist tradition. As he writes, the humanist tradition promotes religiosity but not formal religion. He discusses the relationship of religion and communalism in Section IV and advances the argument that these characteristics of orthodox tradition in religion leads to communalism, causing fragmentation of the nation. He, like many other social scientists, talks about 'real men of God', 'true believer in religion', 'religious people in the real sense of the word' etc. He writes "Indeed communalists become communalists precisely because they are ignorant of the moral teachings and universalist underpinning of their own religion, which makes them in essence, not only irreligious but also anti-national and anti-human". He further writes that communalism is perversion of religion from a moral order to a temporal arrangement of contemporary convenience, from a faith into a constituency. The position advanced here has the advantage of carrying the battle against communalism into the space reserved for specific religious discourses. The disadvantage is that the struggle against communalism and for secularism gets fragmented into the ones waged by humanist and true Hindus against orthodox and ignorant Hindus and another by genuine and real Muslims against irreligious anti-national and anti-human Muslims and so on. There would be as many battles being fought in isolatiion as there are religious faiths and orders or even sects within; the terms of debate and rhetorics would be the separate religious idioms of different religions. The evaluative criteria for deciding as to which interpretation is a 'true' 'genuine' and 'real' and which one 'dubious' 'contentious' and 'ignorant of the moral teachings' of the specific or plainly irreligious, would also be according to the exclusive criteria built within each religious order. A *'fatwa'* declaring Ahmadia Muslims as non Muslims or a *'hukum nama'* from Akal Takht denouncing dissiden individual Sikhs, groups or sects could easily cordon off the dissenting tradition. How reforming Bohras have been punished and paralysed by Syedanna is well known.

It is not being suggested that 'humanist' tradition's struggle against 'orthodox' tradition and structures within religious systems does not contribute to struggle against communalism, or for secularising religion as part of social transformation processes. What is unhelpful is a definitional confinement of communalism and the counter-movement to segmented religious spaces and terms of discourse. Moreover, the ideal types of orthodox and humanist traditions can seldom be identified with empirical positions of living individuals and groups on two sides of a clearly demarcating divider.

Like all social science concepts, the signified and the empirical referents may undergo a change with changing times. Also no two societies throw up exactly identical realities to be conceptualised. Consequently, the concepts through transfer in time and space naturally undergo alteration in nuances associated with the signifier terms. Professor Khan has clearly stated this fundamental theorem about concepts: Secularism in India is an evolving reality through an agonising process, but then that is probably also true of other major ideas before the country. Emboldened by this statement, I would suggest the following definition of communalism in India, to comprehend the contemporary reality.

Communalism is the system of ideas, attitudes, beliefs and behaviour in a multi-religious society, which (1) assigns behaviour in a multi-religious society, which (1) assigns predominant position to interests and identities defined by a commonality of adherence to some specific religion to the relative exclusion of all others, (2) attempts to increase internal homogeneity, and posit other religious faiths, practices and groupings as danger marks to their position on all spheres and therefore deserving a dressing down.

It can be argued that definitional restriction of communalism to systems of ideas alone, as has been done by an eminent historian, fails to underline the mutually supportive relationship of ideas and behaviour, one enforcing the other as happened in the case of religion based 'nationalism' and widespread communal riots in mid forties resulting in the partition and is being enacted in symbiotic growth of Khalistani ideology and terrorist violence in the case of Punjab. On the other hand, when violent behavioural expression of communalism is subdued by administrative measures, the average person is lulled into the illusion that communalism is no more. In the above comprehensive definition of communalism, the incipient communalism that starts with predominant position assigned to interests and identities defined by common religion to the exclusion of other religions, and relatively cross-religion interests and identities, does not go unnoticed, even if antagonism against others may not have surfaced.

The anti-Sikh programs in Bidar (Karnataka) were one traumatic consequences of accepting as permissible communal action, when a Sikh educational trust out-manoeuvered its rivals in cornering a capitation fee medical college, having already established a similar engineering college. Social transformative capacity of the democratic polity in India has been grievously impaired by the erroneous conceptualisation that intrustion by surrogates for religious communities are allowed a growing role in secular educational, political and economic institutions, as long as antagonism against other is dormant. It is time to have a second look at Art. 30(1) and related provisions in the Constitution. An appropriate conceptualisation of communalism would be of help to chart out a practicable programme of realising Art. 44 and other related provisions in the Directive Principles. This will help avoid repeating the kneejerk reactions when events like Shah Bano Judgement by Supreme Court and the following emotional out bursts by 'Shariat in danger', and 'women rights' activists resulted in a backtrack by the Indian Parliament. Any exclusive projection of religion based community interests on to non-religious spheres is but the first step towards antagonism against other and national fragmentation. Incipient and mild variety of communalism need to be dealt with mild and understanding measures but must not be allowed to go undetected.

It seems to me that over emphasising the points of difference, about the religious structures and their role in state and education between India and the West is unhelpful. The intrusion of organised religious bodies in secular education and polity has roots in some indigeneous traditions and was deliberately fostered by the British in the colonial period. So separation of the sacred and the secular spheres remains an important aspect of India's social transformation. Without this, fragmentation of national existence on communal lines cannot be checked. A second aspect of secularism, that needs recognition in the context of social transformation is to build a faith that problems of this world—poverty, ignorance, disease, selfishness, violence, hatred etc.—are not caused by supernatural wrath or punishment for acts of past birth, and that corrections lie in appropriate human efforts. This was the point that Nehru repeatedly harped upon as leader of the national movement. The over zealous assertion of uniquely Indian as against everything happened at ideal, behavioural or institutional level elsewhere gives a handle to those who issue anti-secularist manifestos, talk of genuine secularism, decry Indian Constitution and polity as Western transplant, pit Gandhi against Nehru, Indian tradition against all modernity and science, diversity against unity or heterology against universal rationality etc.

It is my contention that all concepts of secularism in India —Indian tradition spelt out as tolerance for others, Gandhian as equal respect for all religions, Nehruvian as scientific and rational approach in opposition to superstition, fatalism and organised religion, and Marxian as progressive overcoming of the control by supernatural and the Western historical—have their specific emphasis points but carry a lot in common, specially when it secularists and even communalist opposition to democratic social transformation thrive on pitching one conceptualisation of secularism against another to confuse them all and work towards fragmentation of national will for transformation. These different conceptualisations can serve as complementary rather than as adversaries.

DISCUSSIONS

I

Amrik Singh

Prof. Amrik Singh, who presided over the session, made a few initial remarks. First, he pointed out that the partition of the country in 1947 resulted in a significant shift of power. The Muslims who formed one fourth of the population and claimed one third representation, were reduced to 10 or 12 per cent in strength. This change has not been appreciated by the Hindus, who still nurture a feeling of insecurity.

The RSS, Prof. Amrik Singh continued, had gained considerably in strength, but this was due to the bungling and opportunism of the Congress party. As has been pointed out by one of the participants it was during the administration of a Congress Chief Minister that an idol had been planted in the Babri-Masjid to embarrass the socialist leader, Acharya Narendra Deo.

Religion, Prof. Singh remarked, was undoubtedly a private affair but it had social connotation, because it led to the formation of social communities. Communalism was the misuse of religious groups for social purposes. As long as identities are defined by caste or religion, secularism will be subverted, but the rigours of these identities will gradually wear down, though they will still continue. Prof. Singh also forecast that the time will come when Jinnah will be reviled as the man who hurt Muslims the most.

In conclusion, Prof. Singh pointed out that Muslim communalism was certainly a fact, but it was a reaction to majority communalism. The battle of Ayodhya, he thought, was likely to be a decisive battle. If it did result in a Hindu Rashtra, it will be a turning point in Indian history.

II

Rasheeduddin Khan

Prof. Rasheeduddin Khan in presenting his basic paper said that he wished to make four propositions.

First, the term social transformation covered a wide variety of ideas and activities in India. The process of social transformation in a continental polity of the size and diversity of India was different from that in a united, homogenous country.

Secondly, India is the world's most complex federal polity, segmentary, diverse and disjointed in terms of the levels of consciousness of the people.

Third, partition of the country on the erroneous, disastrous basis that religion was the touch stone of state formation was a watershed in Indian history. Its repercussion in India, which still continues, is that communal idioms became acceptable.

Fourth, secularism should be used with great care in India. In Europe, secularism started on two specifications : (a) the Church attempted to encroach on civic authority which had to be fought, and (b) in the established Church there was a dichotomy between orthodoxy and heresy. In Hinduism, on the other hand, unlike in Judaism, Islam or Christianity there is no orthodoxy. Anyone can claim to be a Hindu. In India, secularism ought to mean affirmation and assertion of vertical authority of the Parliament and the State. We must give majestry to the democratic system.

Continuing, Prof. Khan stated that in his opinion India has become neither a Hindu or a secular State but a Hindu interpretation of a secular State.

In conclusion, Prof. Khan pointed out that India was not an agglomeration of nationalities, as the Czarist Russia was. India is a federal nation; a multi-regional federation. Pluralism arises out of regional differences. A Malabar Muslim has nothing in common with an Assamese Muslim, except religion, nor a Kashmiri Muslim with a Muslim of Tamil Nadu.

III

J. S. Bali

Shri J. S. Bali presenting his Critical Note stated that Prof. Rasheeduddin Khan's paper was not only scholarly but erudite. He was, however, of the view that secularism was not the only source or engine of social transformation. He agreed with Professor Khan that while GNP had increased, so had also poverty. There has been a phenomenal increase of the middle class, but that poses its own menace.

Secularism, according to Shri Bali, was supremacy of national over local interests, improvement in the quality of life and of the functioning of a state, and equality of all citizens, irrespective of religion, caste, colour or creed.

Hinduism, Shri Bali thought, cannot be defined as cumulative communalism of the majority community. It has absorbed vicissitudes and has acquired rationality and scientific temper which has made it survive for centuries.

The measures needed for social change, in his opinion, were electoral reforms, including general elections at four instead of five yearly intervals, universal education, with less of university education and more of vocational education and hard work. All religions and all parties, he thought, should arrive at a consensus for social change through institutional processes and democratic means.

Secularism became a bane after Nehru when the largest political party started dividing the line for catching minority votes. Later other parties also followed. Social change cannot be divorced from economic change, Shri Bali concluded. The elites will have to press for such a change and make some sacrifices. He, however, could not understand why a member of a majority community has always to be on the defensive.

IV

R. C. Dutt

Shri R. C. Dutt stated that his differences with Prof. Rasheeduddin Khan were in regard to some matters of detail. He did not agree, for instance, with the Professor's characterisation of the public sector which, according to Shri Dutt, had failed because it was not utilised to determine the pattern of total investment in the country as originally planned.

Shri Dutt agreed with Professor Khan that governments came into existence on popular vote but could not function without upper-class support. He, however, referred to the instances of West Bengal and Kerala, and felt that these two cases should be further studied.

He also agreed that the Centre had a responsible role in co-ordinating the activities of the State, and was of the view that it had failed in this respect for not dismissing the U.P. Government before December 6, 1992, when its actions threatened the Supreme Court and the Constitution.

Shri Dutt asserted that there could be no social transformation except in the context of secularism. He was also of the view that poverty and want encouraged the primordial instincts of religious fundamentalism and ethnic chauvinism. This was indeed well illustrated by the recent experiences of Yugoslavia and the erstwhile Soviet Union where these primordial instincts have manifested themselves on the break-down of their economies.

Finally, Shri Dutt referred to Shri N.K. Seth's paper where the latter had drawn a distinction between academic theories and reality. Religious and ethnic assertions wre realities, according to Shri Seth, in the former socialist countries, but so were death and destruction which have followed, Shri Dutt pointed out. Should death and destruction also be condoned in the name of reality, he asked. Evil must be fought even if it was real, he concluded.

V

V.P.Gupta

Shri V. P. Gupta disagreed with Professor Rasheeduddin Khan that the Congress with its multi-party attitude had helped to stabilise the polity. If this was the stability that Congress had brought, only Heavens could save India, Shri Gupta exclaimed.

There has not been much growth either. Shri Gupta concluded, and the growth, such as it was, had not trickled down. The great majority of the population living in the villages are in much the same condition as before. The working classes too were no better off. He disagreed with Prof. Khan that pre-occupation with wages and conditions of service was counter productive.

There has been little of social transformation, Shri Gupta concluded. This was, in his view, due to over-protection of the minorities. We would have been better off, he thought, if we had adopted the melting-pot process of absorbing the minorities.

VI

P. G. Menon

Shri P. G. Menon further to his written Note, added the following oral comments :

1. Professor Rasheeduddin Khan seemed to have deliberately pulled his punches, perhaps because a really scholarly exposition would, at the present moment, have provided fuel to bigots and mischief-makers.

2. In regard to "social transformation", we must consider who is to be transformed, and into what, and whether the transformation is as per the choice of those to be transformed.

3. It is near impossible to become a Hindu except by

birth; and it is equally difficult to opt out of Hinduism, as Dr. Ambedkar and his community found. A "Hinduvta State", as a definition, has internal contradictions to which we have not addressed ourselves.

VII

Nirmal Singh

Prof. Nirmal Singh was of the view that while the growth-poverty model had been rightly criticised by Prof. Khan, the implications thereof had not been brought out. In Prof. Singh's opinion, somewhere in the mid sixties further growth on the lines adopted until then became impracticable. This alienated not only the poor, but the affluent sections of the population too. In the face of this failure populism became prevalent, and populism of one type took the form of communalism. Unless some alternative method of growth was found, Prof. Singh thought, we shall continue in the quagmire of poverty.

Continuing, Prof. Singh pointed out that secularism was necessary but not a sufficient condition of development. In this connection he regarded as important the distinction drawn by Prof. Khan between orthodoxy and humanism which existed in all religions. In Prof. Singh's view, those representing the humanist aspects of all religions should join forces and work out a common approach to secularism.

Prof. Singh concluded by saying that the spheres should be separated, and religion removed from economic and social activities.

VIII

N. K. Seth

Shri N.K. Seth was not interested in academic discussions. He wanted to be realistic. The problem of implications of secularism existed, in his opinion, and we must not shirk a debate on this issue.

However, unfortunate, it was a fact, Shri Seth pointed out, that multi-ethnic, multi-religious societies were today breaking up as in Yugoslavia and the erstwhile Soviet Union. Why were the Muslims being persecuted in Bosnia, he asked. Shri Seth was of the view that the onus of coming to a settlement in their own interests, rested on the minorities. According to Shri Seth, unfortunately, the image of a Muslim that has been created is that of a bigot. Most of the Islamic countries were theocratic, Shri Seth pointed out in support of his view.

In India, Shri Seth thought, the psychological fact had to be appreciated that after being at the receiving end for a thousand years the Hindus now find themselves at the giving end, and they are asserting this position, unfortunately aggressively. This psychological fact, whether justified or not, was there and some solution will have to be found. Shri Seth had indeed come across many young and rational Muslims who were prepared for any sacrifice, even to give up Babri Masjid, to live peacefully and amicably with the majority community and improve their quality of life by modernisation and competition.

IX

Amrik Singh

Prof. Amrik Singh, Chairman, intervened to say, that Shri Seth's assertion that the Hindu majority wanted to assert themselves was precisely the problem. There could be no co-existence, the Chairman said, if the majority did not consider it their duty to protect the minority. It was not for the minorities to prove their *bonafides*, he added. It was the lack of scruples of the ruling party, according to Prof. Singh, that had led to this position.

Secondly, Shri Seth had referred to thirty odd Muslim countries. These countries, Prof. Singh said, had an acute crisis of identity, and anxiety born out of the fact that they had lost their primacy in the world to the European powers. These thirty odd countries might be Islamic, but that has not stopped them fighting one another.

After a thousand years, Prof. Amrik Singh concluded, Hindus are now the rulers, but they have not appreciated this fact. They still want assurances for their protection.

As Prof. Amrik Singh had to leave for another engagement, Dr. A. Rahman took the Chair and called on Shri Badruddin Tyabji to speak.

X

Badruddin Tyabji

Shri Badruddin Tyabji while complimenting Prof. Rasheeduddin Khan on his excellent paper pointed out that the paper had failed to mention why secularism was necessary, and what would happen to the country if it abandoned secularism.

India is a democracy, Shri Tyabji asserted. He thought it was a prime necessity for good government that various sections of the population should be represented in all activities of the State in proportion to their relative strength.

Another omission in Prof. Khan's paper, according to Shri Tyabji, was that he had failed to mention that a civilisation gap existed between the Hindus and the Muslims. During Muslim rule this gap was sought to be bridged by building up a composite culture. This attempt has now been abandoned, and even a composite language like Urdu has been marginalised.

XI

Ramaswamy R. Iyer

Shri Ramaswamy R. Iyer was of the view that the concerns which gave rise to the adoption of the idea of 'secularism' could have been met without using the word "secular" which, in European history, came into currency in the context of the conflict between Church and State. This word was chosen by our leaders in their concern to ensure that the State had no special affiliation to any one religion. The term, however, according to Shri Iyer, tended to downgrade religion. Along with what he described as a naive belief in rationalism and the scientific temper, it had, in his opinion, had an unfortunate effect. It created a discomfort with our past religious texts and our traditions.

Sarva Dharma Sambhava, Shri Iyer thought, was an appropriate response to the post-partition scenario, and need not be identified with the theosophical outlook.

What Professor Khan seemed to be suggesting, Shri Iyer continued, was not merely a secular State, but a secular society. But religion was an important aspect or determinant of the way of life of the people. When millions congregated at the Kumbh Mela, or thousands at Mecca, or at the Vatican to receive the Pope's blessings, the phenomenon could not be regarded as merely the affair of individuals.

Shri Iyer thought that 'secularism' had nothing to do with social transformation which had to be decided separately. To summarise, he stated :

1. A secular state may be desirable, but not necessarily a secular society.
2. Aganist the backgournd of religious and communal conflicts we must emphasise the need for a non-sectarian State with complete equality and no discrimination against anyone.
3. Secularism need not be stretched beyond this to include an advocacy of rationalism and the scientific temper, which are matters for separate discussions.
4. Religion is a social phenomenon and not merely the personal affair of individuals.

XII

V.G. Bhatia

Shri V.G. Bhatia considered secularism to be safe in India. Concern about secularism was expressed by politicians, according to him, only to attract popular attention. India is secular, Shri Bhatia was of opinion, because of the Hindu way of life, whose cardinal principle is tolerance. The concept of pluralism was inherent in Hinduism, he thought.

Shri Bhatia conceded that the concern for harmonious living was genuine, but was of the view that our approach to secularism, both before and after independence, had been erroneous. Why does one have to consider oneself as a Hindu or a Muslim and then talk of Hindu-Muslim unity, he asked ? Religion is a private affair, he thought, and the social affairs of a community should be looked after by the community concerned.

Shri Bhatia agreed with Shri R.C. Dutt that economic prosperity was a remedy for communalism, but thought that our economic policies had been wrong and our economists had failed us.

XIII

Saheb Singh

Shri Saheb Singh wished to make four points :

First, India was partitioned, he pointed out, on the basis of the two-nation theory, but Indian leaders have stated that they did not accept this theory. In that case Pakistan should still be considered as part of India.

Second, many individuals who were staunchly secular were turning communal. Why, he asked? This fact should be considered along with the reality of what was happening in the world. India cannot isolate herself from the rest of the world.

Third, when a community defies the orders of the highest court in the land, the only way out is to amend the Constitution.

Fourth, Shri Singh referred to the case in Kerala where some school children, at the instance of Islamic Sevak Sangh, refused to put on school uniforms and insisted on wearing their distinctive dress.

XIV

Baren Ray

Shri Baren Ray thought that secularism had become a formula which prevented full understanding of the concept.

He referred to the lectures of Chaturvedi Badrinath on the Mahabharata and pointed out that the story of the Mahabharata was not that of an ideal society, but that in narrating the story the author or authors had put in enlightened ideas. To that extent Hinduism is indeed pluralistic, but there is another aspect of Hinduism enshrined in *Manu Samhita* which, according to Shri Ray, was probably more reactionary and more unjust than any thing contained in any other literature in the world.

We merely fool ourselves talking of Hindu pluralism, Shri Ray thought. The Bhakti cult and the liberal ideas of Kabir and Nanak no doubt testify to the liberalism of Indian thought, but so great is the tenacity of Hindu society that these enlightened ideas have been deleted.

The real discussion should now be, Shri Ray concluded, about the inbuilt nature of injustice in our society.

XV

Balraj Mehta

Shri Balraj Mehta in his initial remarks pointed out that the underlying thesis of Prof. Khan's paper was that the majesty of the Indian State and its acceptance were to be regarded in the Indian context as secular. At the same time, Prof. Khan was not in a position to define the precise character of the Indian State which he described as a Hindu version of a pseudo-secular state. This was confusing, Shri Mehta thought. How can the majesty of the Indian State, unless properly defined, be related to social transformation, he asked.

Shri Mehta did not also agree with the proposition that while growth had taken place in post independence India, poverty had not abated. The increased prosperity of the middle class whose number was said to be about 300 million was cited as evidence of growth. Shri Mehta thought this number was highly exaggerated and that not more than 40 to 50 millions could afford to buy refrigerators or private cars, and even if capacity to buy scooters was regarded as sufficient for middle class status the number would not exceed 100 million.

Finally, Shri Mehta observed that we were greatly, concerned with Indian identity and Indian unity which were regarded as essential for the stability of the Indian State. We are worried about political destabilisation. Shri Mehta, however, thought this had nothing to do with the vast majority of the poor. Their life was lawless, and they lived in a state of perpetual destabilisation. It is not unity of the State and political stabilisation, Shri Mehta concluded, but the struggle of the people outside the mainstream of Indian politics that could bring about social transformation.

XVI

Ajit Mozoomdar

Shri Ajit Mozoomdar referred to two basic aspects of the concept of secularism as it had developed in the Western context.

The first is religious tolerance. There is no established Church in India as in the West, but the fundamental basis of the concept is that the State does not act on behalf of any religious body.

The second aspect is that of minority rights. Shri Mozoomdar was of the view that in a plural society the rights of the majority and those of the minority could not be treated as entirely at par. The majority had the obligation to protect the minority. Uniformity in such matters as personal law could not be forced on the minority.

Referring to the basic paper, Shri Mozoomdar thought that Prof. Khan's observations on the two aspects of all religions was philosophically correct, but it ignored the social aspect which gave rise to antagonism. Shri Mozoomdar also felt that by attaching undue importance to the concept of nation state Prof. Khan had overlooked differences within the regions. Regional identities,

Shri Mozoomdar pointed out, did not supersede indentities like religion, language and caste within the regions.

Finally, Shri Mozoomdar emphasised the fact that poverty was not the cause of communalism. Communalism arose, he thought, from partial development, not absolute poverty.

XVII

Indiresan

Shri Indiresan asked :

i. Is our problem basically social, or is it political? The Hindu society, he pointed out, was divided within itself, with the result that the minority community provided the balance. The politicians, he thought, took advantage of this, and created tension.

ii. Could it be a fact that the Constitution did not treate all communities alike? Was this the reason for the tension ?

iii. Or, is the failure of the judicial system to punish or restrict political misbehaviour the reason for social flare-ups not being contained?

XVIII

S. S. Rao

Shri S.S. Rao pointed out that Prof. Khan had not defined secularism. Did secularism mean, Shri Rao asked, neutrality towards all religions, or did secularism envisage a homogeneous society. In Shri Rao's opinion secularism should include castes also, and not religion alone.

Shri Rao disagreed with Shri R.C. Dutt who had suggested that the Centre should have taken action against the U.P. Government under Article 356 of the Constitution. Shri Rao thought that the issue was social and should be settled socially.

XIX

Ashis Banerjee

Shri Ashis Banerjee thought that Indian intellectuals were not paying sufficient attention to global developments in the current phase partly due to the pre-occupation with pressing domestic compulsions relating to the Ayodhya issue. That is why the shifts that have occurred in the relationship between religion and politics have perhaps eluded them. Whether we like it or not religion has acquired fresh acceptability in recent years. In some cases it is the basis on which ethnicity, or even nationality is being defined, while in other cases religion is serving as an inspiration for political and social transformation. In the emerging context we need to see that the defining characteristic of secularism as separation of State (or politics) from religion cannot work in any simple sense. The State in India, which is under great pressure at the moment, will have to develop greater sensitivity towards religion based mobilisation and acquire better skills for the reconciliation of different religion based (political) interests.

Reacting to a suggestion made by one participant (Shri Seth) to the effect that the religious minorities in India should not be allowed (by the majority) to take shelter behind favourable judicial decisions, Shri Banerjee concluded that such challenges were an indication of the dangerous trends with which the State will have to cope with in times to come.

XX

A. Rahman

Dr. A. Rahman, chairman, wished to place on record his personal views as a participant. He thought that three major factors, fear, intolerance and violence increasingly governed human relations now. This had happened because personal relations had been commercialised and society technicalised. Easy availability of weapons of destruction had further added to this tendency.

The second proposition, Dr. Rahman wished to advance, was the clear dichotomy of the people who manned the freedom struggle. At the top of the movement were the English speaking elite who talked of liberalism and democracy. At the district level, on the other hand, the leadership was of indigenous people. The result was that there were two clear planks of the movement—anti British on the one hand, and revivalist on the other. The non-cooperation movement thus resulted in the establishment of the Kashi Vidyapith at Banaras to propagate the Hindu values, and the Jamia Millia at Delhi based on Islamic culture.

The third proposition of Dr. Rahman was about the influence exerted by non-resident Indians. During the fifties and the sixties, the U.S., Britain and France promoted a large number of research projects in India which collected sectarian data about religion, caste et al. Taking advantage of this data the Indian residents in these countries formed centres based on religious issues. No wonder the Canadian Sikhs propagated Sikhism in India, ISKON taught Krishna consciousness to the Hindus, and the Muslims from Algeria and France taught Islamic culture to the Muslims of India.

Dr. Rahman wanted Prof. Khan to take these factors into account and comment on them.

XXI

N. K. Seth

Shri N. K. Seth reiterated that he was not interested in a theoretical discussion of secularism. There was a communal problem in India, he said. He was interested in discussing how this problem could be solved; how communal harmony could be achieved.

According to Shri Seth, the Muslims were nursing a sense of grievance against the Hindus, though he felt that this was so with the older generation and not with the younger generation of Muslims. The latter were not interested in religious strife. They focus their attention on modernisation, education and competition so that they could lead better lives. He quoted a young Muslim journalist to say: "Wherever we are in the majority, we want theocracy, and wherever we are in the minority, we want secularism."

Shri Seth was of the opinion that the Muslims should now do some introspection. They should also try to recognise the psychological urges of the Hindus, who after having been ruled over by the Muslims for seven hundred years, were now in a position to dominate in India after the creation of Pakistan on religious basis.

In conclusion, Shri Seth agreed with the remark of Karl Marx that religion was the opiate of the people, and of Johnson that politics was the last refuge of scoundrels. Both should be shunned, Shri Seth thought, and a solution found by discussion with ordinary people.

Prof. Nirmal Singh was of the view that secularism and social development were inter-related processes. Deformities in one, he said, distorted the other. Something went wrong in the development process in the mid-sixties. Prof. Nirmal Singh would like Prof. Khan to consider what exactly went wrong and how it affected secularism.

Secondly, Prof. Singh pointed out that we have been influenced by the West not only in our thoughts and even in matters of communicaton like language, and even the address system we use in meetings. There is no point, therefore, in rejecting secularism because it was first conceived in Europe.

The term Hindu, Prof. Singh continued, has been used in more than one sense. The term included all those who lived in India. In this sense the Muslims, the Jains, the Buddhists and the Sikhs were all Hindus. But the term has also been used to run down other communities. Anyone who spoke for Hindus in this narrow sense, however, Prof. Singh warned, should speak for himself, for the majority among the Hindus, as among the Muslims, the Sikhs and other communities still think in terms of secularism.

We cannot accept the suggestion, Prof. Singh concluded, that the State should not interfere with religious beliefs even in public affairs. The State certainly has a responsibility to ensure that places of worship are not demolished. The State should also reconsider the idea of Hindu or Muslim universities of Khalsa colleges.

XXIII

V. P. Gupta

Shri V. P. Gupta had three points to make :

1. In his opinion secularism had no direct relationship with development, though development might be affected by secularism. Communities such as Parsees and Gujaratis, whether secular or not, he pointed out, were developing. So was Punjab in spite of the turmoil.
2. According to Shri Gupta, India never had secularism in the way the term was now being used. The partition of the country on the basis of religion had been accepted by both parties throwing secularism over board.

Our ideal, Shri Gupta continued, was not secularism, but peace, tranquillity and development, in other words, pragmatism. If secularism created mass discontentment and hampered development then it was of no use, he thought.

3. In Shri Gupta's view there has been over protection of minorities. Protectionism has become a vested interest, and the minorities feel they can get away with anything, he concluded.

XXIV

Kartar Singh

Dr. Kartar Singh was of the view that the discussions so far had highjacked the real issue. The Congress alone, he thought, was not the villain of the piece. All political parties, including the left parties, were responsible for the present situation. Not finding issues of development and social transformation, politicians of all hues had resorted to casteism, criminalisation of politics and communalism.

Will the new economic policy strengthen or weaken communalism, he asked. Does more poverty mean more communalism?

Communalism did not merely mean one community against another. It meant negation of democracy. It meant neo-fascism, Dr. Singh warned. This could be avoided, Dr. Singh concluded, if the State was not influenced by any religious community.

XXV

Prem Singh

Shri Prem Singh wished to make four points :

1. If regional identities had been powerfully developed the country would not have been partitioned. Regional identities, according to him, have their limitations. They may become divisive too but they have not so far been developed as much as communal identities.
2. Some scholars working on the subject have felt that the Sikhs formed a nationality, if they were not a nation, or even if they were not a nationality they were in the process of becoming so. But it has not been explained that if this were so what the position of the Punjabi Hindus were.
3. A lot of work still needs to be done about the partition of the country. Was it still possible in the late forties to avoid partition? No convincing answer to this was forthcoming yet.
4. The intelligentsia of the country should realise that the wrongs of history cannot be put right now by political means.

In conclusion, Shri Prem Singh welcomed more discussions on the roles of political parties, and called for an end to the thinking that the past wrongs should be corrected now.

XXVI

B.R. Nanda

Dr. B.R. Nanda, referring to the British policy of "divide and rule", cited two letters. One was written in July 1909 by Lovat Fraser, the Editor of the *Times of India,* to the Private Secretary to the Viceroy, (and really meant for the latter) in which he stated "Men like the Aga Khan plainly feel that in pressing for separate treatment for Mohammedans, they were fighting our battle much more than their own. We have far more to lose than the Muslims by an *entente* between Islam and Hinduism". The second letter, date 14th November 1912, was from Lord Hardinge, the then Viceroy, to Sir Ali Imam, a member of his Executive Council in which he described Britain as "the greatest Mohammedan Power" and the Government of India as "the greatest safeguard of Muslim religion".

There was thus no doubt about the colonial policy of "divide and rule", but Dr. Nanda pointed out, that Muslim leadership from the Aga Khan to Jinnah was only too willing to accept British blandishments. The elections in 1946 fought on the issue of Pakistan, Dr. Nanda continued, resulted in all the seats in the Central Assembly and 90 per cent of the seats in the Provincial Assemblies being won by the Muslim League. This final result was not wholly the result of British manoeuverings.

Dr. Nanda disagreed with Prof. Khan that the two nation theory had been accepted by the Congress. The Congress never accepted it, Dr. Nanda asserted, though in the circumstances prevailing in 1947 it resigned itself to the partition of the country as an alternative to civil war and anarchy.

XXVII

Paulose Mar Gregorios

Dr. Paulos Mar Gregorios drew distinctions between the terms 'Secular', 'Secularism' and 'Secularisation. The word "Secular", he pointed out was 2,000 years old while secularisation was an 18th century, and secularism a 20th century word. Each had its own historical context which should not be distorted. Nehru, he pointed, had used the term "secular" as an adjective qualifying the State, but he had never talked of promoting secularism.

Dr. Gregorios agreed with Prof. Khan that secularism now meant multiple communalism. What we really wanted, he pointed out, was a commitment larger than to one community. Secularism was not the answer to communalism. It (secularism) was a wrong concept, he said.

Proceeding, Dr. Gregorios stated that our difficulty was that the trust we had placed in the Central Government had been betrayed during the last several decades. The Central Government had shown partisanship in favour of those with voting or lobbying power. That is why religions have now retreated to smaller identities. There was no one at the national centre, he stated, who could reassure the people about social and economic equality and justice.

Dr. Gregorios explained the ancient Indian (Jaina) concept *Anekanta Vada* and stated that that was what pluralism meant—no particular position can claim to be absolute. Pluralism meant larger commitment which ultimately covered all humanity.

XXVIII

Arshi Khan

Shri Arshi Khan did not agree that the minorities, especially the Muslims, had been getting special privileges. There may have been some effort to appease the Muslim elites, but if the Muslim masses had really been given protective cover they could have come up to a balanced social, cultural and political level.

Secularism, to Shri Khan was a social philosophy of a humanistic character. There was nothing foreign about it. It is a valuable gift of the Indian civilisation which had been marked by accommodation, tolerance and peace. Our culture and history, both ancient and medieval, have proved this.

Continuing, Shri Khan suggested that there should be a mechanism in the Constitution to arrest the growth of communal forces. He referred in this connection to the 1982 Constitution of Turkey which disqualified parties that favoured particular religions and denominations.

In conclusion, he appealed to the media in general to show greater awareness of the danger of communalism.

XXIX

Balraj Mehta

Shri Balraj Mehta was shocked to hear one of the speakers say that religious revivalism had become a global phenomenon and that we should, therefore, accept it. Was this what globalisation implied, Shri Mehta asked.

There was a tendency, Shri Mehta continued, to regard this group or that as communal. The fact, however, is that communalism has become pervasive. The communists are not infected by it, but all major political parties including the Congress are.

Shri Mehta regarded as very perceptive the observations made by Prof. Khan in his paper about public promises and private betrayals. It is true that a party could be voted to power by the people on public promises, but could stay in power only with the support of vested interests. This, however, has its own implications. There have been only two non-Congress Ministries at the Centre since independence, but neither could stay in power for more than a year. This implies that while all parties make public promises, only one party enjoys the confidence of the vested interests.

As regards political instability, the problem needs to be studied. It was Shri Mehta's thesis that though the British were forced to quit as a result of a mass movement, it was only a small proportion of the population that came to power and had a part in the productive and social processes. If this caused political instability Shri Mehta wondered what the situation would be like when the masses participated in these processes.

XXX

Ramaswamy R. Iyer

Shri Ramaswamy R. Iyer commenced by stating that his reservations about secularism were in some ways similar to those of Dr. Gregorios.

Prof. Khan had referred to the absence of an organised Church both in Hinduism and in Islam. This created an impression that the two religions were similar. In Shri Iyer's view they were not.

Prof. Khan had also referred to the loyalty to the State being supreme. Shri Iyer felt that there were different spheres of loyalty, the State, the Community et. al, but not necessarily a hierarchy of loyalties.

Prof. Khan had drawn a distinction between the orthodox and the humanistic traditions of all religions. There could indeed be a difference between the liberal and the rigid traditions in many (not necessarily all) religions, but Shri Iyer found it difficult to accept the term "humanistic" which generally carried the connotation of being distinct from "religious". He preferred to think of pluralism, which was not necessarily humanistic, to accommodate the liberal traditions of various religions.

If, however, "orthodox religion" conveyed the sense of a religion which was exclusive in spirit and regarded itself as superior to other religions. Shri Iyer thought that there was no such tradition in Hinduism. Hinduism did not claim to be inexclusive possession of truth. There could, therefore, be strictly speaking, no Hindu 'fundamentalism'. Bigotry had indeed entered into the Hindu fold, but these are instances of militancy, not fundamentalism. They arise out of grievances, real or imagined, and are exploited for political purposes.

Continuing, Shri Iyer observed that according to Prof. Khan 'Pseudo-secularism' meant the lack of a scientific temper, while according to the B. J. P. it meant placating the minorities in the garb of secularism. Shri Iyer was not in sympathy with the B. J. P., but wished to point out that instances like the Shah Bano case and the attitude that no one in official position and no official media should refer to the Hindu past created a senses of grievance which helped the B. J. P.

Finally, while agreeing with Prof. Khan's questioning of the proposition that to be Hindu was to be secular, as bigotry and intolerance were clearly to be found among the Hindus too, Shri Iyer pointed out that *"Sarva Dharma Samabhava"* was indeed a Hindu concept. Neither Islam nor Christianity accepted the validity of other faiths. Neither Pakistan nor Bangladesh had proclaimed itself as a secular State. India could do so only because it was a Hindu majority State.

XXXI

Ashis Banerjee

Shri Ashis Banerjee, clarifying the statement he had made earlier in the seminar, said that in Eastern Europe, for instance, religion was playing a greater part now than before. Also, in Latin America, Liberation Theology was speaking on behalf of the poor and the deprived. In the changed climate, when religion was playing a complex variety of political and social roles, the state has perforce to take cognisance of these factors. The older theoretical model of secularism faithfully adhered to by a section of India's intelligentsia does not seem to have the range of inventory necessary to engage with these developments. That is an important aspect of the present crisis.

XXXII

Rasheeduddin Khan

Prof. Rasheeduddin Khan in replying to the discussions said he felt gratified that his paper had evoked a plurality of responses on the interlinked subjects, socialism and social transformation. He pointed out that the formulations by the author were transmuted in communication to the moulds of the listeners, according to their perceptions. He felt bewildered that some words he had used meant different things to listeners, like for instance Shri Ramaswami Iyer.

Prof. Khan wished to confine himself to four points :

First, he agreed that certain terms that were used required further clarification. The terms as used were mere approximations. How is a State which is not dominated by any religion, organised or unorganised, to be defined, he asked. It is true a term like secularism had some universal features which are important, but this should not be pushed too far. The term also has a historical context and an ethnic background. Prof. Khan asserted that he was not equating Hinduism and Islam. He was merely stating that neither had an organised Church.

In referring to the majesty of the State, Prof. Khan observed, he was not referring to a pseudo-Hindu State. He was referring, on the other hand, to the State as defined in the Preamble of the Indian Constitution. India had embarked, he pointed out, on a experiment, unprecedented in history, by trying to make a single democratic State out of an ancient civilisation which was plural and diversified. Even the October Revolution had failed to build up a democratic State.

Our main concern, Prof. Khan continued, was not to build up a Hindu Pakistan, but to follow up the ethos of the national movement in which people of all religions had participated. He had referred to the State, sought to be built up, as a secular state. He had not spoken of secularism, of whose positive and negative contents he was aware, and which in fact he had described in his paper. Nevertheless, he was glad Dr. Grogorios had used the term "democratic pluralism". The concept certainly deserved to be examined. Whatever term is used, however, the problem is how to build a State where pluralism is not merely tolerated, but is honoured as an integral part of the mosaic.

Secondly, on the concept of *multiple communalism* advanced by him, Prof. Khan stated that he disagreed with the proposition that since Hinduism was plural and, therefore, secular, the introduction of secularism amounted to intrusion of an extraneous factor. There was a lot of confusion in the Hindu tradition, he pointed out, and cited Manu and his code as a instance of intolerance. Islam and Christianity too had similar traditions.

Prof. Khan was of the view that a good religious man, whether or not one agreed with his philosophy, was a good human being. One must, however, draw a distinction between the corpus of religion as a moral order and the use of religion in politics.

The image created by the Head of a State prostrating himself before an idol gave a wrong signal. When it was made up by going to a Darga and placing a chaddar on it provided an instance of multiple communalism. The latter act was not a concession to the Muslim masses. It was a concession to the Muslim obscurantists. It is not enough to have equal respect for all religions (*Sarva Dharma Samabhava*) at the rhetorical level and equal confusion at the operational level.

Thirdly, the first monotheistic project in the world had been in Hinduism as Moulana Abul Kalam Azad and several savants before him had pointed out. Monism and universalism came first to Hinduism, but Hinduism also had multi-layer institutionalism. There were two types of Hindus, Prof. Khan said, Mohandas Karamchand Gandhi, who was deeply rooted Hindu culture, represented one, and Nathuram Godse the other.

Fourthly, Prof. Khan stated that there was no reason for the Hindu psyche to be hurt by the so-called domination of the Muslims, and later, the British, for 700 years. The administration during the "Muslim" period was dominated by Rajputs, Kayasthas and Banias and presided over by the derelict Sultanate, and later by Mughal Emperor. During the British period, it suited imperialism to be strongly anti Muslim from 1857-1885. It was when the Congress was formed, that the imperialists tried to keep the Muslims away from the Congress and turned anti-Hindu. It was all a matter of imperialist policy.

A great experiment is on, Prof. Khan concluded, to build a sovereign, democratic, secular republic in India. One would need to have both compassion and clarity of mind to appreciate this experiment.

INDEX